Moving Aboriginal Health Forward

Moving Aboriginal Health Forward

Discarding Canada's Legal Barriers

YVONNE BOYER

PURICH
PUBLISHING
LIMITED
SASKATOON, SK. CANADA

Purich Publishing Ltd.
Box 23032, Market Mall Post Office, Saskatoon, SK, Canada, S7J 5H3
Phone: (306) 373-5311 Fax: (306) 373-5315 Email: purich@sasktel.net
www.purichpublishing.com

Library and Archives Canada Cataloguing in Publication

Boyer, Yvonne, author
    Moving aboriginal health forward : discarding Canada's legal barriers / Yvonne Boyer.

Includes bibliographical references and index.
ISBN 978-1-895830-79-8 (pbk.)

    1. Native peoples — Health and hygiene — Law and legislation — Canada. 2. Native peoples — Medical care — Law and legislation — Canada. 3. Native peoples — Legal status, laws, etc. — Canada. I. Title.

KE7722.H4B69 2014   342.7108'72   C2014-900069-3

Edited, designed, and typeset by Donald Ward.
Cover design by Jamie Olson, Olson Information Design.
Cover photograph of Fort San (Fort Qu'Appelle Sanitorium) by Henry "Harry" Saville (1886-1948), Saskatchewan Bureau of Publications, 1928. Courtesy Elizabeth Saville McKenzie.
Cover photograph "Pavilion Balcony" at Fort San [R-B7903] courtesy Saskatchewan Archives Board.
Index by Ursula Acton.
Printed and bound in Canada by Houghton Boston Printers and Lithographers

Purich Publishing gratefully acknowledges the assistance of the Government of Canada through the Canada Book Fund, and the Creative Industry Growth and Sustainability Program made possible through funding provided to the Saskatchewan Arts Board by the Government of Saskatchewan through the Ministry of Parks, Culture, and Sport for its publishing program.

Printed on 100 per cent post-consumer, recycled, ancient-forest-friendly paper.

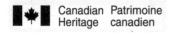 Canadian Patrimoine
Heritage canadien

 Saskatchewan
Ministry of
Tourism, Parks,
Culture and Sport

 SASKATCHEWAN
ARTS BOARD

ACKNOWLEDGEMENTS

I would like to thank the people who have generously contributed to this work.

Thank you to my mother, Norma May Boyer, for always believing; my Aunt Lucille DuBois, for sharing her Fort San stories with me as a child; and thank you to my friend/sister Wanda McCaslin.

I want to thank some of the people who have been inspirations in my life-long learning: Dr. Joan Boyer, Dr. Gail Valaskakis, the Honorable Mary Ellen Turpel-Lafond, and James Sa'ke'j Youngblood Henderson.

My husband Marv Fletcher has given many years of patience, love, and support, as well as my four children, Kyle, Kurt, Erin and Jade. Without them none of this work would be possible.

Contents

Part One

PART ONE

Introduction

HISTORICAL FACTORS AND EVENTS have contributed to the shaping of Aboriginal[1] health through laws, legislation, and policies that were detrimental not only to the social fibre of Aboriginal people in Canada but to their physical health as well. Today, there is a stark difference between the health of Aboriginal and non-Aboriginal people in Canada, with alarming rates of chronic diseases and socio-economic ills among the Aboriginal population. It is well documented that risk factors and chronic conditions among Aboriginal people show that, compared with the rest of Canada, their health is clearly worsening. Evidence of a health crisis includes a wide range of problems, many of which are less common or serious in non-Aboriginal society. For example, obesity is more common among Aboriginal people, and diabetes and cardiovascular disease are far higher in Aboriginal populations.[2] The Health Council of Canada reports that life expectancy for First Nations, Métis, and Inuit is far lower than non-Aboriginal peoples at the national, provincial, and territorial level.[3]

While certain health indicators, such as mortality and morbidity, are important, it is equally important to look at economic measures that determine health outcomes, such as clean water, adequate and available housing, sewage, food security, environmental contaminants, and access to basic health care services. These are services that the majority of Canadians take for granted, but are inadequate or missing in urban and reserve Aboriginal communities. For these reasons, a study of Aboriginal health must reflect a holistic approach that considers the importance of key health determinants, including historical legal relationships.

The shaping of health of Aboriginal people began with the early Crown/Aboriginal relationship. The assertion of Aboriginal rights and the signing of treaties that deal with health care reaffirmed this relationship. Aboriginal and treaty rights are entrenched in the *Constitution Act, 1982*. The inherent right to health and traditional health care practices is simply part of a broader conception of Aboriginal rights.[4] Certain health practices were integral to all Aboriginal peoples, both as individuals and as communities and societies. Various healing practices were in place pre-contact and have devolved to modern practices today; this is a critical factor in fulfilling Supreme Court of Canada tests to prove Aboriginal rights. Battiste and Henderson wrote that "the Supreme Court acknowledged that these cultural rights arise within a system of beliefs, social practices and ceremonies of Aboriginal people. They are traced back to their ancestral Indigenous order and their relationship with ecology."[5] Although not all people who possess Aboriginal rights also possess treaty rights, the *Constitution Act, 1982* confirms that anyone who possesses treaty rights also possesses Aboriginal rights (if these rights were not extinguished or modified by treaties). While entrenched in the *Constitution Act, 1982,* Aboriginal rights are inherent to all Aboriginal people in Canada and are passed down from generation to generation. They are derived from Aboriginal knowledge, heritage, and law.[6] It is important to review Aboriginal and treaty rights to determine if there are breaches of these constitutionally protected rights and if the breaches may have contributed to poor Aboriginal health status today.

The Context, Themes, and Structure of this Book

It is noted throughout this book that federal policy and institutions contributed to the crisis in Aboriginal health. The failure of Aboriginal health policies resides in the false assumptions that Aboriginal people were biologically predetermined to vanish, were inherently unhealthy and inferior, and that their culture caused them to pursue harmful lifestyles. This book reviews a selection of Canadian policies and laws which embrace these false assumptions and highlights some of the historical points in Aboriginal health that led to the creation of current federal Aboriginal health policies.

In 1969, Canada's Medical Liaison Officer, Dr. Graham-Cumming, reported that Aboriginal people had few health problems before contact, and noted that "surprisingly little evidence has been found to suggest that the Eskimo and the Indian Populations did have any major health problems before the intrusions of venturing Europeans."[7] Graham-Cumming also noted that, "before the arrival of foreigners, health problems in the Far North had probably been largely reduced to getting enough to eat, keeping warm and avoiding being killed. Even tooth decay does not appear to have been a problem."[8] The *Royal Commission on Aboriginal Peoples* remarks that, prior to European arrival, Aboriginal people enjoyed remarkably good health. They suffered few of the illnesses common today:[9]

> There was no plague, cholera, typhus, smallpox or measles. Cancer was rare, and even fractures were infrequent. . . . There were, apparently, no [skin tumours]. There were no troubles with the feet, such as fallen arches. And judging from later acquired knowledge, there was a much greater scarcity than in the white population of . . . most mental disorders, and of other serious conditions.[10]

Through archeological studies of tissue from bones, teeth, and mummified remains, it is documented that in the pre-contact period Aboriginal people were a relatively healthy and disease-free population. Coupled with effective health practices and ongoing healing methods, the near absence (except for internal parasites and some types of warts and venereal disease) of lethal pathogens allowed Aboriginal people to survive and thrive until contact.[11] For instance, in 1796, Duke de la Rochefoucalt noted that, while local Indians at Niagara had access to a physician paid for by the government, they preferred to treat themselves, and "more frequently take draughts which they prepare themselves."[12]

Author John McLean wrote in the early 1800s that, in spite of being in Canada for twenty-four years at various Hudson's Bay posts, he had never known "a single instance of an Indian being retained at any inland post for medical treatment."[13] Instead, "[t]he knowledge the natives possess of the medical virtues of roots and herbs is generally equal to the cure of all their ailments; and we are, in fact, more frequently indebted to them, than they to us, for medical advice."[14] Healing was viewed as an internal process, whereas sickness was seen as generated externally. Sickness in a person indicated the presence or location of an external force. Waldram, Young, and Herring explain that "the world is seen as a place in which harmony and balance exist between and among human beings and spiritual or 'other than human' entities, and serious illness is indicative of a disruption in this balance."[15] Images of pre-contact good health and health care contrast starkly with the post-contact decimation wreaked upon Aboriginal populations. Diseases imported from overseas produced epidemics that forever altered the "social and biological structure of Aboriginal communities."[16]

Aboriginal knowledge and heritage reveal that the healing environment pervades every community. Each has the capacity to renew itself by daily practices. However, certain families and healers act as animators, focusing or harnessing the healing energy that is already present.[17] It is further suggested that early Aboriginal societies developed their medicine societies and created a complex pharmacopeia. They also refined their ability to call applicable unseen spirits through complex and elaborate ceremonies. All together, these ways ensured health and a relatively balanced lifestyle for individuals, families, and communities.

Traditional approaches to health and well-being are rich and diverse. For instance, the medicine societies manifest vast differences—from the Ojibwa *Midewiwin* to the Cree of Northern Saskatchewan to the Métis of Manitoba to the Inuit *angatquq* (shamans). Yet, they also hold many principles and values in common, including a commitment to healing, well-being, and balance. They practise preventative models, which have their roots in holism as a fundamental principle. Aboriginal peoples used their medicines to assist not only their individual well-being but also healthy relationships amongst each other, within their communities, and between their nations.

The World Health Organization acknowledges the importance of traditional health care as "the sum total of knowledge, skills and practices based on the theories, beliefs, and experiences indigenous to different cultures, whether explicable or not, used in the maintenance of health as well as in the prevention, diagnosis, and improvement of treatment of physical and mental illness."[18] The *Royal Commission on Aboriginal People* also defined traditional healing:

> Traditional healing has been defined as practices designed to promote mental, physical and spiritual well-being that are based on beliefs which go back to the time before the spread of western "scientific" biomedicine. When Aboriginal people in Canada talk about traditional healing, they include a wide range of activities, from physical cures using herbal medicines and other remedies, to the promotion of psychological and spiritual well-being using ceremony, counseling and accumulated wisdom of elders.[19]

Traditional healing and health practices, medicines, and medical applications for the prevention and promotion of good health are ways through which Aboriginal people manifest or express an inherent right to health. In addition to defining the terms of "health," it is helpful to define the application of western law in relation to those rights: jurisdiction over health and health matters for First Nations, Métis, and Inuit may be seen as law-making powers that affect Aboriginal health; the provision of medical care by the federal government (ties back to jurisdiction); the ability to practice and maintain traditional health care free from Canadian interference (meaning legal sanctions) and the ability to seek and maintain good health within all realms. The physical repercussions are disease. The body breaks down as stresses compound and intensify. Under these conditions, the options for sustaining healthy lifestyles and the ability to acquire help in health crises narrow. Illness and death are far more likely for those who are poor and marginalized. People who are not marginalized, who are not living in poverty, who enjoy adequate housing, who are educated, and whose cultural identity is not under attack have better states of health.

This book charts the development of ill health from pre-contact Aboriginal society, and provides a general description of the state of Aboriginal health today as well as what factors influence and determine or affect the outcomes of Aboriginal health. Part 1 also provides the foundation for the factual evidence that pre-contact healing sources not only existed but flourished. The historical descriptions are critical for the analysis in Part 2, as it concludes that these practices were in place and thrived before Europeans arrived, which is an elemental Supreme Court of Canada test that must be met to determine Aboriginal rights.

Part 2 provides an analysis of the constitutional status of Aboriginal and treaty rights, and considers if there are any breaches that may have contributed to the poor health status of Aboriginal people today. Part 2 also deals with Aboriginal and treaty rights that review the oral and written clauses of the treaties that are closely aligned with medicine and medical care, the provision of services, and access to those services. *Moving Aboriginal Health Forward: Discarding Canada's Legal Barriers* explains how policies and laws can be influenced and reshaped to transform them into useful tools for community and national development that will provide the structure for good legislative and policy development. The aim of this work is to move the dialogue toward new ways to deal with old problems, and offers hope for change and practical solutions that may provoke thought and real differences in the lives and generations of Aboriginal people to come.

Chapter One

Health Determinants

A HUMAN IS NOT ISOLATED LIKE AN ISLAND, but is interconnected with families and communities. Certain factors inevitably have an impact on individuals, their communities, and their nations. These determinants also have an impact across generations. Their widespread effects force us to think about the indivisibility and interconnectedness of health and society. Chronic diseases, for example, correlate with social, economic, and environmental factors. The rise of chronic diseases in Aboriginal communities has jeopardized not only the health and lifespan of Aboriginal people but also the core strength of Aboriginal communities and the endurance of Aboriginal languages and cultures.

Health is obviously central to the total well-being of Aboriginal peoples. This includes environmental factors, connection to the land, culture and language, social/economic factors, mental/psychological factors, access to services, family/child/kinship relations, as well as the practice of self-determination and self-governance as a Nation and a people.

In 1946, the World Health Organization (WHO) adopted a broad definition of health. It transformed the concept of health from an "absence of disease" model to an understanding that encompasses "[a] state of complete physical, mental and social well-being and not merely the absence of disease or infirmity."[1] The emergence of the WHO definition not only iterated an Aboriginal approach; it "defined an integrated approach linking together all the factors related to human well-being, including physical and social surroundings conducive to good health."[2] The WHO also confirmed that the health and well-being of all people come from their living circumstances and their quality of life — in other words, their social determinants. If people have control over their living circumstances and quality of life, then they are self-determining. They exercise voice and power over the social determinants of their health, as individuals, communities, and peoples.

Indigenous people throughout the world are burdened disproportionately not only with the social determinants of ill health but also with the conditions that result from these socioeconomic determinants, such as poverty, low household incomes, lack of adequate housing, lack of good nutrition, and homelessness. In fact, "social inequality, whether measured at the population or individual level, is the single leading condition for poor health."[3] Social and economic disadvantages vastly increase the risk to the health and well-being of Aboriginal people. The negative impacts of these socioeconomic factors extend further and damage the biological development of Aboriginal children and youth, reducing their immunity to disease. The consequences of weakened health accumulate across individual life spans as well as through succeeding generations. Colonization policies and tools of assimilation have had both a direct and indirect effect on the state of Aboriginal health which are directly linked to "the corrosive effects of poverty and economic marginalization."[4] It follows, then, that the damage caused by colonization is directly related to and intertwined with the risks to health caused by socioeconomic disadvantage.

The social conditions of many Aboriginal communities show the results of colonization in the form of addictive behaviours and violence. Alcohol and drug abuse are the most prevalent types of addictive behaviours in Aboriginal communities, and they are associated with a range of serious physical and mental health problems.[5] Women face additional problems by being affected more severely and in a shorter time by intensive substance abuse.[6] There are a myriad of other dangers, including HIV, osteoporosis, and coronary disease that have particularly harmful effects on women.[7]

The following health determinants are highlighted to illustrate their intergenerational impacts on Aboriginal health.

1.1 POVERTY

Poverty increases an individual's, a family's, and a community's risk of developing chronic diseases that lead to death.[8] Being deprived of the basic necessities of life, in addition to unhealthy living conditions and poor access to health care services, predispose people to developing chronic diseases and health-risk behaviours. Ill health is the inevitable result. The WHO reports that "the poor and people with less education are more likely to use tobacco products and to consume energy-dense and high-fat food, be physically inactive, and be overweight or obese."[9]

The link between poverty, fast food, and obesity has been correlated, and childhood obesity has become an epidemic. For instance, the Public Health Agency of Canada has provided a strategy to curb childhood obesity through the Federal, Provincial, and Territorial Framework for Action to Promote Healthy Weights. Obesity leads to many chronic diseases and negative health outcomes, including hypertension, type 2 diabetes, heart disease, gallbladder disease, stroke, and certain types of cancer, including breast and colon cancer.[10]

1.2 SHELTER, HOUSING, AND OVERCROWDING

Income directly affects shelter and housing, and housing disadvantages negatively affect health. Although substandard housing is a grave concern, the most detrimental impact of low income on housing is the lack of a home. Homelessness poses severe health risks: exposure to the elements, poor nutrition, lack of support, and poor access to health services. Clearly, these factors negatively affect the health and well-being of people living on the streets. Homeless people are more likely to have chronic and severe medical conditions than the general population.

Aboriginal people who are homeless also suffer high levels of substance abuse. For example, the 2007 Street Health survey in Toronto reported that 92 per cent smoke cigarettes. Of those, 89 per cent smoke daily. Among Aboriginal people living on the street, 77 per cent used an illicit drug other than marijuana regularly in the past year, 26 per cent had injected drugs in the past year, 29 per cent had five or more drinks on one or more occasion at least once a week in the past year, and 15 per cent had consumed non-beverage alcohol in the past year.[11]

Not only are chronic physical and mental diseases prevalent among Aboriginal homeless people, but these diseases often remain undetected for years and may be poorly controlled. Both of these conditions can lead to premature mortality and excess morbidity.[12]

For the Inuit, homelessness is particularly harsh. The Inuit Tuttarvingat Centre at the National Aboriginal Health Organization identified three characteristics: 1) homelessness is hidden, in that Inuit cultural values ensure that those who have houses will share them; 2) housing design is based on a southern Canada model, as houses that are being shared are prefabricated structures designed in sizes usually not larger than four bedrooms, a condition that easily leads to overcrowding; 3) the Arctic climate requires humans to have shelter, as life for humans is possible only with shelter. This means that we do not see "absolute homelessness" — i.e., someone living on the street — because a person will freeze without protection against weather.[13]

The Inuit experience a severe housing crisis in both shortage and quality. A shortage of housing leads to overcrowding, deficient sanitation and ventilation, the spread of infectious diseases, psycho-social stresses, and violence. Housing problems have been associated with low achievement levels in schools, spousal abuse, respiratory tract infections among infants, depression, and substance abuse.[14] The overcrowding situation is desperate for Inuit:

> As a group, Inuit suffer the worst overcrowding in Canada. It is estimated that 53 per cent of Inuit households are overcrowded, and it is not uncommon for seven or more people to inhabit a single household. Fifteen per cent of Nunavut's population is on waiting lists for public housing.[15]

First Nations housing is generally old and decrepit. Houses need to be upgraded and better maintained. According to the 2008/10 Regional Health Survey, over one-third (37.3 per cent) of First Nation homes are in need of major repairs. Another third (33.5 per cent) need minor repairs. A high percentage of First Nations living in band owned houses reported that their home was in need of major repairs (41.8%). While the existence of household incomes below $25,000/year indicated that their home was in need of major repairs, rates of houses needing repair varied with income brackets and were still high (26.4 per cent) in more moderate income brackets ($50,000 to 79,999/year).[16]

Substandard housing creates prime conditions for mould growth, poor air quality, poor ventilation, and a breeding ground for contagious diseases. These factors contribute to environmental toxins, affect the respiratory system, and lead to chronic respiratory problems. Overcrowding also leads to chronic diseases and higher rates of tuberculosis. Health Canada notes that the housing density for the Canadian population is 0.4 persons per room, while for First Nations on reserve it is 0.7 persons per room.[17] A house is considered to be overcrowded if the density exceeds one person per room. This means that, on average, about 2.6 people live in a house in the non-First Nations population, whereas 4.8 people live in a single house on First Nations reserves. In some cases, overcrowding in First Nations communities is so severe that as many as 23.4 people per house has been reported. Clearly, homes in Aboriginal communities have more people per room than the Canadian population.[18]

Research has also shown that the high rates of overcrowding affect both individual and community health and well-being. For instance, First Nations Regional Longitudinal Health Survey (RHS) statistics indicate that one in three of all respondents diagnosed with tuberculosis live in an overcrowded house. The fact that 37.5 per cent of the homes with Aboriginal children that were surveyed for the 2008/2010 RHS were overcrowded raises concerns about the long-term impacts of crowding on the health of new generations of Aboriginal people.[19]

Housing shortages and poor quality housing are an urgent public health priority for all Aboriginal people in Canada. Substandard housing creates a myriad of problems, including overcrowding, deficient sanitation and ventilation, the spread of infectious diseases, psycho-social stresses, and an increase in violence.

1.3 WATER QUALITY

Results from the RHS in 2008/2010 confirmed serious concerns about water quality and identified 21 communities that are at high risk. The Regional Health Survey report found that over one third (35.8 per cent) of First Nations adults consider their household water unsafe to drink, while 86.1 per cent resorted to using bottled water for drinking. Along with the high number of people who considered their water unsafe to drink, they also reported their water/sewage systems as sub-standard and a low level of trust with respect to general water safety.[20]

Attawapiskat First Nation in northern Ontario has been on a boil-water advisory since 1989. This is just one of 118 Aboriginal communities that are on boil-water advisories.[21] Worse yet, many communities have not been assessed by Health Canada and are drinking water and raising their children on water that may be unfit for human consumption.[22]

On February 29, 2012, Bill S-8, the *Safe Drinking Water for First Nations Act,* was introduced in the Senate. This Bill is currently under review by the Senate Standing Committee on Aboriginal Peoples following second reading on November 1, 2012. A similar Bill (Bill S-11) was introduced in the last session of Parliament, but did not proceed past committee review owing to the election.[23]

There are legally enforceable drinking water and wastewater standards in the provinces and territories, but these protections do not exist for drinking water and wastewater for reserve lands. Aboriginal and Northern Development Canada (AANDC)[24] states that in 2009, the federal government commenced the National Assessment of First Nations Water and Waste Water Systems to conduct an assessment of existing public and private water and wastewater facilities operating on First Nation lands. Recommendations were released on July 14, 2011, and stated the need for a water and wastewater regulatory regime on First Nation lands.[25]

1.4   GEOGRAPHIC FACTORS AND ACCESS

In addition to the economic status and housing conditions of Aboriginal people, geographic location can negatively affect overall health and well-being by reducing access to facilities, supplies, and support services. The location of a community may correlate with the health of the community. Aboriginal people live in every province and territory and comprise the majority of the population in Nunavut and the Northwest Territories; large portions of the Aboriginal population are in the prairie provinces.[26] Aboriginal peoples living in rural or remote regions of the country may not only lack access to healthy and affordable food but also may be exposed to health threats arising from their geographic location. In these areas, access to quality and appropriate health care is critical. In rural and remote areas, lack of local services, lack of access to a physician or other health provider, and the need to travel to a health facility in order to receive medical treatment form major barriers to adequate health care for Aboriginal people.[27] Transportation, child care, and the direct costs of some health services compound the challenges Aboriginal people face. Cultural barriers, such as the lack of culturally appropriate or relevant care and lack of traditional care, are further issues. A large problem that seems to be unaddressed is access to health care for people with disabilities. High rates of diabetes and the resulting effects of poor circulation mean that a high percentage of Aboriginal people may be either missing limbs or using a prosthesis and unable to access health services without aids such as wheelchairs, ramps, sidewalks, or even accessible doorways.

In the North, many Inuit communities are served by nursing stations. Doctors are available in larger centres, and specialized services are offered in southern centres. Many Aboriginal patients must travel great distances to access these services, and therefore must cope with delays or even lack of access to various critical health services.[28] These factors and many others affecting Aboriginal health are tied to the geographic locations of many Aboriginal communities.

1.5 ENVIRONMENTAL FACTORS

Environmental contaminants from hydroelectric, mining, energy, and forestry projects; chemical pollution; nuclear energy and weapons testing; toxic waste mismanagement; depletion of the ozone layer; and global warming — these are critical environmental problems facing Aboriginal people. The far-reaching impacts of environmental damage and contamination confirm what has been long understood: human health is intertwined with and indivisible from the natural environment.

Industry releases contaminants into the air, water, and soil. Traditional foods and medicines are affected by industrial contamination, which wreaks damage on the habitats of wildlife as well. Traditional Aboriginal lifestyles depend on the purity of the land, the water, and all living things. The environmental impact of industrialization constitutes a brutal assault on Aboriginal ways of being.

Household mould, poor sanitation systems, contaminated drinking water, and unsafe disposal of waste and refuse are significant problems for crowded Aboriginal communities. Contaminated water spreads infectious diseases, such as cryptosporidiosis and shigellosis. Pesticides and fertilizers sprayed on land around rivers or lakes carry contaminants that seep into the water.[29] AANDC is charged with protecting First Nations' environment, yet they have not been addressing the many landfill sites, sewage treatments, and other disposals that pollute on reserves. Many operate without required permits, according to Auditor General Sheila Fraser.[30] Septic systems, water treatment facilities, waste water discharges, and hazardous waste, which are strictly controlled by provincial and municipal laws, are not subject to any regulations on reserves because of jurisdictional issues. In her report, the Auditor General commented that there are few federal regulations that apply to environmental protection on reserves, and the federal government has taken little action to change this. Fraser stated that the federal government is aware of the problems but does not or cannot monitor and enforce compliance of the few regulations that exist. Fraser's report also found that, while AANDC wants to encourage First Nations to manage their own land, it will train only one person per community. This lack of regulatory backup leaves Aboriginal communities vulnerable to duties being forgotten if that person dies or leaves the reserve. AANDC blamed a lack of funding for its failure to meet its obligations.[31]

For many Aboriginal communities, harmful pollutants may include everyday substances such as cigarette smoke. Nunavut has the highest smoking rate in Canada, with 54.2 per cent of those over the age of 12 smoking either daily or occasionally as compared to the Canadian average of 21.4 per cent in 2007. It is also suggested that more than 80 per cent of Inuit women in Nunavut smoke during pregnancy. In May 2010, Mary Simon, president of Inuit Tapiriit Kanatami, accepted $350,000 in federal funding for smoking-cessation programs aimed at expectant mothers in four Inuit regions of Canada, and commented that many children have respiratory problems which could be related to smoking. Simon notes that "in one study, more than 80 per cent of Inuit women were shown to smoke during pregnancy. Another concluded that 85 per cent of infants in Nunavut's capital, Iqaluit, were exposed to second-hand smoke in the womb."[32]

1.6 COLONIALISM AS A DETERMINANT OF HEALTH

Prime Minister Stephen Harper addressed the media at an international press conference in September 2009 and stated, "We also have no history of colonialism. So we have all of the things that many people admire about the great powers but none of the things that threaten or bother them."[33] In contrast to Harper's views, the health problems Aboriginal people face can be traced directly to colonialism. Colonialism has caused acute trauma to the health and social fibre of Aboriginal people and their communities.

The mechanisms of law, institutions, and public policies — the *Indian Act*, residential schools, and other assimilation projects — have been driving forces behind the colonization of Aboriginal people in Canada. Professor Sa'ke'j Youngblood Henderson describes Eurocentrism as a "dominant intellectual and educational movement that postulates the superiority of Europeans over non-Europeans," and the source of colonialism.[34]

Colonization came to North America with European settlement and subsequent industrialization. Colonization continues today and is evidenced by the marginalization of Aboriginal people in Canada. Professor Sharlene Razack explains that a "white settler society" is one that Europeans set up on non-European soil.[35] The origins of this society lie in the Europeans' multi-century campaign to dispossess and exterminate Indigenous populations. As white settler societies have grown, they have continued to enforce a racial hierarchy. Their state mythologies claim outright, or tacitly assume, that European people have a superior intellect and create superior social structures. The Europeans imported hierarchical socio-economic structures, which have been forced onto Indigenous society. Aboriginal people were relegated to the role of secondary or non-persons; the classification was considered temporary, because Europeans presumed that Aboriginal peoples were mostly dead, dying, or soon to be assimilated. European settlers thus established themselves as the privileged inhabitants and the ones most entitled to the fruits of the "new" lands. By imposing colonization on every facet of life, white settler societies claimed control over unimagined wealth, political power, human labour, and natural resources.[36]

Globally, the similarities are striking between the health issues of Aboriginal peoples in Canada and the health issues of Indigenous peoples throughout the world — Australian Aboriginal, Torres Strait Islander, Maori, Kanaka Maoli, American Indian, and Alaskan Native peoples. The International Network for Indigenous Health Knowledge and Development commented:

In each country the legacies of colonial dispossession, land alienation, forcible relocation, suppression of indigenous cultural practices, values and beliefs, loss of language, disruption of families, violations of indigenous inherent sovereignty and right to self-determination, treaties, international law and indigenous cultural law, and other factors, have resulted in indigenous peoples experiencing a deplorable health status compared to non-indigenous settlers.[37]

Taiaiake Alfred and Jeff Corntassel comment on how far-reaching colonization is:

There are approximately 350 million Indigenous peoples situated in some 70 countries around the world. All of these people confront the daily realities of having their lands, cultures, and governmental authorities simultaneously attacked, denied, and reconstructed by colonial societies and states. This has been the case for generations.
...
[In Canada] the results are measured in losses of cultural identity,

marginalization and health status that fall well below that of main-stream Canadians.[38]

The health statistics concerning Aboriginal people living in Canada provide abundant information about the challenges Aboriginal people face. The statistics paint a grim picture, especially given all the factors that converge to endanger Aboriginal health.

Restoring health for Indigenous people worldwide and in Canada involves a holistic approach that builds on balance and harmony, including recognizing harms resulting from colonization. The immense job of restoring Aboriginal health requires collaboration to generate an analysis that eventually will change and influence government policies in ways that will positively affect the health of Aboriginal people.

1.7 The Current State of Aboriginal Health

The overall health status of Aboriginal people falls well below that of other Canadians, and large inequities in health exist between Aboriginal people and the rest of the population. Aboriginal people continue to die at higher rates and younger ages than the general Canadian population. The infant mortality rate for First Nations on reserve is seven times higher than the national average.[39]

The 2008/2010 First Nations Longitudinal Regional Health Survey indicates that 27.9 per cent of First Nation adults report that they have a disability. Compared with one in four Aboriginal men, nearly one in three First Nation women have disabilities. Disability becomes more common as people age. Half of First Nations people over 60 years of age have a disability, compared with 13.1 per cent in the 18 to 29 age group. This increase of disability with age can be explained, in part, by increased exposure to factors that place people at risk of disability across a lifespan, such as accidents, exposure to environmental toxins, stress and anxiety, addictions, the aging process, illnesses and other chronic conditions (e.g., arthritis, heart conditions, progressive hearing loss).[40]

The highlights of the 2006 Aboriginal Peoples Survey (APS) showed that Métis have higher rates of chronic conditions than the total population of Canada. Arthritis is the most common at 21 per cent, higher than the 13 per cent for the rest of Canada. High blood pressure was the second most common condition, reported by 16 per cent of Métis compared with

12 per cent of the total population. Asthma and diabetes are nearly double for Métis over the rest of the population. More Métis women (57 per cent) than men (50 per cent) reported having a chronic health condition.[41]

The realities of health care in the North differ greatly from southern Canada. Overcrowding, geography, the harsh climate, and smaller populations make access to services extremely difficult. The most commonly reported diagnosed chronic conditions among Inuit adults were arthritis/rheumatism (13 per cent) and high blood pressure (12 per cent). Inuit children aged six to 14 suffered from ear infections (15 per cent), allergies (10 per cent), and asthma (seven per cent).[42]

The average lifespan for Inuit women is 14 years less than that of the average Canadian woman;[43] suicide rates in Nunavut are six times the national average.[44] On most indicators where there is health data available for Inuit, they fare far worse than not only their non-Aboriginal Canadian counterparts, but their First Nations and Métis counterparts as well.[45]

Drawing from the 2006 Statistics Canada census data, the Native Women's Association of Canada compiled some important but basic health statistics on Aboriginal women. The life span for Aboriginal women is 76.8 years on average while 82 is the norm for non-Aboriginal women. Suicide for Aboriginal female youth is eight times higher than other Canadian youth, while for Aboriginal women the rate of suicide is three times the national average for non-Aboriginal women. In addition:

- Aboriginal women are almost three times more likely to contract AIDS than non-Aboriginal women (23.1 per cent versus 7.2 per cent).

- Seven per cent of Aboriginal women over the age of 15 have been diagnosed with diabetes compared to three per cent for the rest of the female population of this same age category.[46] The rate of diabetes increases with age. Twenty-four per cent of Aboriginal women over the age of 65 have diabetes compared to 11 per cent for the rest of the senior female population in Canada.[47]

- Between the ages of 25 and 44, Aboriginal women are five times more likely to die as a result of violence than non-Aboriginal women.[48]

Aboriginal women are critical in determining the health of a community. They are often the centre and anchor of the household. They may be the primary caregivers of children, families, and the elderly, and they most often deliver health care services to family and community members. When women break down the family unit breaks down.

1.7.1 Mental Health

The rate of suicide among Aboriginal people is about twice that of the total Canadian population.[49] The Regional Longitudinal Health Survey notes that both depression and drug and alcohol abuse are strongly correlated with suicide and suicide attempts. "[I]ndividuals who had experienced feeling sad or depressed for at least two weeks in a row in the previous year were more than twice as likely as others to report suicidal ideation or a suicide attempt."[50] Noted mental health expert Dr. Lawrence Kirmayer reports that suicide does not have one single cause. However, he states that the most important factor is the mental health of the individual. Kirmayer observes that "many studies concur that the majority of people who die by suicide suffered from a psychiatric disorder that contributed to their death."[51]

1.7.2 Chronic Diseases

Only in the past 50 years has type 2 diabetes been detected in Aboriginal populations in Canada. The steady increase in Aboriginal communities is the root cause of serious health complications. These affect the circulatory system, eyes, kidneys, and periodontal and nervous systems. Complications can result in premature death, disability, and a compromised quality of life. The disease has a serious negative impact on quality of life and is associated with premature death.[52]

In Canada, the rate of diabetes among Aboriginal people is three to five times higher than in the general population.[53] They also suffer high rates of complications and a younger average age of onset.[54] The prevalence of diabetes among the Métis is comparable to the rates in First Nations in most age and sex groups.[55]

Type 2 diabetes among the Aboriginal population occurs for a multitude of reasons, including genetic factors such as ancestry and family history, coupled with detrimental lifestyles.[56] Diabetes correlates with the harsh socio-cultural changes that Aboriginal peoples have experienced. It also reflects harsh social conditions, such as poverty, lack of education, stress, and depression, all of which can lead to obesity (a predisposing factor for diabetes and heart disease). Under these circumstances, the genetic susceptibility for diabetes interacts with the environmental stressors of changing nutrition and a sedentary lifestyle. These, in turn, lead to increased chances of obesity and related chronic conditions.[57]

1.7.3 HIV/AIDS and Hepatitis C

Tuberculosis is the leading cause of death in HIV/AIDS-infected individuals.[58] HIV/AIDS is another serious and increasing concern within the Aboriginal population. The Canadian Aboriginal Aids Network reported grim statistics on Aboriginal people and HIV/AIDS:

- Aboriginal people experienced HIV at rates about 3.6 times higher than other Canadians in 2008.

- Even though the Aboriginal population only represented 3.8 per cent of the general Canadian population, Aboriginal people represented about eight per cent of all people living with HIV and AIDS, and about 12.5 per cent of new HIV and AIDS cases diagnosed in Canada in 2008.

- Between 1979 and 2008, 19.3 per cent of reported AIDS cases among Aboriginal people were between 15 and 29 years old, compared with 14.8 per cent of reported AIDS cases among non-Aboriginal people in the same age group.

- HIV affects Aboriginal women at higher rates than non-Aboriginal women. Between 1998 and 2008, Aboriginal women represented 48.8 per cent of all the HIV test reports within the Aboriginal HIV/AIDS statistics as compared with 20.6 per cent of reports among those of other ethnicities.[59]

For the Inuit, HIV/AIDS present additional problems. Pauktuutit, the Inuit Women's Organization, reports that the most common route of HIV infection for Inuit is through unprotected sex, while high rates of pregnancy as well as sexually transmitted infections, such as chlamydia and gonorrhea, are evidence that Inuit are engaging in behaviour that puts them at risk for HIV infection. Because many Inuit youth move south, their risk of contracting HIV is increased. Similarly, with increased travel between Arctic communities and southern centres, the risk of HIV and Hepatitis C being introduced to a Northern community also increases. The increase in population with these diseases requires community members and health staff to have a basic understanding of precautions and treatment.[60]

In 2010, the Correctional Service of Canada reported that the HIV prevalence rate in federal prisons "rivals those of many countries in sub-Saharan Africa and is greater than the HIV prevalence rates in all other regions of the world":

> At 4.6 percent, the rate of HIV infection in federal prisons is 15 times greater than that in the community as a whole. As for hepatitis C in federal prisons, the 31 percent rate of infection is 39 times greater than the population as a whole. In both cases, incarcerated women and especially Aboriginal women — of whom 11.7 percent are infected with HIV— are disproportionately infected with HIV and hepatitis C.[61]

Hepatitis C is a chronic liver disease caused by the Hepatitis C virus (HCV). Health Canada estimates that 250,000 people in Canada are infected with HCV. HCV in Aboriginal people is seven to nine times higher than in non-Aboriginal Canadians.[62]

Extreme health disparities in the forms discussed in this chapter exist in Canada between Aboriginal people and the rest of the population. Arguably, the simplest way to address the inequities in Aboriginal health may be to reduce the inequities in the health determinants — the social inequities. This strategy could catalyze any number of opportunities for improving the grim health outcomes that Aboriginal people face today.

Chapter Two

Aboriginal Society and Good Health

Many different types of healing practitioners exist today and have existed since pre-contact times; they include herbalists, ceremonialists, midwives, spiritualists, diagnosis specialists, medicine men and women, and healers. Aboriginal societies make important distinctions among healers based on their knowledge and skills. For example, some are skilled in first aid, which requires that a person possess a generic knowledge of medicinal plants and methods that heal. Others are specialized healers. They use spiritual assistance, often in combination with botanical substances. A medicine man or woman denotes a healer who uses supernatural forces to heal.[1] Shamanism was and is common among Aboriginal peoples. The shaman is a doctor who heals people through contact with spirits. The cause of most diseases is thought to be an imbalance between an individual and the world around him or her. The shaman uses music, herbs, plants, dreams, visions, and ceremonial dances to restore a balance.[2] The work of the shaman is differentiated from that of a medicine man or woman in that "the ordinary medicine man may certainly heal the sick while in a light trance, but he does not sink down into the deep trance that is necessary for making contact with the supernatural world."[3] In reality, these differences are much more complex. In general, though, the difference between practitioners lies in the extent to which spiritual help must be invoked. For instance, "Eurocentric researchers may know the name of an herbal cure and understand how it is used, but without ceremony and ritual songs, chants, prayers, and relationships, they cannot achieve the same effect."[4] In 1886, Dr. Robert Bell explained these differences among the Cree:

> [T]he term "medicine" does not mean strictly material remedies or the practice of the healing art, but rather a general power or influence, of which that of drugs is only one variety. Hence a "medicine

man" is not simply a doctor of medicine, but a sort of priest, prophet, medium and soothsayer. He is also a juggler, conjurer, sorcerer or magician and general dealer in the supernatural. A mere knowledge of medicine proper is rather one of the lower or accessory branches of his profession, and it is often practiced by those who have no pretensions to be considered full-fledged medicine men. Even women sometimes obtain great reputations as doctors. To the medicine man a knowledge of drugs is valuable, principally to enable him to carry out different kinds of poisoning as may best serve his ends. His most important function and the secret of his power is his dealing in occult influences.[5]

Each Aboriginal group uses a variety of methods with its diverse populations. The following section provides some examples of healing methods that have been witnessed and documented by various individuals, such as Jesuits, explorers, traders, anthropologists, and social scientists. Eurocentric bias is woven through many of these early accounts, but important information can be gleaned nonetheless. Practices described in this section should properly be viewed as medicinal treatments and practices which meet the legal requireme nts for proving that such healing practices were in place before European control.

2.1 EARLY HEALING PRACTICES

2.1.1 Sweat Lodge

The process of sweating cleanses the body of toxins and boosts the immune system. The sweat lodge has been used across many different Aboriginal groups for centuries. It is used to facilitate prayer, to maintain health, and to address particular health or social concerns. Among the many health problems that the sweat lodge addresses are febrile symptoms, rheumatism, headache, fast pulse, catarrh, and sore muscles. In fact, the sweat lodge has been used for most health problems.[6] It was usually located in a separate structure, sometimes built into the side of a hill or made from wood and was heated with hot stones. "Into this the patient creeps naked, and the heat soon throws him into such a profuse perspiration that it falls from him in large drops. As soon as he finds himself too hot . . . he immediately plunges into the river."[7]

The sweat lodge is a method of health practice that was in place before contact. The Jesuits recognized its healing properties among the Montagnais as early as 1730, and noted that "this method of producing perspiration is a sovereign remedy for languor, rheumatism, inflammation, pains in the side, and minor aches; in a word, it is worth many baths."[8]

Part of the initiation ceremony of the Midewiwin includes a visit to the sweat lodge for "vapour baths" to purify the spirit before the initiation can occur. The candidate for initiation is seated in the sweat lodge and is given water to pour over the hot rocks to create the vapours. The vapours are purifying agents that help the candidate ponder the serious nature of the upcoming initiation.[9]

The Jesuit priests described what they witnessed of the Algonquin people following the sweat lodge when they visited New France:

> They keep themselves well (principally in Summer) by the use of hot rooms and sweat boxes, and by the bath. They also use massage, afterwards rubbing the whole body with seal oil, causing them to emit an odor which is very disagreeable to those not accustomed to it. Nevertheless, when this oiling process is over, they can stand heat and cold better, and their hair is not caught in the branches, but is slippery, so that rain and tempest do not injure the head, but glide over it to the feet; also that the mosquitoes (which are very vicious there in Summer, and more annoying than one would believe) do not sting so much in the bare parts, etc. They also use tobacco, and inhale the smoke as is done in France. This is without doubt a help to them, and upon the whole rather necessary, considering the great extremes of cold and bad weather and of hunger and overeating or satiety which they endure; but also many ills arise from it, on account of its excessive use. It is the sole delight of these people when they have some of it, and also certain Frenchmen are so bewitched with it that, to inhale its fumes, they would sell their shirts. All their talks, treaties, welcomes, and endearments are made under the fumes of this tobacco. They gather around the fire, chatting and passing the pipe from hand to hand, enjoying themselves in this way for several hours. Such is their inclination and custom.[10]

Not only did the hot baths and sweat lodge predate contact, but they also evolved with the environmental and health changes that the Europeans brought. Their use continues today.

In addition to the practical aspects of the hot baths and sweat lodges, Waldram describes Andrew's observations in the late 18th century. He pays special attention to "conjurors" or "jugglers" who were highly involved with spirits and the spiritual aspects of healing.[11]

2.1.2   Conjurers and Jugglers

The ability to contact spirit helpers to assist in diagnosing and treatment was important in early society. The degree to which a person could summon spirits denoted a certain standing in society. Graham described this practice in the later 18th century:

> Jugglers or conjurors are very numerous amongst them (Cree). They are generally men who are good hunters, and have a family; some of them are very clever at it. They are supposed to have intelligence with the Evil Spirit [actually the Creator], and by that means can procure anything to be done for the good or injury of others, foretell events, pacify the malignant spirit when he plagues them with misfortunes, and recover the sick. They have also several tricks of sleight of hand; such as swallowing a string with a musket ball hanging to it; taking it directly out at the fundament; pretending to blow one another down; swallowing bear's claws, and vomiting them up; extracting them from wounds, or the breast, mouth etc. of a sick person; firing off a gun and ball to remain behind; and a thousand other pranks which make them be held in great esteem by the rest.[12]

In 1771, Samuel Hearne described the effects of jugglery or conjuring as an important aspect of physical healing among the Dene:

> Though the ordinary trick of these conjurers may be easily detected, and justly exploded, being no more than the tricks of common jugglers, yet the apparent good effect of their labors on the sick and diseased is not so easily accounted for. Perhaps the implicit confidence placed in them by the sick may at times, leave the mind so perfectly at rest, as to cause the disorder to take a favorable turn; and a few successful cases are quite sufficient to establish the doctor's character and reputation.[13]

In 1823, among the Potawatomi of Muskwawasepeotan (town of the old red wood creek) near Fort Wayne, Indiana, American explorers confirmed the Potawatomi's use of healing practices that were distinct from jugglery:

> Among the Potawatomi, the practice of medicine is considered quite distinct from that of jugglery. Both are in great repute, but it appears that there is not interference. The man of medicine has, it is true, recourse to spells and incantations to add to the virtue of the plants which he uses: but this is totally unconnected with the avocations of the sorcerer and juggler whose object is amusement.[14]

In his seminal work on the Midewiwin, Walter James Hoffman reviewed the work of Baron Lahontan, an early explorer (1703). Lahontan described some of the health practices of the Algonquin peoples, and the overlap between ceremony and the application of medicinal plants:

> When the Quack comes to visit the Patient, he examines him very carefully; If the Evil Spirit be here, says he, we shall quickly dislodge him. This said, he withdraws by himself to a little Tent made on purpose, where he dances, and sings houling like an Owl; (which gives the Jesuits Occasion to say, That the Devil converses with 'em.) After he has made an end of this Quack Jargon, he comes and rubs the Patient in some part of his Body, and pulling some little Bones out of his Mouth, acquaints the Patient, That these very Bones came out of his Body; that he ought to pluck up a good heart, in regard that his Distemper is but a Trifle; and in fine, that in order to accelerate the Cure, 't will be convenient to send his own and his Relations Slaves to shoot Elks, Deer, &c., to the end they may all eat of that sort of Meat, upon which his Cure does absolutely depend. Commonly these Quacks bring 'em some Juices of Plants, which are a sort of Purges, and are called Maskikik.[15]

It appears that the spirit helpers often assisted the medical doctors for a holistic cure.

2.1.3   Sucking Doctors

Another healing practice has been referred to as "sucking" or "cupping," and its practitioners are referred to as "sucking doctors."[16] The technique is generally used when it is believed that the problem is caused from an object entering the body or if an internal poison or tissue is implicated:

> Most accounts suggest that a sucking horn or tube of some sort is used, although the healer may place his or her lips directly onto the flesh. By sucking and blowing, the object is ultimately removed, and is usually shown to the patient and the others attending. The ceremony involves prayer and singing, sometimes blowing on a whistle, all designed to summon the supernatural assistance required to locate and extract the object.[17]

Among the Chippewa in 1763, Alexander Henry recorded this practice:

> After singing for some time, the physician took one of the bones out of the bison; the bone was hollow; and one end being applied to the breast of the patient, he put the other into his mouth, in order to remove the disorder by suction. Having persevered in this as long as he thought proper, he suddenly seemed to force the bone into his mouth, and swallow it. He now acted the part of one suffering pain but presently finding relief he made a long speech and after this returned to singing, and to the accompaniment of his rattle.[18]

The Jesuit priests recorded:

> All that they do for their sick is to suck them Until Blood comes. I saw one in the hands of the old Medicine-men; one whistled and played on a gourd; another sucked; while the third sang the Song of the Crocodile, whose skin served him as a drum.[19]

Dr. Robert Bell noted in 1823:

> In regard to the practice of medicine proper, the common Indian notion of disease is that it is caused by some evil influence, which must be removed, either by driving off its spirit with the tom-tom and sing-

ing, or by a charm, and by sucking or blowing upon the affected. The idea of drawing or sucking out the evil is the prevailing one in their theory of the practice of medicine.[20]

It appears that, historically, the method of sucking and/or blowing was useful as a healing art throughout various pre-contact Aboriginal societies.

2.1.4 Botanical Cures

There are many useful sources on the botanical medicines and complex pharmacopeias. As the scholar Olive Dickason notes, Aboriginal peoples were by nature physicians, apothecaries, and doctors. They had a large knowledge of "certain herbs, which they use successfully to cure ills that seem to us incurable. . . . The process by which the Amerindians acquired their herbal lore is not clearly understood, but there is no doubt about the results. More than 500 drugs used in the medical pharmacopoeia today were originally used by Amerindians."[21] A testament to the importance of Aboriginal medicinal knowledge lies in the fact that, when Europeans arrived in North America, the fur traders, whalers, missionaries, and traders all turned to the Aboriginal people and their medicines for help. There are numerous examples:

> [P]revent scurvy by brewing teas from spruce bark (rich in Vitamin C); they were able to reduce pain by using Willow extract, which contains salicin (similar to the product aspirin); they had various kinds of anesthetics, emetics, diuretics and medicines that could induce labour or numb labour pains. Plant extracts also acted as antibiotics when applied to wounds.[22]

There were cures for other ailments. Blood-root was said to be an "infallible cure for rheumatism" and was infused in whiskey for that purpose.[23] The root was the only part used in the medicine. It worked as a "powerful and valuable remedy, acting in small doses as a stimulant and expectorant, in over doses producing nausea and vomiting."[24]

Other medicinal plants included spignet, alecampaine, wild turnip, coltsfoot, skunk cabbage, lady's slipper, poke-root, gold thread, liverwort, white root, milkweed, white pond lily, and thistle, as well as pennyroyal, lobelia, balm, winter green, Oswego bitters, white oak, butternut, elder, hemlock, spotted alder, red willow, wild cherry, iron-wood, slippery elm, sumac, beech, hemlock, and basswood.[25] The seeds and plant of the lobelia were used and were said to have been "a favourite with the medicine man among the Indians long before the settlement of Canada by the whites. . . . They are emetic and in small doses expectorant and diaphoretic."[26]

The inner bark of the slippery elm was used by the Montagnais as a "valuable demulcent and emollient, and in the form of effusion has been found highly beneficial in inflammation of the stomach and bowels."[27] Wild cherry bark was strongest when gathered in the fall and acted as a tonic and a sedative.[28] Balsam was considered an excellent remedy for frostbite.[29]

The M'ikma'q used a drop of "the secretion of skunks" to treat toothache and rheumatism, while the Montagnais used the roots of the white water lily and rushes both as a food and a medicine, along with the roots of the thistle. "[W]hen these fail they have recourse to the conjuror's arts, for with many of the Montagnais Indians, when in the woods, the conjuror [medicine man] is still much esteemed and feared."[30] The red willow was also used as a medicine by the Montagnais, who used it as a purgative, and by the Cree, who smoked the inner bark.[31]

In 1823, Dr. Bell noted the use of plant material among the Cree and listed their uses:

> Their *materia mediea* is divided into two branches, good medicines and bad. Among the Crees, if not among other Indians, twenty classes of drugs are recognized. The first nine are all good or beneficial medicines, and the rest are all more or less bad or injurious. The student is first made familiar with the good medicines and then the bad, the worst of all being taught last.[32]
>
> ...
>
> The great majority of their medicines are vegetable, but some are derived from animals, as the beaver, the musk-rat, the skunk, the deer, toads, snakes, insects, etc., while others are mineral, as iron pyrites, gypsum, salt, ochres, clays, ashes, etc. Parts of rare animals, impossible to obtain at the time, may be prescribed as the only means of saving a patient, who appears sure to die in any case.[33]

2.1.5   Other Cures

It is interesting to note how the Potawatomi used the rattlesnake in healing:

> They are often bitten by rattlesnakes; the wound is cured among the Potawatomi by poultices of Seneca snake-root, draughts of violet tea and *Eupatorium perfoliatum*; they have other remedies which they keep secret; the venom of the snake is considered greater at some periods of the moon than at others; in the month of August it is most so. These Indians entertain a high degree of veneration for the rattlesnake, not that they consider it in the light of a spirit, as has frequently but incorrectly been asserted, but because they are grateful to it for the timely warning which it has often given them, of the approach of an enemy. They therefore seldom kill it.[34]
>
> ...
>
> The fang of the snake is held to be a charm against rheumatism and other internal pains; the mode of applying it consists in scratching the affected part until it bleeds. In their rude midwifery, they use the rattle to assist in parturition; it is then administered internally. It is not however, used as an emmenagogue.[35]

The Ojibway people used "Seneca snake," (Seneca snake root) as a "sure remedy for the bite of the rattlesnake."[36] Anthropologist Dr. Frank Speck noted that the Montagnais used snakes for rheumatism and sometimes carried them around in their shirts:

> [A]ccording to the Penobscot belief [a snakeskin] becomes a cure for rheumatism when bound around the infected part. Such a skin must have been taken from a living snake. The idea is no doubt derived from the feeling in the native mind that a creature with so pliable a frame is not only free from stiffness himself, but that contact with him can cure stiffness in others. Similarly a snakeskin, the Malachite say, worn around the head or hatband, will ward off enemies. A snake's tongue taken from a living snake, dried and carried about, will both cure and prevent a toothache. Further south the Mohegan and the Iroquois believe that a toothache can be cured by gently biting the body of a living Green snake.[37]

In relation to the multifaceted turtle, explorer John Josselyn noted in his records of his voyages in 1638 and 1663 that the Massachusetts Indians used the land turtles for the "Ptisick [cough], Consumption [tuberculosis], and some say the Morbus Gallicus [venereal disease]." Josselyn also noted that if the turtle was consumed for a 12-month period that the Consumption and "Great pox" [smallpox] would definitely be cured. The sea turtle mixed with oil or bear grease would make the hair grow; the shell or flesh of a land turtle burned and dissolved in wine and oil would heal sore legs; the shell and egg whites, burned together and pounded, healed chapped nipples in women; if the turtle head was pulverized with it, then the falling out of hair would be prevented; hemorrhoids could be cured by using this mixture if the hemorrhoids were first washed in white wine.[38] Dr. Bell further suggests that the Cree had surgical skills that surpassed "present day skills":

> In surgery, the medicine-men confine themselves to setting bones, dressing wounds and ulcers, and alleviating pain by any means in their power. They never attempt any grave operation, although their general knowledge of anatomy is not to be despised. They resort to cupping by means of sucking-tubes. They sometimes bleed by opening a vein in the arm with a sharp chip of flint. I have some evidence, in the shape of relics discovered in mounds, which leads me to think that certain of the ancient Indians had a better knowledge of surgery than those of the present day.[39]

In 1830, explorer James A. Jones described how "quacks or physicians" were able to set broken bones in a manner that allowed them to heal perfectly and "solid" within eight days. He also recalled how a French soldier in Acadia, suffering daily seizures from epilepsy, was treated by an Indian woman with "two boluses of a pulverized root, the name of which she did not disclose" and thereafter enjoyed a perfect state of health.[40]

2.1.6   The Shaking Tent

The "shaking tent" or "conjuring lodge" had a variety of functions, including the diagnosis of the cause of illness. It seemed to be common in a large geographical range in Canada, particularly among the Montagnais, Northern and Plains Cree, Ojibwa, Saulteaux, Blackfoot, and Assiniboine.[41] In 1823, trader George Nelson described Northern Cree techniques:

[F]requently the shaman was bound hand and foot by his assistants before being placed in the lodge; sometimes he was gagged as well. Shortly after the commencement of the ceremony, with assistants and community members seated around the outside, the ropes that bound the shaman would be thrown out the door or the top of the tent. Then the shaman would sing and invite his spirit helpers, and indeed any spirits to enter the lodge. When they did so, the lodge would often shake violently back and forth. The people outside would then hear a succession of voices of the spirits as they entered and communicated with the shaman. These were not in the voice of the shaman, however, and were sometimes in a language unintelligible to those on the outside (often considered an ancient language). Some of the discussion in the tent was jovial with the spirits and the shaman exchanging jokes, but the spirits also provided important information at the shaman's request. On occasion, an outside participant, such as the sick person, would be invited to enter the tent to see the spirits.[42]

Nelson's reactions showed his exuberance for the ceremony:

I am fully convinced, as much so as that I am in existence, that Spirits of some kind did really and virtually enter [the shaking tent], some truly terrific, but others again quite of different character. I cannot enter into a detail by comparison from ancient and more modern history, but I found the consonance, analogy, resemblance, affinity or whatever it may be termed so great, so conspicuous that I verily believe I shall never forget the impressions of that evening.[43]

The shaking tent ceremony that Nelson witnessed obviously left a deep impression. Each Aboriginal culture determines how one views illness and, thus, one's choice of healing. Some ancient healing rituals that are used in a contemporary mode include the Sun Dance, Yuwipi, Ojibwe Healing Ceremony, Shaking Tent and Shaker Healing Ritual.[44] The ancient knowledge garnered through these ceremonies is important in today's contemporary society.

2.1.7 The Pau Wau

The term "powwow" is a European term. "Pau Wau" means medicine man or conjurer, but it was misconstrued by European settlers. When they witnessed the healing practices of the village shaman, they thought the word referred to "the gathering of natives" who surrounded the medicine man during the healing practices, rather than to the individual healer.[45] On the east coast, shamans were called "powwow" from powin, meaning "shaman."[46] A powwow has also been defined as a "medicine-man; the conjuring of a medicine man over a patient; a dance, feast or noisy celebration preceding a council, expedition, or hunt; a council; or a conference."[47] Rev. Peter Jones was a member of the Midewiwin and an Ojibwa Episcopal clergyman who describes the healing properties of the powwow as "persons who are believed to have performed extraordinary cures, either by the application of roots and herbs or by incantations."[48]

The powwow has been practised historically for its healing powers and the ability to invoke special magic. It is practised today throughout various parts of Canada, and the ceremony continues to hold special healing and health powers.

2.1.8 Traditional Midwifery

The many types of Aboriginal healers across North America included men as well as women. For instance, at times the wife of the medicine man learned healing secrets by healing with herbs. In other communities, they learned medical care from their mothers and grandmothers. Often their powers had to be validated by a dream where a spirit gave them personal healing knowledge. Early Plains Indian medicine women were noted to have a special connection to the spirit world that empowered them to heal.[49]

Interestingly, the function of clan mothers in Iroquois culture and political systems (as important as it is in history and in Iroquois society) was not mentioned in the *Jesuit Relations*,[50] which recorded the interaction between missionaries and the Iroquois in the 1600s. Neither was it mentioned in the journals of any of the other early historians of New France, such as La Potherie[51] or Charlevoix.[52] Either they were unaware of the role of clan mothers, or it was not of importance to them. Yet, few would argue that Iroquois society could have flourished as effectively without clan mothers.[53]

While First Nations, Métis, and Inuit people had important ceremonies and rituals around childbirth, the women mostly assisted other women in birthing. Many may have turned to medicine men (and medicine women) for help as well. The women and midwives who were experienced with childbirth passed on the knowledge needed to ensure a safe birth. The historical evidence shows that pre-contact Aboriginal societies designated midwives formally as well as informally. The Nuu-chah-nulth people translated their word for midwife as "she can do everything." The Coast Salish translated midwife as "to watch, to care," and the Chilcotin people translated the word as the "women's helper."[54]

Inuit families often accompanied women throughout the birth process in a separate snow house.[55] "No one was sheltered from birthing knowledge. Children and young adults gained experience from watching, and men often assisted their wives."[56] Inuit women gave birth "in either a squatting or kneeling position with the midwife behind them, [and the] midwife would often enlist the help of the pregnant woman's husband and female relatives, thus involving the whole family in the process of childbirth."[57]

In 1823, a government expedition to the Lake of the Woods observed that, among the Dakotas, "there are professed midwives but the women are sometimes delivered by their husbands, brothers, sisters; the medicine man is generally present but never operates, his only business is to sing, and to assist by his prayers and incantations. They never bleed during labour."[58]

The same government expedition reported that the Potawatomi had "professed midwives, who are paid for their attendance; these are principally old women. Men are never allowed to assist at the delivery of a woman."[59] Childbirth was seldom fatal, but when it was, "it is attributed to ignorance or carelessness on the part of the midwife."[60]

In 1866, it was reported that midwifery was never practised by Ojibway medicine men but was "left entirely to the female [Ojibway] doctors." It was said that among the "Outchipwais," (Ojibway) that some women held "great reputations as doctors."[61]

In the 1600s, the "Gaspesian" or Acadian Indian (M'ikmaq) women in labour called on medicine men and medicine women. Isobel Dodo was an "Indian doctoress" who lived near Halifax[62] and was a well-known "Indian doctor woman." Isobel was so well-known that the Chain Lakes near Halifax were called "Isobel's Lakes" by the M'ikmaq.[63] M'ikmaq women had specific positioning and places for delivery — in the woods at the foot of a tree, where, "[i]f she suffers pains, her arms are attached above to some pole, her nose, ears and mouth being stopped up. After this, she is pressed strongly on the sides. . . . If she feels it a little too severely, she calls in the jugglers, who come with joy, in order to extort some smoking tobacco. . . ."[64]

"Jugglers" was a term used by Europeans to describe medicine men, demonstrating that men were also sometimes involved in the birthing rituals. As James A. Jones wrote in 1830, the "chief of the village was commonly invested with this dignity. The ceremonies and practices observed by the Acadian jugglers being common to the 'profession' throughout the Indian nations."[65]

Midwifery practices among the British Columbia tribes were highly developed. Before contact with Europeans, midwives were held in high regard among their people. The midwife was trained through a long apprenticeship and was knowledgeable about birth as well as cultural traditions associated with birth.[66] Many of the early visitors to British Columbia commented on the midwives in Aboriginal communities. In 1825, on a coastal visit by a whaling ship, Captain Beechey referred to the Aboriginal women on some islands he visited as having "all learned the art of midwifery: parturition generally takes place during the night-time; the duration of labour is seldom longer than five hours, and has not yet in any case proved fatal. There is no instance of twins, nor of a single miscarriage, except from accidents."[67] It was recorded in 1868 of the Nootka that "[t]hey suffer little during pregnancy or at childbirth, but seldom bear children after the age of about twenty-five. As a rule they have few children and, I think, more boys than girls. Their female relations act as midwives."[68]

In the late 1880s, a committee looking at the northwest tribes in British Columbia observed that the Tlingit used midwives,[69] as did the Kwakiutl.[70] Like many First Nations women, the Kwakiutl woman giving birth was also isolated from others in the community during her labour, with the exception of the "professional midwives" who assisted her.[71] The Bilqula, one of the Coast Salish tribes, had "professional midwives to assist the woman, who is delivered in a small house built for this purpose."[72] The Heiltsuk women gave birth in a special house as well.[73] Many rituals surrounded the midwives' attendance at these births. As Professor Cecilia Benoit notes, traditional techniques and tools used by Aboriginal midwives included, among many others, herbal medicines, seal skins, string, and blades.[74]

In 1900, the Squamish people would engage three or four midwives to attend a birth, and each had specific duties, ranging from cutting the umbilical cord to looking after the mother:

It was customary among the Sk'qo mie [Squamish] women to retire to the woods when they were about to give birth to their children. Usually a woman went alone or accompanied only by her husband. Midwives were called in for the first child, but afterwards only in cases of difficulty or when the labour was unduly prolonged. Usually the woman would fulfill her daily duties to within an hour of the child's birth and be ready to take them up again a few hours afterwards. In the case of first children, parents of standing would engage three or four midwives or experienced women for the occasion. Each had her own special duties to perform. These were prescribed by long-established custom. It was the office of one to sever the umbilical cord and dispose of the after-birth; of another to watch and care for the baby; and of another to "cook the milk" and generally look after the mother.[75]

There were medicines specific to childbirth. The Potawatomi used pieces of the rattlesnake's rattle to induce labour by administering it internally,[76] the Dakota also used the rattlesnake to "administer medicines in such cases, and among these, the rattle of the rattlesnake, in doses of one segment at a time."[77] The M'ikmaq used a small bone from the heart of the moose to aid them in childbirth, "they reduce it to powder and swallow it in water, or in the soup made of the animal."[78]

Medicines were also used to assist with the delivery of the afterbirth. The Dene used a plant they called *hwujrej*, believed to be devil's bush (*fatsia horrida*), to assist in expelling the placenta. The bark of the plant was mashed "while fresh and taken internally with a few drops of water by women just delivered of a child but whose after-birth had not, or could not otherwise, be expelled."[79] If a Potawatomi woman had not expelled the placenta and if the medicines that were provided had not had an effect after several days, her husband would "[take] his wife upon his shoulders and carr[y] her about for some time; the motion is said to assist in its expulsion."[80]

2.2 THE MIDEWIWIN

The Midewiwin is a highly evolved Indigenous hierarchal, religious, and medical system and is sometimes referred to as the "Grand Medicine Society." It is comprised of a society of individuals who gather periodically to perform various healing ceremonies. These practices were recorded as early as 1666, when Father Claude Allouez arrived at Shagawaumikong. The Grand Medicine Society was practising its "greatest purity."[81] The Midewiwin spread from the Ojibwa to neighbouring nations, including Woodlands and Plains Indian groups such as the Saulteaux, Dakota, and Plains Cree.

Based on traditional Ojibwa beliefs, the Midewiwin was integral to the maintenance of health and the instruction of novices in identifying and preparing botanical medicine.[82] Frances Densmore explained that the concept of the Midewiwin "is not so much to worship anything as to preserve the use of herbs for use in prolonging life."[83] The Grand Medicine Society included instruction on how to commune with the spirit world to enhance individual powers to heal. It also taught methods of health maintenance by maintaining harmony with the world and by refraining from breaking social norms. The society taught that the "rectitude of conduct produces length of life and that evil inevitably reacts on the offender."[84]

Chippewa scholar Dr. Gail Guthrie Valaskakis describes the Midewiwin as "more powerful and impressive to the Indian than Christianity is to us today."[85] The Midewiwin is based upon the mythical life of "Manabush,"[86] who secured secrets from the underworld. The secrets contain the purposes of prolonging life and the use of herbs and medicines and spiritual power to cure illness. Although the Midewiwin has other purposes, the primary purpose is to cure the ill. The person who wishes to join the Medwewin is usually ill and will apply to the Mide priest for membership in the hope of being cured. Other reasons to become a Mide priest include replacing a deceased member of the society, being accidently "shot" with the Megis shell while watching a ceremony, or responding to a dream or vision that directed the person to join.

The person wishing to join must apply to a Mide priest, who then presents the request to the Mide council. If accepted, the council sets the fees for initiation, and an instructor is appointed to teach the applicant the Midewiwin. During this period, the applicant is on probation. The applicant must collect his or her fees through blankets, pails, and other material possessions to pay the priests for their services while learning the rituals and medicines of the society. Normally, this probation period lasts for a year. Then the applicant has four or more degrees of initiation, each more complex than the previous one. If the applicant is seriously ill, then he or she has great incentive to progress rapidly. Attendance at Midewiwin rites is compulsory for applicants. Each member of the society owns a medicine bundle or bag made of a pelt (usually otter) that contains sacred objects. During a curing or initiation, an initiate or patient was "shot" with the medicine bag (the pelt of an otter or other animal) containing the sacred white Megis shell in an elaborate ceremony. The patient then spit the shell out of his or her mouth at the end of the ceremony as proof that supernatural power had been carried into their bodies.[87]

The Midewiwin went underground for many years but has since resurfaced, particularly among the Saulteaux of Manitoba. Currently, Midewiwin ceremonies are held yearly in Manitoba and Minnesota.

2.3 Métis Healing

The term Métis refers to persons of mixed Indian and European blood, particularly of French Roman Catholic background. Over the years, various organizations and governments have proposed different criteria for who is Métis. For this reason, it is important to have a more in-depth explanation of who the Métis are in order to effectively examine their healing practices. It is extremely important not only to acknowledge that the criteria for Métis healing practices differ from those of Inuit or First Nations, but the tests that the courts have developed for Métis are different and are included in this section for clarity in understanding their healing activities.[88]

The Métis used a variety of herbs to alleviate physical and other ailments, although some Métis healing practices may have subsided with the arrival of modern medicine. Métis Elder George McDermot says, "If you want to learn about medicines, then you have to come for a walk with me in the bush." Elder McDermot may introduce you to a plant and tell you what it is; it is then up to you to get to know it and to give it an offering. He explains:

> When you pick medicine, you must pick it clean. Talk to it, my little brother. You do not step all over the medicines. You do not disrespect any plants, whether they are big or small, because a small plant can be just as powerful as a large plant. That plant's life is a whole new world to people not familiar. It is a different life altogether, it is a different world view. There is nothing to be afraid of in the bush.[89]

The criteria for Métis healing practices are different from Inuit or First Nations, since the Métis people came into being post contact. The healing practices of the Métis developed through the guidance of First Nation grandmothers long before the Europeans established political or legal controls and before the Supreme Court of Canada articulated tests to prove these rights.

2.4   Inuit Healing[90]

Author John O'Neil suggests that the Inuit sought explanations for their illnesses that were grounded in their relationships with the physical, social, and spiritual environment.[91] The Inuit have a holistic view of health care: "mind, body and spirit are intrinsically linked, and a weakness in one will surface as a weakness in another aspect."[92]

For many Inuit, health signifies the link between the soul (*tanniq*) and the body (*tiimuit*). Consuming country food builds this connection. The belief is that country foods strengthen the Inuit and connect them with the land. It reinforces a spiritual connection between health and the land. Hunting and eating seal, in particular, is essential for the life of the soul and the body.[93] Hunting has always been critical to the Inuit for maintaining good health.[94]

Professor Michele Therrien notes that, among the Inuit of Povurnituq, three forces contribute to their good health. The body is the outcome between the *anirniq* (breath which confers vitality, energy, and warmth), the *tarniq* (the immortal soul of a person), and the *atiq* (name and assurance of one's intellectual development and identity).[95] Therrien states that "the Inuit continue to believe that the *anirniq* disappears upon death, the *tarniq* continues on to survive beyond the individual's passing, and the *atiq* remains a direct bond to their ancestors, the source of life."[96] The balance for Inuit healing was maintained between life, breath, soul, and identity as well as by relying on marine mammals and the goodness of plants.[97]

The Nunavut Arctic College Report, "Interviewing Inuit Elders: Perspectives on Traditional Health," provides an interesting study on healing methods used by the Inuit before contact. The report illustrates the Inuit use of seal and other mammals as well as their use of the plants to create a healthy balance. This healthy norm went "out of balance" only after European diseases were introduced.[98] For instance, Ilisapi, an Inuit elder, spoke about not just the medicinal uses of the seal for cuts and wounds:

What we thought of first was oil for the *qulliq*, the lamp, as that was our only source of heat. The thin layer beneath the blubber would be saved for the dogs. The blubber around the flippers was saved entirely for the lamp. Oil would also be used as ear drops for children with earaches to help them feel better. If a wound was too dry, oil would be applied to keep it moist. I do not know how this was done as I was born after *qallunaat* were already present. Sometimes, when new skin was being formed over a wound and it cracked, oil was applied. It was also applied to skin that had been sunburnt. We would not put much on; just enough to keep the skin from cracking. We grew up around the R.C.M.P. base so we had ointment. If it was packed away in the sled, then we would use seal oil to protect our skin from cracking while we were travelling.[99]

Although Ilisapi grew up around the RCMP base camp, the uses of the seal remained central in Inuit knowledge and practices, and the RCMP acknowledged the Inuit source of this knowledge.[100]

The healing therapies used by the Inuit vary. Some involve touching or breathing upon an individual. Other methods engage a group of people, who accompany the healing process with songs, drums, dance, and spoken words:

The cure has equally a dimension of power. Not the unilateral power of healing but of participatory power in a context known to all: the power of evil spirits possessing the body, or that of a theft of one of the constituents of the person: the power of the *angakkuq* to do away with the illness affecting the body's integrity through the intermediary of his spirit helper; the desire of the illness to submit to the cure and to his prescriptions; to engage not only the individual in the healing but also the participation of the family group and of the community as a whole in the cure; to call out to the animals and the participatory forces of the external world to man through an association of the illness to the excesses found in nature.[101]

In 1823, Dr. Robert Bell noted:

The wild Eskimo appear to suffer fewer diseases that Indians or Whites. . . . They also have a class of medicine-men whose pretensions to perform all kinds of miracles are one of the most extravagant character. They appear to deal almost entirely in the supernatural, and to make little use of medicines. They have no hesitation in declaring to their own people that they can cure all kinds of disease and prolong life indefinitely, if they only choose to do so. They account for their own death by saying that they wish to die, or that that they are overcome by a still greater, but unseen, medicine-man. They say they can and do make themselves larger or smaller at will, or change themselves into some other animal, or enter into a piece of wood or stone; that they can walk on the water or fly in the air; but there is one dispensable condition, — no one must see them. They find themselves powerless to perform these miracles if anyone is looking on.[102]

Connecting medicinal plants to good health, Dr. Bell noted:

The Eskimo, who live entirely on raw animal food, appear to regard any edible vegetable substance as medicine. They eat with great relish the northern blueberries and cranberries, and where they cannot get these, they take the leaves of the dwarf willows, a plant of the parsley family, called "scurvy-grass" (*Lingusticum*), and almost any kind of seaweed. On the shores of Hudon's Straits they collect and eat the starchy roots of *Polygonum viviparum*, which grows there in considerable abundance. It is a singular circumstance that, notwithstanding the sameness of their food, and the fact that they never wash either their bodies or their clothing, the Eskimo appear never to be afflicted with scurvy, whereas white men, under a similar regimen, would be almost certain to be attacked.[103]

In a study on the Inuit use of plants to maintain good health and treat sickness, Professor Paleah L. Black reports that, prior to the arrival of mass medical evacuations and nursing stations, Inuit elders described their health practices as involving the mind, body, and spirit. In fact, the four Inuit elders interviewed in the Black Study recalled a detailed pharmacopoeia. In 2006, Black *et al* noted the Inuit uses of plants in their ethnobotanical Nunavut study of 13 species. The study assessed the level of consensus among the elders for their medicinal uses of the plant species as well as for the use of a particular plant for a particular illness.[104]

The elders in the study stressed the importance of these plants as part of their regular diet to maintain health. One elder stated, "We were very rarely sick before we moved into settlements. I was taught to eat some plants from the land so I was not sick."[105] Because the Inuit existed largely on an animal-based diet, the use of plants to maintain general health would have been important, as plants contain antioxidants.[106] Additional studies confirm that willows and lichens contain antioxidant and antimicrobial properties,[107] brown algae possess antiviral properties, and fucoidan provides additional food components.[108]

The results of the Black Study are important because they conclude that Inuit medical knowledge is well preserved and was in existence before European contact. The Inuit developed knowledge over generations about how to survive and stay healthy under harsh conditions, and how to make the best use of the overall species diversity, which is limited compared to the south. The Inuit's ability to use these sources came from their traditional knowledge of how to practise good health in the land of their ancestors.

2.4.1   *The Inuit Sled Dog and Healing*

The *qimmiq* is also known as the Canadian Inuit dog, Inuit dog, Canadian Eskimo dog, or *canis familiaris borealis*. This topic is important because of the close human connection to dogs, the dog being the non-human person, the counterpart of the Inuit. The dog served critical functions in Inuit health, not only by providing hunting methods but also as a vital aid in healing the sick. Author Frances Lévesque describes the origins of the *qimmiq* as arriving in North America about the same time as humans did, or right after them. "[T]he *qimmiq* is, with the Malamute, the only dog breed that came into the world on the American continent. While the Malamute originated in Alaska and remained there until today, the *qimmiq* migrated towards Canada from Alaska with its Thule masters towards the year 1000."[109] An Inuit elder comments:

> The most important part of the dog is that way back from the beginning of the world the Inuit have been having dog teams and they have saved lives from starvation and the dog team helped a lot to the Inuit, and that's the most important part of dog team.[110]

The elder is clarifying the fact that the Inuit sled dog has existed as long as the Inuit have. The dog was used for a variety of purposes, yet the connection between human health and the Inuit sled dog was the most important. The *qimmiq* take part in many aspects of Inuit daily life and survival: hunting, clothing, warmth, hauling, and transportation. As a result, the dog team is intimately tied to the physical, emotional, psychological, and spiritual health — indeed, the total well-being — of the hunter and the hunter's family.[111] Lévesque notes some of the utilitarian purposes of the sled dog, not just for transportation but for hunting; for many Inuit populations, the dog may have been more useful for hunting than for transportation. When dogs who have outlived their usefulness are killed, their fur is used for mitts or other clothing. In cases of famine, dog meat was eaten as a last resort.[112]

The cultural aspects of the dog team and the dog/Inuit relationship are important: "Dog teams are more than just a form of transportation; they are an integrated part of Inuit life."[113] Quite simply, the Inuit could not have survived as a society without the sled dog. The purposes fulfilled by the sled dog go to the core elements of Inuit-ness. The *qimmiq*-Inuit relation marks the central reality of Inuit society. Examining the role the dog plays in the Inuit mythical universe, Lévesque reports that the dog has a place at both the origin and the end of Inuit life.[114] Direct evidence confirms that the *qimmiq* originated in North America and was not introduced from Europe, and has always had an integral role in Inuit society. The dog forms a spiritual, symbolic, and economic whole with its master, and this bond can be traced to the dog's place in the ancestral Inuit order and relationship with the ecology. Shannon offers the concept of sled dogs as non-human persons:

> The reason for calling an animal a non-human person is to emphasize the relationship the animal has with human society according to some peoples' particular perceptions of the natural world.[115]

> He or she must be willing to accept that social life and communication among subarctic hunter-gatherers include a wider range of "persons" than the language and culture of social science generally admit.[116]

In Inuit society, the *qimmiq* is distinguished as a member of human society: it is the only animal that is given a name (*atiq*); it has a social identity. Inuit children are also given an *atiq*. Lévesque argues that because the dog is given an *atiq*, it is accorded the same social standing as a human being.

As such, the dog is acknowledged as a vital and equal part of Inuit society:

> The *atiq* of a dog is just like the *atiq* of a human being. It is an autonomous entity with its own characteristics, allowing the dog that carries it to integrate into a particular social network. Since it has an *atiq* as humans do, the dog is part of human society. By giving it an *atiq*, the dog is part of human society.[117]

Lévesque explains the significance of the *atiq*:

> The *atiq* is an autonomous and immortal entity carrying a group of qualities, abilities and desires. Guemple writes that the *atiq* incorporates the status, the nature and the attributes of the one who possesses it. In fact, the *atiq* gives the one who holds it a defined social status within society.
>
> Without an *atiq*, a human being is nothing, both at the personal and at the social level. As such, the *atiq* is the symbol of social continuity.
>
> The *atiq* always comes from a deceased person or a person who is about to die. As a result, an elder may share with future parents the desire for his or her *atiq* to be attributed to the child about to be born. *The deceased who wants his or her atiq to be given to a child will appear in the dreams of the parents or the relatives of the new parents. In this way, elders and deceased people may decide to live again, through their* atiq, *in the bodies of newborns.*[118]

Dogs may be named after humans, deceased relatives, aunts, uncles, or grandparents. These deceased relatives may "decide to live again, through their *atiq*." In these cases, the Inuit will therefore not only respect the social relationship through the dog's *atiq*[119] but may also consider the dog as a deceased ancestor.[120] Lévesque explains:

> Hadwen points out that the Inuit from eastern Arctic Canada, for instance, did not want to sell or trade their dogs because of the "cultural attachment" they feel towards them. In terms of the Polar Inuit, a part of their population being relatives originally from Baffin Island, trading and selling dogs only occurs among close relatives. To this end,

Freuchen recounts that one day an Inuk refused to sell him a dog telling him "I cannot sell it, for it is my grandfather."[121]

It is interesting to note that when Christianity was brought into Inuit communities, at least in Repulse Bay, some sled dogs were also Christianized. In Naujaat (Repulse Bay), Freuchen reported that the sled dogs had to wear crucifixes on their necks. In the town of Iglulik, the Christian leader Umik asked that all visiting people shake hands with the dogs.[122]

2.4.2 Connection to Human Health

Some Inuit believe that the relation between humans and dogs makes the difference between health and sickness. In his article, "Adaptive Innovation Among Recent Eskimo Immigrants in the Eastern Canadian Arctic," Freeman claims that Inuit from Port Harrison (relocated to Grise Fiord in the 1950s) believe deeply in the correlation between human health and the dog.[123] Similar to Freeman's and Taylor's accounts, some Inuit spoke of the connection between human health and the dog: when an illness came to a household, it would be better if the sickness was taken by a dog rather than by any of the people. An elder recalled that his father used to tell him to always have a dog in case of sickness coming to the household so the dog could take it from the people in the house.[124] It was clarified that "dogs should not be beaten for biting a human. If the dog was beaten the wound would become worse because the *inua* [spirit] of the dog would be angry."[125] It was also noted that some Inuit use hair from the dog to dress the wound of a dog bite.

In Northern Baffin Island, it was believed that the death of a dog that bit a person would prevent the person from healing; therefore, dogs that had bitten people were killed only after the victim healed.[126] If the owner was ill, dogs could also be mutilated or killed to heal their owner; for instance, an Inuk Elder from Salluit recalls:

[W]hen a person or other members of his/her family became sick they would kill sometimes their most valued dog and subsequently would be healed from their sickness. . . . Whenever someone, an adult or a child was very ill, a dog had to be killed in hopes of becoming healed as we value people more than a dog and whenever they killed a dog that sick person would be healed.[127]

Laugrand and Oosten also recall that Reverend Edmund James Peck, a missionary in Nunavik during the late 1800s, noted a similar circumstance: an Inuk who was ill killed his beloved dog in hopes of recovering from his illness.[128] Laugrand and Oosten also report that, when the dog is mutilated and killed for the purpose of healing its master, the assumption is that this works because the dog is part of society and forms a whole with the master.[129] The mere fact that the dog and its owner are one makes it possible for a transfer of relations between them: "by killing the dog or destroying part of the dog, significant others (spirits, enemies) will consider the patient as dead and there is no need to kill him anymore."[130] These relationships occur within a whole, therefore the transfer between the dog and its master is possible: "the dog substitutes itself for its master and dies instead of him. This way, the master may heal. Therefore, it is only because the master and his dog form a whole that this transfer of relation is possible and that the mutilation or elimination of a dog can help its master to heal."[131]

Peck also reports that, west of Hudson Bay, "the angakkuq questions the sick man of his past life and deeds. After confession the conjuror orders one of the sick man's dogs to be shot,"[132] quite likely for the same reasons as Laugrand and Oosten described. In another story, when a woman went back for a dog that was lame, the dog uttered a song in response:

My dog's down there
Its skin down there
Its foot-sole down there
My gift, my present,
The one without a pattern, ajai
There, there, yonder
A skin boat put off from land
At (the spirit) Manilik's he was born
Aijauna uwshale-una
Ufvatitaujaq
Niklatitaujaq
Poq poq poq![133]

The last few lines are "special dog words that cannot be turned into comprehensible human speech, but they are of powerful effect, driving out evil spirits, when uttered by a sick person."[134] It may be that the song was a gift from the dog to the woman for her to use for future healing purposes.

Many healing substances are derived from the dog, such as urine, saliva, and excrement. According to Salumi Ka&&ak Qalasiq from Kangir&iniq (Rankin Inlet), the urine of old dogs was used to cure patients. Felix Pisuk, from the same community, tried the remedy as a child, but he immediately threw it up. Pisuk stated, "I have heard that some people when they are sick cut themselves a little, then get the dog to lick them because of its healing power."[135] Manilaq, a Netsilik woman, explained to early explorer Knud Rasmussen:

> When I was a girl my grandmother took me out with her and found old dog turds for me. Every single turd I had to wet with my tongue, and when it was softened I had to rub myself with it all over my breast and stomach. That made me vigorous, for the old shaman told me that dog turds, used in the right way, possess magic powers and a kind of fountain of youth.[136]

Among the Copper Inuit, Rasmussen noted that the "saliva of a dog is good for certain ailments, especially those of long duration. The saliva must be swallowed, and then something must be given to the dog in payment, for instance a handsome collar of skin."[137] Diamond Jenness referred to the healing qualities of dog saliva. He related that his dog was thought to restore lost souls of patients; a white caribou fur was attached to its neck in recognition of this.[138] The head of a dog could also be used for its healing properties: "in Mittimatalik, a dog's head was given to a boy to eat when he is one year old, so that he will have a strong head."[139] Another Inuit healing method to ward off disease is to consecrate him as a dog to Sedna. In this case, he would get a dog's name and would be required to wear throughout life a harness over his inner jacket.[140]

These reports of the healing properties of the *qimmiq* give indisputable evidence that the *qimmiq* is not "just a dog" as far as the Inuit are concerned. The sled dog is more than a beloved family pet or a loved sub-member of the family or even a working dog. It is a part of the circle of the Inuit family, an integral family member that is connected holistically to the individual, the family, the community, and Inuit society. The Inuit and dog live in a symbiotic interdependence: neither is able to exist without the other. One may even say that the Inuit consider the dog as an ancestor. The life of the dog may be sacrificed in certain circumstances to heal its human companion and family. The existence of the *qimmiq* bores directly into the Inuit's root of being and embodies a core value of Inuit society. Its existence and its use for purposes of health and healing can be considered an inherent right to life for the Inuit. It is also understandable that when the RCMP slaughtered the Inuit sled dogs in the 1950s to the 1970s that the core and spiritual being of the Inuit was torn and deeply affected, causing great stress on the human body.[141]

CONCLUSION

In summary, although Aboriginal medical systems have often been misunderstood and undermined, they embody "sets of coherent beliefs and practices that were well integrated within society which served important social, religious, as well as medical functions."[142] As O'Neil and Postl note, much of what was written by the explorers and missionaries was presented from their vantage point. They did not share the world view of those they observed. As a result, they often failed to see Aboriginal medicine in its own terms — as practised by its own practitioners.[143]

These healing practices were comprised of intricate ceremonies, which served to cement them into the laws of their respective societies. Documented evidence amply supports the conclusion that the therapeutic ceremonies and healing practices were integral to the existence of Aboriginal societies. The Jesuits, the explorers, and the traders who witnessed and wrote about these practices acknowledged their importance. The documented operations of these practices affirm an Aboriginal right to health and an Aboriginal right to achieve and maintain health by traditional Aboriginal means. Europeans did not teach Aboriginal people how to heal or practise healing methods; these methods of healing and health-preserving ways were already in existence when the Europeans arrived in North America.

A large body of historical evidence confirms that the explorers, missionaries, and traders witnessed healing practices by the people they encountered. Aboriginal healing practices cannot be dismissed as merely incidental to Aboriginal society in the pre-contact or pre-control period. Nor were the practices common to all societies — another test outlined by the courts. Instead, they differed nation to nation. They are distinct, integral aspects of distinct Aboriginal societies. As such, they stand as generic rights under the larger umbrella of Aboriginal rights. Unfortunately, with the influx of European settlement, the diseases that they brought caused death, destruction, and a legacy of ill health.

CHAPTER THREE

Historical Health Influences

3.1 HISTORICAL DETERMINANTS OF HEALTH

Following European contact, the health of Aboriginal peoples declined dramatically. A number of factors contributed to this, including epidemics of new diseases; the loss of traditional lifestyles; the change to a nutritionally inadequate diet; the depletion of food resources; the dislocation of life styles; confinement to reserve land; and the implementation of laws to force assimilation, the residential school system in particular. Correlating these historical health influences to current Aboriginal health is the focus of this chapter. Maureen Lux's *Medicine That Walks*[1] and the *Report of the Royal Commission on Aboriginal Peoples*[2] document how federal government policies caused suffering, hunger, starvation, disease, and death to Aboriginal peoples. The following section will highlight some events and time frames that influenced current federal Aboriginal health policies. It will also indicate how these historical events and policies have played a critical role in shaping the health of Aboriginal people today.

3.1.1 Epidemics

Documentation confirms that the Aboriginal population must have been large enough to allow smallpox and other infectious diseases to spread far from their origins on the southern extremes of North America.[3] Although other diseases were also spreading at the time — measles, influenza, typhoid, and typhus — none were as virulent as smallpox. Epidemics that cycled every seven to 14 years meant that the existing population had no time to reproduce a fully immune generation — or even to reproduce minimally.[4] Babies born to survivors died in subsequent epidemics. In this way, population levels were depressed for centuries.[5]

At least until 1918, epidemics devastated Aboriginal people as far north as Alaska and as far west as British Columbia. Death occurred in ninety to ninety-five per cent of the Indigenous population "by epidemic disease, warfare, slavery, starvation and complete and utter despair, with most dying within one hundred years of contact."[6] High smallpox mortality continued among North American Indians of the northern Plains and Upper Great Lakes in 1781 to 1782, with as much as 60 per cent of some groups succumbing to the disease.[7]

Besides smallpox, other diseases spread rapidly: tuberculosis, cholera, scrofula, chickenpox, diphtheria, pertussis (whooping cough), venereal disease, and poliomyelitis.[8] These diseases could not sustain themselves in small groups of hunters and gatherers, but their impact on larger groups who lacked immunity was enormous. Graham-Cumming describes the European races as being "heavily infected and had been for centuries. Chronic rather than acute cases were extremely common among them, persons not seriously incapacitated by the disease but still capable of actively spreading the infection."[9]

Death rates were high, as smallpox ravaged the Indigenous peoples after contact.[10] In 1612, the Jesuits reported that the Indians were

astonished and often complain that since the French mingle with and carry on trade with them, they are dying fast and the population is thinning out. . . . "One by one the different coasts according as they have begun to traffic with us, have been more reduced by disease. . . ."[11] Between 1634 and 1640, a series of epidemics broke out, with smallpox being a principle component. . . . By 1640 there were only 10,000 Huron left out of an estimated 20,000 to 35,000 in the early 1600s. . . . The Iroquois themselves suffered a similar fate two decades later.[12]

In 1843, Indian Agent Moses Perley told the Nova Scotia legislature that he had spoken with many older Indian people who said that they were childless. In reality, all of their children had died from these diseases:

[T]hat they had had from 8 to 12 Children each, who had died in infancy from Measles, Whooping Cough, Scarlet Fever, Croup, Typhus, Small Pox and a variety of other Diseases to which Children are subject. The Infants are much exposed by the wandering habits of their parents, who rely almost entirely upon their own modes of treatment with roots and herbs.[13]

In 1849, the Shubenacadie chiefs signed a petition to the Queen indicating that with death and disease, and having been driven off their lands, their nation was "like a withering leaf in the summer sun."[14] The petition pointed out that "[b]efore you came we had no sickness, our old men were wise, and our young men were strong, now smallpox, measles and fevers destroy our tribe."[15] The suffering was described:

> The disease began with serious pains inside the intestines which made the liver and the lungs rot. It then turned into pox that were so rotten and poisonous that the flesh fell off them in pieces full of evil-smelling beasties. . . . the skin and flesh of the sick often remained stuck to the hands; and the smell was too strong to endure. . . . This was a form of smallpox or pox so loathsome and evil-smelling that none could stand the great stench that emerged from them. For this reason many died unattended, consumed by the worms that grew in the wounds of the pox and were engendered in their bodies in such abundance and of such great size that they caused horror and shock to any who saw them.[16]

Tuberculosis ran rampant throughout North America. Some reports claim that tuberculosis may have been present among the ancient inhabitants of North America prior to the arrival of Europeans. Deformities in the bones of some very old skeletons (Huronia and Inca) suggest that they may have resulted from tubercular lesions. These findings have led some anthropologists to assume that tuberculosis has always existed in Aboriginal society.[17]

However, Indian people had not completely developed an immunity to the disease. If the Indian population ever had tuberculosis, they eradicated the disease through attrition and the natural elimination of the infected. At contact, exposure to the bacteria was followed by a reduction of the antibodies against it, which resulted in a low resistance. Evidence further suggests that, over centuries, Aboriginal populations eliminated most infectious diseases. The survival of the fittest created a race of healthy human beings who were, however, extremely vulnerable to alien invading organisms.[18] The Jesuits noted that, "with the coming of the whites; however the disease (tuberculosis) appeared in a virulent form and early in the seventeenth century the Jesuits recorded in the *Relations* the presence among the natives of the glandular type — scrofula."[19]

The Plains Indians stayed remarkably healthy until the end of the 18th century, when they also were ravaged by smallpox, measles, whooping cough, and venereal disease. Tuberculosis was not cited until 1800, when it surfaced along the Red and Saskatchewan Rivers. Tuberculosis became epidemic, destroying those unable to build up a resistance to it and lingering among those who could. All forms were present, but glandular and pulmonary dominated.[20] The first case was recorded by H. Y. Hind in 1857.[21] By the time of the Northwest Conflict in 1885,[22] tuberculosis was killing Indian and Métis people on the prairies at an epidemic rate.

In 1878, immigrants began entering Canada in large numbers and settling close to the Indian reserves, bringing latent tuberculosis. Forced attendance at poorly ventilated residential schools not only facilitated but ensured the rapid spread of tuberculosis.[23]

i) Tuberculosis in Residential Schools

In 1897, Inspector Benson, head of the Department of Indian Affairs school branch, wrote to Indian Affairs Department Secretary J. D. McLean about the dangerously unhealthy conditions at the schools. He followed up with another report about the deplorable building conditions, including extremely poor ventilation systems that should have been remedied immediately. Inspector Benson's recommendations were not heeded:

> Outlets for the escape of foul air are provided in some rooms at a few schools but without adequate provision for the admission of fresh air, and it is scarcely any wonder that our Indian children who have a hereditary tendency to phthisis, [tuberculosis] should develop alarming symptoms of this disease after a short residence in some of our schools, brought on by exposure to draughts in school rooms and sleeping in over-crowded, over-heated and unventilated dormitories.[24]

Tuberculosis was widespread in the residential schools. From 1884 to 1890, tuberculosis specialist Dr. R. G. Ferguson reported a mortality rate of the Qu'Appelle and File Hills Cree at 90 deaths per 1,000.[25] It was not until the early 1900s that the federal government finally acknowledged something was gravely wrong with the health of Aboriginal people in Canada. In 1904, Dr. Peter Bryce was appointed General Medical Superintendent of the Department of Indian Affairs.[26] He was the first to notice that cancer and kidney diseases were rare, and that venereal disease and alcoholism were not as rampant as believed. He did, however, discover that the mortality rates of many bands were extremely high, and concluded that tuberculosis was an epidemic in progress. In 1906, Bryce issued a report to the government that stated that the "Native people had a death rate more than double that of the general population and in some provinces more than three times."[27]

In 1910, Duncan Scott introduced some measures to combat the conditions that were exposed by Bryce and others. However, as scholar Brian Titley clarifies,

> The elimination of the worst of the industrial schools and the new regulations introduced by Scott in 1910 did not entirely eradicate the hazards of residential education. Ill-health, for instance, persisted at unacceptably high rates in places.[28]
>
> . . . .
>
> [S]tudents with contagious diseases were often enrolled merely to secure the per capita grant. Within the institutions, poor ventilation, inadequate diet and little medical attention combined to create the prime conditions for epidemics.[29]

Government records noted that "regarding Jesse Williams, she appears to need a lot of hospital treatment, I am inclined to think that the state of her health is such that it might be wise to discharge her, she is becoming an expensive pupil."[30] The federal government's severe underfunding of health-related problems was one direct cause of student illness and death.

In 1918, the year the Spanish flu epidemic hit Canada, Duncan Scott eliminated the medical inspector position "for reasons of economy."[31] Prairie schools in Alberta were some of the hardest hit by both the flu and tuberculosis:

> Not surprisingly, the Spanish influenza epidemic that hit Canada along with most of the rest of the Western world at the end of the First World War proved devastating, particularly in prairie schools. The degree to which residential schools were not equipped to cope with a pandemic can be measured in the words of the principal of

the Methodist Red Deer school, who described "conditions at this school" as "nothing less than criminal" and "a disgrace." Like almost all boarding and industrial schools, Red Deer had "no isolation ward and no hospital equipment of any kind. The dead, the dying, the sick and the convalescent were all together."[32]

In 1922, Dr. Bryce released *The Story of a National Crime: An Appeal for Justice to the Indians of Canada*, a report on the conditions of the disease-infested residential schools. Bryce reported that, "regarding the health of the pupils, the report states that 24 per cent of all the pupils which had been in the schools were known to be dead, while at one school on the File Hills reserve, which gave a complete return to date, 75 per cent, were dead at the end of the 16 years since the school opened."[33]

Dr. Bryce analyzed these shocking statistics from every perspective: the influences of climate, economic conditions, income, diet, and housing. He printed circulars in Cree and published a textbook on hygiene, which was distributed to Indian Agents throughout the country.[34] Although Dr. Bryce's report made recommendations to improve the health of the children in the schools, the federal government refused to act on them. It claimed the costs associated with such improvements were too high. In addition, the churches involved opposed such reforms.[35] Apparently, they did not consider the cost effectiveness of shutting down the schools altogether. Bryce left his position as Chief Medical Officer in 1921 and his position was not staffed again until 1927. During this six-year gap, no efforts were made to contain the numerous epidemics that were spreading through the Aboriginal population in Canada.[36]

In 1924, the Canadian Tuberculosis Society reported that, while Aboriginal people comprised 1/22nd of the total population of British Columbia, they accounted for one-quarter of all deaths in the province.[37] In 1934, the Department of Indian Affairs admitted that "it is impossible to admit to a sanatorium more than a very small proportion of Indians who are recommended for such care."[38] In 1937, an editorial appearing in the *Canadian Tuberculosis Association Bulletin* commented, "the facilities for early diagnosis, treatment and prevention that have been used to such good advantage in the White population have never been made available for the attack on the Indian problem."[39]

At that time, official government procedure demanded that an Indian agent give permission for an Indian to be hospitalized and permission from the head office in Ottawa was a prerequisite for an Indian to be admitted to a tuberculosis sanatorium.[40] The high rates of tuberculosis among the Indian population were submitted as proof that "Native people were incapable of making the transition from nomadism to 'civilization.'"[41] Before tuberculosis was unmistakably evident as the cause of death and was shown to be killing Aboriginal youth in epidemic proportions, the medical profession did little to curtail its spread. The cost involved in treating Indians was clearly a factor behind this inaction, again, because the government claimed it lacked the funds to deal with the situation.[42] It was not until anti-tuberculosis campaigns pressured the Medical Branch that they finally took action to curb the disease. Maureen Lux explains:

> The increasing cultural and professional authority of medicine in the first half of the twentieth century worked to construct Native people as biologically inferior and disease-prone. In the same vein, the anti-tuberculosis campaigns in Canada framed Native people as a disease menace to themselves and others. Although living conditions were often pointed to as a health concern, it was Native people's lack of resisting power that identified them as inferior. From this, it followed that what the people [Aboriginal people] most needed were those inherited qualities that separated the civilized races from the primitive — qualities that were subsumed in Dr. Ferguson's phrase "white blood." That prescription for good health, coming from one of the country's leading medical authorities on tuberculosis, lent medical certainty to what the department had always contended: that Native people would only gain the good health enjoyed by non-Native Canadians when they ceased being Native.[43]

Although in Treaty 6 it was clear that the federal government had an obligation to provide health services, the government rejected any legal or treaty requirements to provide health services to Aboriginal people, arguing that they did so "for self-protection."[44]

While the Indian population was regularly screened for tuberculosis, the Métis population was not. The rate of tuberculosis among the Métis, however, was high and remained so until the early 1960s, when the government's health advisors realized that the rate of tuberculosis might not be associated with the biological factor of having "Indian blood" but might be due to socioeconomic conditions, such as poverty. The 1963 report, *The*

Métis in Alberta Society, suggested that the Métis occupied a class position of poverty within the context of the larger Euro-Canadian structure. It further suggested that the solution to the disease problem lay in "extending civilization northward and increasing Métis participation in it."[45] In other words, if the Métis were "civilized" like the Euro-Canadian settlers, they would enjoy a comparable health status.

By the end of the 19th century, most western Métis could be found living on the margins of First Nation and Euro-Canadian societies. Many lived on lands adjacent to First Nation reserves. Others lived along road allowances on the outskirts of Euro-Canadian settlements, and were considered squatters on provincial lands. Although most held strong ties of kinship with people on reserves, they were denied treaty and other benefits and services because of their ambiguous legal status. The northern Métis settlements were impoverished. Infectious diseases, particularly tuberculosis and syphilis, became rampant.[46] The federal government denied the Métis the provision of health services, and the provinces provided services only when it was evident that the good health of the non-Aboriginal population was threatened.

As early as 1895, the first Métis settlement, St. Paul des Métis, was established by the federal government; ten years later it was abolished in favour of public homesteading. The 1938 *Population Betterment Act* was passed by the Alberta Legislature that formed 12 Métis Settlements. This region is now home to eight communities, known collectively as the Métis Settlements of Alberta.[47]

The Ewing Commission was created in 1935 to examine the problems of health, education, and general welfare of the Métis population in Alberta. The Métis Association of Alberta produced evidence of widespread infectious diseases from six doctors and Indian agents in the Grouard area. However, they noted that "the reliability of these testimonies was challenged by the Alberta government by Dr. Harold Orr, a physician employed by the Alberta Department of Health. Earlier, Dr. Orr had alerted his minister to the political implications of increased health expenditures on the Métis."[48]

When the Ewing Commission report was released, it reported that the Métis did, in fact, experience ill health. The commission noted that "many Métis lived far from any health professionals and lacked money both to cover travel costs to consult them and to pay for medical services rendered. Traveling doctors and nurses, who commonly visited 'Indian reserves,' rarely came to these Métis communities." The commission further noted the "poor sanitary conditions which characterized Métis homes and the lack of proper food (implying in fact that some Métis were, in effect, periodically starving)."[49]

The commission stated that, as a result of the federal government scrip policy,[50] "large numbers of the Métis population are at this time, in this Province, destitute, and their health is jeopardized, their education neglected, and their welfare in the worst possible condition."[51] Further, a Métis "is an outcast, and he is in far worse plight than the Indian, the Indian is far better treated than the Half-breed."[52] However, the report concluded that, while the health problems were serious, they were not any more serious than among the white settlers. The commission advised against making the Métis wards of the state, as the Indians were, but the commission recommended that parcels of land be set aside for the Métis where hospitals could be constructed and the services of a travelling physician could be provided. Métis colonies were established under the authority of the *Métis Population Betterment Act of 1937*.[53] Some of these recommendations were carried out, but it remains unclear to what extent the Métis were required to pay for medical services.

For the Inuit, tuberculosis was particularly virulent.[54] The disease came to them from missionaries, whalers, and growing numbers of European settlers. In 1969, Dr. Graham-Cumming, the medical officer of National Health and Welfare, noted, "Surprisingly little evidence has been found to suggest the Eskimo and Indian populations have had any major health problems before the venturing Europeans."[55] Yet by the 1950s, at least one-third of all Inuit had tuberculosis; in 1956, one in seven Inuit, or approximately 1,600 people, were in a sanatorium in southern Canada. The average stay was two and half years, although many stayed longer. At the time, bed rest, fresh air, and seclusion in sanatoria miles away from home and family were considered the cure for tuberculosis patients.

The Inuit were considered untreatable in their tents and snow huts. They were also the last of the three groups of Aboriginal people to be provided tuberculosis treatment by the federal government.[56] From 1950 to 1969, the *C. D. Howe* coast guard ship made annual summer trips to the Eastern Arctic. It contained a small hospital, which included an operating room, a sick bay, a dental office, an X-ray machine, and a darkroom. The ship also removed TB patients from their communities and took them to the south for treatment. This treatment proved devastating for individuals, families and communities:[57]

When the doctors made their final decision on whether an individual should go to the hospital for treatment or stay in the North, the evacuees were sent down to the Inuit quarters in the prow of the ship and the rest were sent ashore. The evacuees were not allowed to go ashore to collect belongings, to say goodbye, or to make arrangements for their families or goods. If a mother was judged sick but her children were not infected, the children (sometimes including unweaned babies) were given to an Inuk women going ashore. Fathers had no chance to arrange for someone to hunt for food for their families or to look after their dogs and equipment, mothers had no chance to arrange for someone to care for their children or to sew and process the skins needed to keep the family warm, virtually nothing was done from the social side. Those needing hospital treatment were kept on board, the rest sent ashore and on sailed the ship to the next settlement.[58]

Waldram, Herring, and Young describe the appalling conditions that the federal government subjected the Inuit to:

It was not uncommon for individuals to board the medical or patrol ships for x-rays, and then be refused permission to return to shore when the results positively indicated tuberculosis. They were simply taken away. . . . The Inuit people were treated like cattle. . . . To the bulk of the federal staff in Ottawa they were just numbers. But these numbers kept getting mixed up. . . .

Other patients were not even lucky enough to be returned to their families; in some cases they were dropped off at settlements hundreds of kilometres from home, often with little recollection of their families.[59]

On the totality of Inuit deaths, CBC reported:

When a TB patient died in the south, the hospital notified the Indian Health Service, which notified the Department of Northern Affairs. Northern Affairs then contacted someone in the patient's community — a missionary or RCMP officer — who was charged with telling the family that their loved one had died. Often, however, the message never got through.

These patients were buried in paupers' graves in a southern cemetery at the expense of Northern Affairs.[60]

No one knows how many Inuit are still buried in exile. Frank Tester reports that "records show that between 1953 and 1961 a total of 5,240 Inuit, from toddlers to elders, were sent south, sometimes plucked right out of hunting camps on the land. The entire Eastern Arctic Inuit population at the time was only about 11,500."[61]

It must be noted that in southern Canada in 1953, there was a peak of 19,000 sanatorium beds, rising from 9,000 in 1937. Although Inuit seemed to have a longer stay of up to three years, it is reported that patients in southern Canada reached a peak of just over one year in the mid-1950s, although some stayed longer.[62] The treatment appears to be similar for the Inuit and non-Inuit; however, there may have been a difference upon completion of treatment and/or death. It is abundantly clear that the federal government had the discretion whether to return the patients home or not.

3.1.2   Nutrition

Aboriginal people sustained high levels of health by maintaining complex relationships between the land and how food was obtained and prepared, their culture, and the transmission of knowledge between generations. Colonization profoundly interrupted these relationships and introduced new crops; it appropriated land; and it moved Aboriginal people into the wage economy. In all these ways, colonization eroded Aboriginal hunting and food gathering, which affected the lifeblood of Aboriginal autonomy and self-determination.

Cutting Aboriginal peoples off from their traditional foods also cut them off from their medicines, which had been part of the food security system. For Aboriginal peoples, food security and food sovereignty[63] were solidly in place before contact. Colonization damaged, and in many cases destroyed, these processes.

The Coast Salish people of southern Vancouver Island are one example. Scholar Kathleen Turner examines the profound impacts of colonization on diet and cultural practices relating to food production, preparation, and consumption. The blue camas is a blue flowering plant of the lily family that has an edible bulb when properly cooked. It was a staple on the Northwest Coast. However, owing to a confluence of colonial pressures, the blue camas was eliminated from the diets of the Coast Salish peoples.

Before colonization, the Coast Salish held control over their food system and "derived their food security through a rich knowledge of their environment, passed down through oral tradition and longstanding land stewardship and plant cultivation practices."[64] According to the elders, the blue camas was held to be the "Queen Root" and the "Number One vegetable."[65] It was a principal carbohydrate and a valuable source of fibre, vitamins, minerals, and protein.[66] The harvesting, preparation, and consumption of the blue camas were critical components of Coast Salish knowledge and what was transmitted to subsequent generations.

The camas disappeared from Coast Salish society after the Europeans arrived around 1827. The Europeans imposed "real farming" as part of the colonial mission to "civilize" and assimilate First Nations.[67] The pressures on First Nations to abandon their traditional foods led to the loss of many dietary traditions, including the camas. European foodstuffs became the norm.[68]

The Coast Salish Nation is but one example. Every nation in North America could undoubtedly provide many examples of how their nutrient-rich diets were depleted or destroyed and replaced by European diets. The following section describes the results of these changes from a nutrient-rich diet of sustainable food autonomy to a nutrient-depleted diet of unsustainable food dependency.

i)   Hunger, Starvation, Disease, and Death

As Canada was colonizing and industrializing, the Indians and Métis living on the western prairies experienced severe hardship. While tuberculosis rates were climbing, the buffalo also disappeared. The tuberculosis epidemic coincided with a complete dietary change as well as a transition from an active migratory lifestyle to a non-nomadic one. The buffalo had provided a food staple, yet the herds started declining in 1870. Smallpox, which surely affected the health of the hunters and their ability to hunt, began to rage through the people. When the famine came in 1878 and 1879, the buffalo went south for the final time. In Blackfoot lands, six hundred people starved to death.[69] Starvation further reduced resistance to disease.

In an attempt to force them to farm and feed themselves, the federal government issued rations of white flour and salt pork and settled Indian people on reserves. This transition from a nomadic and migratory lifestyle to a sedentary one further exacerbated health problems. While Aboriginal people were attempting this agricultural way of life, the numbered treaties were being negotiated. Some agricultural provisions were specified in the treaties. Aboriginal people negotiated the treaties, accepted the "Queen's hand," and were promised government support to facilitate their transition from hunting buffalo to farming. Yet, the buffalo provided much more than meat. They also provided clothing, warmth, housing, medicine, and a range of tools — all essential to sustaining health. A field of wheat or a vegetable garden could not provide all that the buffalo provided. Once the buffalo disappeared, Aboriginal people were left without the basic necessities of life that the buffalo had once provided.

Bent on "discouraging indolence," the government issued rations to the starving.[70] The Indian agent, acting on behalf of the Crown, provided rations to Indian bands. Yet, the rations they provided were nutritionally inadequate. They consisted mainly of white flour, bacon, and a little fresh meat.[71] Before long, the teeth of the children began to rot, tonsils and adenoids became enlarged, and profuse nasal discharge became common, all of which indicated a lower resistance to disease. Rickets appeared from lack of Vitamin D and the rapid change in diet.[72] Maureen Lux elaborates on the purpose of the rations and their devastating effects:

> The starvation at Fort Walsh was a cynical and deliberate plan to press the government's advantage and force the Cree from the area to allow the government a free hand in developing the prairies.[73]

The department was well aware of the horrific effects of its policy. The year before, Dr. John Kittson of the NWMP had warned the Indian Department that the rations were inadequate for subsistence. Working from figures he received from prisons and asylums in Europe, Kittson reckoned that a minimum daily ration for a man in moderate health with an active life should be one pound of meat, 0.2 pounds of bread, and 0.25 pounds of fat or butter. State prisoners in Siberia were given more than twice the ration. In severe weather or hard labour, the NWMP minimum daily ration was 1.5 pounds of meat, and 1.25 pounds of bread, plus tea, coffee, sugar; and abundant beans and dried apples. The daily ration for Native people of a half-pound of meat, and half pound of flour was, according to Kittson, "totally insufficient." And the consequences were appalling:

> Gaunt men and women with hungry eyes were seen everywhere

seeking or begging for a mouthful of food — little children . . . fight over the tid-bits. Morning and evening many of them would come to me and beg for the very bones left by the dogs in my yard. When I tell you that the mortality exceeds the birth rate it may help you to realize the amount of suffering and privation existing among them.[74]

For those who survived, the transition from a high protein diet to one of limited nutritional value had a devastating and long-lasting intergenerational impact. Not only was illness present, but some evidence suggests that these rations may have been deliberately or inadvertently poisoned. Lux notes that Treaty 7 oral history states that the rations were intentionally poisoned. The Indian Agent directed the Indians to "mix a yellow substance into the flour. . . ." Lux cites Tom Yellowhorn:

The people who lived around the agency camp were those that got sick. Those who were away did not get sick. . . . So many died so fast they did not have time to bury them; they just left the bodies on top of the ground. Today this place is known to the Indians as Ghost Coulee. . . . The Indians always used "The time the flour burned" for a counting date; that was around 1882.[75]

Peigan Elder Alan Pard explained that the substance in the flour was believed to be sulfur. Bluestone and lye were allegedly found in the meat (bluestone is also called blue vitriol and is used as an insecticide or fungicide). Elder Pard's grandfather confirmed that it was sulfur in the rations, and "Belly sickness" was the term used for the distended abdomens resulting from eating these rations. Rations on the Blood Reserve were also contaminated: "the food was treated with a kind of chemical. The Indians believed it was a poisonous substance. The meat discoloured with the use of this substance that was mixed with flour. The people who died from this food poisoning were all buried at the Belly Butte site."[76] Blood Elder George First Rider corroborated these stories:

The meat was treated with some kind of chemical. Shortly after it would turn blue and not be eatable. Those were the days when people were dying off. Bodies were hauled out of the camps at a high rate and carried to the burial grounds. During the time of issuing the rations, many people got sick and very many died. . . . That was the first time we were poisoned by the Queen and the government. Those people were just about wiped out by the first ration.[77]

Although it is difficult to say what the purpose of the substances mixed with the rations were, the elders generally viewed the contaminations as deliberate acts. Even if the rations were not deliberately poisoned, diets were not markedly improved over the next 40 years. Canada's Medical Officer, Dr. Graham-Cumming, reported that, in 1927 and 1928, only 13.9 per cent of the Native people living in the west lived on a "white man's diet" of milk, butter, eggs and meat, vegetables, and fruits. On the other hand, 34.7 per cent of Aboriginal people lived on a monthly ration of 50 pounds of flour, two pounds of tea, and three pounds of rice, and thirty pounds of bacon in the summer, or thirty pounds of beef in the winter. Also, 34.7 per cent of Aboriginal people lived on a slightly "better" diet, adding either vegetables or milk and eggs. The remaining 25.3 per cent of Aboriginal people lived on the same rations with two of the following added: milk, eggs, or vegetables.[78]

Dr. Graham-Cumming noted that, because of the poor diet, the tonsils and adenoids of Aboriginal people were enlarged, and constipation was a problem. He also noted that, before the buffalo disappeared, dental caries were non-existent. Scurvy became a problem in the northern residential schools, where it was difficult to get fresh fish and meat most of the time. Graham-Cumming stated in his report that the federal government sent canned goods to the children who suffered, therefore preventing the deaths of many of them. Before iodine was added to salt, a lack of iodine in the diet caused goiter, which was endemic in several areas.[79]

ii)   Sickness and Residential School Hunger

In the residential schools, the children were hungry. A survivor recalls that hunger was the first and last thing he remembered about the residential school he attended.[80] Another student commented:

The only time I did not feel hunger during those two years was when my grandparents came. . . . When they came they brought deer meat and bannock and other real food you could get full on. Nobody thought to want candy when we had not seen meat for so long. For weeks before they would come I could not think of anything besides the food they would bring with them. The food always crowded out the people. It was not my grandfather who was coming. It was meat, dried fruit, and roots. Hunger like that numbs your mind.[81]

Cree leader John Tootoosis recalled that the pots that clothes were washed in were the same pots that food was cooked in. He noted, "this one spring the meat was probably thawing and about to get bad. Didn't they go and boil the meat in these pots and that's what they tried to feed us. It was very difficult to eat the food."[82] Historian John Milloy cites;

The Sisters didn't treat me good — they gave me rotten food to eat and punished me for not eating it — the meat and soup were rotten and tasted so bad they made the girls sick sometime. I have been sick from eating it. . . . I used to hide the meat in my pocket and throw it away. I told the Sisters to look at the meat as it was rotten, and they said it was not rotten and we must eat it. The Sisters did not eat the same kind of food as they gave the girls. If we didn't eat our porridge at breakfast, it was given to us for our dinner, and even for supper, and we got nothing else till it was eaten.[83]

A very different story appeared when school inspectors visited, according to Métis scholar Agnes Grant: "schools were inspected at intervals and inspection meant that food would temporarily improve. The children viewed these inspections with considerable cynicism as corn flakes, oranges, toast, and eggs would suddenly appear at breakfast time, and thick, wholesome stew appeared for lunch and supper."[84]

For the Inuit who attended residential schools:

Between 1955 and 1961, on advice from the Department of Health and Welfare, the mission schools decided what food should be given to the Inuit. The churches in Inuvik and Chesterfield Inlet decided on a combination of traditional and Western foods for their students. The Department of Northern Affairs agreed that Inuit students could be fed a traditional diet. By 1961, with allegations of smaller caribou herds and more Inuit going to school, less traditional foods and more Western foods were being served at the schools. In this same year, the Department of Health and Welfare advised the Department of Northern Affairs to ban the eating of raw meat in the schools and to teach the students that eating raw meat was the cause of sickness.[85]

Children died in large numbers because of malnutrition. The scarcity of food contributed to the students' susceptibility to disease, and has led to long-lasting effects for future generations.

3.2   How Federal Government Policies Affect Aboriginal Health

3.2.1   *Provision of Health Services*

Early government policies implemented health care to Aboriginal people on an *ad hoc* basis. Care or lack of it was wholly dependent upon the contagiousness and severity of the diseases that might have an impact on the non-Aboriginal population. Health policies were geared toward protecting the good health of non-Aboriginal people. This motive, coupled with the complex jurisdictional conflicts arising over the provision of health care to Aboriginal people, has also contributed to a disjointed policy framework for Aboriginal health. It is noted that "the experience of Aboriginal people as they access health care services has been described as an encounter of isolation, alienation, and marginalization and health care systems are seen as 'powerful colonial forces' and agents of social control."[86]

Before Confederation, Indian agents, missionaries, traders, and the Hudson's Bay Company provided periodic medical services to Indian people.[87] The term "Indian agent" was used to describe the person who was responsible for administering treaties on behalf of the Queen. The agents worked closely with physicians, missionaries, and the police. The physician was paid from treaty money to provide vaccinations, medical examinations, and dental extractions.[88] These health services have been described:

> Indian agents, missionaries, traders and the Hudson Bay Company provided periodic medical services to Indian people. In 1873, the North West Mounted Police (N.W.M.P.) was formed and began providing some services as agents for the Department of Indian Affairs. Besides their role in controlling Indian access to alcohol, N.W.M.P. surgeons provided routine medical services to Indians into the early part of the twentieth century. The N.W.M.P. also played a significant role in the quarantine of groups of Indian people when smallpox,

whooping cough, influenza, and tuberculosis swept through the Indian populations.[89]

Over the years, nurses and doctors who were employed full or part-time by the federal government were placed in Aboriginal communities. They either replaced or worked in conjunction with the Indian agents. In 1930, the first on-reserve nursing station opened in Fisher River, Manitoba.[90]

Following the Second World War, the organized medical services available to Inuit and Indian people increased. In 1944, the National Health and Welfare Department (NHWD) was formed and the Department of Indian and Northern Health transferred all aspects of Indian health services to the NHWD. All other administration of "Indians and lands reserved for the Indians" remained with the Department of Indian Affairs. Indian agents were renamed Superintendents. They retained control over health by virtue of their designation as Health Officers on reserves, even though a different department was now delivering the actual medical services:[91]

By the 1950s, the federal department of National Health and Welfare was operating a network of 33 nursing stations, 65 health centres, and 18 small regional hospitals for registered Indians and Inuit. This undertaking was motivated by the post-war spirit of humanitarianism that propelled the emerging Canadian welfare state and by fear of the threat posed to Canadians by sky-high rates of tuberculosis in Aboriginal communities.[92]

In 1956, the NHWD had grown sizably due to a funding increase of more than $17 million dollars and a corresponding increase in medical professionals employed. In 1962, the Medical Services Branch of the NHWD was created, which assumed responsibility for all Indian and Inuit health services. Federal government expenditures to Indian health increased, and by the end of the 1960s the budget was more than $28 million, compared to $4 million in the 1950s.[93]

The government health system operated on the assumption that Aboriginal peoples would welcome Western-style health care services. Even in cases where this may have been true, Aboriginal people faced some basic and severe functional problems, as at the time Aboriginal people with serious illnesses were often sent unaccompanied to medical facilities far from their homes for treatment and placed alone in strange and often hostile environments. If they remained in their own communities, they were offered health care services without any relation to their values, traditions, or conditions. Some Aboriginal people were forced (or convinced) to suffer invasive medical procedures, including sterilization.[94]

In 1979, the *Federal Indian Health Policy* (Three Pillars Policy) was released. It strengthened community development and clarified the relationship between Indian people and the federal government. Relative to Canadian health services, the Three Pillars Policy required those provincial governments, municipal governments, the private sector, and Indian reserves to work together to achieve higher levels of health in Aboriginal communities. The Policy stated:

> "[T]he first, and most significant, [pillar] is community development, both socio-economic development and cultural and spiritual development, to remove the conditions of poverty and apathy which prevent the members of the community from achieving a state of physical, mental and social well-being." Indeed, the overarching goal of the new federal policy was to "achieve an increasing level of health in Indian communities, generated and maintained by the Indian communities themselves."[95]

The goal of this policy was to integrate Aboriginal health services with the standard health care system in ways that were positive and collaborative for Aboriginal people. It began to involve First Nation and Inuit communities in the delivery of health care services.[96] Yet, this step alone was not enough.

The same year, Canada adopted the international *Alma-Ata Declaration,* which defined and acknowledged the basic requisites of health, equitable distribution, community involvement, multisectoral approach, and implementation of appropriate technology.[97] The hope was that this Declaration would help reduce health inequities. However, it, too, was not enough. In 1980, Justice Thomas Berger issued a report that called for a consultative process to transfer the control of health services to First Nation communities.[98] In 1983, the Report of the Special Committee on Indian Self-Government (also known as the Penner Report) also advocated for improvements in Aboriginal health care. The report stressed the need to take a more holistic approach to health care by incorporating traditional with Western approaches as well as by focusing more on preventative measures.[99] Transferring health services to Aboriginal control became the new hope for achieving more equitable health results for Aboriginal people.

The first steps toward "health services transfer" began in 1982 with the *Community Health Demonstration Program*. This program experimented with different models of health service delivery and different levels of control.[100] Again, the goal was to lead to more positive health results for Aboriginal people.

In 1986, "the Sechelt Indian Band signed the first Self-Government agreement in which a First Nation community assumed control of their health services."[101] In 1989, with the approval of both the Canadian cabinet and the treasury board, the federal government proceeded with its health transfer policy. This involved assigning control of resources allocated for health-based programs to communities south of the sixtieth parallel. In the fall of 1989, 58 pre-transfer projects were underway, involving 212 Aboriginal communities in Canada.[102] The same year, during a national conference on health transfer, First Nation delegates called for the removal of some of the constraints built into the process. By the fall of 1990, an additional eight transfer agreements had been signed, and 67 more First Nations were involved in pre-transfer planning.[103]

To help move the transfer along, in 1995, the federal government published "The Government of Canada's Approach to Implementation of the Inherent Right and the Negotiation of Aboriginal Self-Government."[104] One aspect of negotiations involved the transfer of health services from the federal government to Aboriginal communities, and jurisdiction over health.

On September 11, 2000, the First Ministers agreed that "improvements to primary health care are crucial to the renewal of health services," and emphasized the importance of multi-disciplinary teams.[105] The Government of Canada then established the $800 million Primary Health Care Transition Fund (PHCTF). Over a six-year period (2000–2006), the PHCTF funded provinces and territories in their efforts to reform the primary health care system. The PHCTF itself had a time-limited mandate. The programs and services it supported were intended to have a lasting and sustainable impact on the health care system. The Aboriginal envelope of the PHCTF was open to application from federal, provincial, and territorial governments, First Nations and Inuit communities and health organizations, and not-for-profit non-governmental organizations.

In addition, all the initiatives that applied for funding had to address one or more of the common objectives of the PHCTF. They also had to complement provincial/territorial direction in primary health care reform. Health

Canada selected the initiatives to be funded by consulting with provincial and territorial governments.[106]

Today, the government department responsible for health services to First Nations and Inuit people is the First Nations and Inuit Health Branch (FNIHB) of Health Canada (formerly called the Medical Services Branch). Their mandate includes:

- ensuring the availability of, or access to, health services for First Nations and Inuit communities;

- assisting First Nations and Inuit communities in addressing health barriers and disease threats and in attaining health levels comparable to other Canadians living in similar locations; and

- building strong partnerships with First Nations and Inuit people to improve the health system.[107]

FNIHB provides primary health care for community-based health programs and services. FNIHB works with First Nations and Inuit organizations and communities to carry out activities that keep people healthy and prevent chronic and infectious diseases. FNIHB supports community-based programs on-reserve and in Inuit communities. It provides drug, dental, and ancillary health services to First Nations and Inuit regardless of residence (as long as First Nations have status). They also provide primary health care services on-reserve in remote and isolated areas where provincial services are not available.

The Non-Insured Health Benefits Program is available through FNIHB. It offers a safety net to ensure that basic needs are still met if they are not met by other private or public insurance plans. The program states it provides a range of "medically necessary goods and services to status Indians and Inuit that supplement benefits provided by private or provincial/territorial programs including: dental and vision care, prescription drugs, medical supplies and equipment, transportation to medical services, short-term/crisis mental health counselling and payment of health insurance premiums in British Columbia and Alberta."[108]

FNIHB provides community care in over 600 communities, and primary health care in over 200 remote communities. It also maintains 223 health centres in semi-isolated communities and nursing stations in 74 remote and semi-remote areas. Public Health programs monitor communicable diseases, drinking water on reserves, and environmental health issues (waste water management and mould).[109]

On the surface, it appears that the health system should be effective, at least for First Nations and Inuit people, with the changes every decade or so in government programs and initiatives that have been underway. However, it is abundantly clear that it is not, evidenced by poor Aboriginal health.

i)   Status of Midwifery in Canada for Aboriginal Women

In the North, childbirth has been medicalized. Pregnant women are evacuated thousands of miles from their families and homes to give birth in southern hospitals. This forced separation from families has been linked to increased stress and lower birth weights, an increase in birthing complications, an increased likelihood of post-partum depression, and unnecessary strain on family relations.[110] A smattering of centres throughout the North, covering different Inuit regions, offer varying degrees of access to childbirth programs and services.

Nunavik's *Innulitsivik* midwifery service and education program have been providing childbirth services in Inuktitut to the communities of the Hudson Bay region since 1986. Three maternity centres serve seven villages on the Hudson Bay Coast. The midwives who are involved with the women in this region are both traditional Inuit midwives and Western medical practitioners. An interdisciplinary council sets the protocols for maternal care. *Innulitsivik Centre* also provides on-the-job midwifery training. Inuit midwives are the lead caregivers for maternity clients, including pre-natal and post-natal care. They have access to a variety of Western medical services with onsite physician services. Specialist consultations are conducted by phone or by medevac. The Centre also provides well-woman and baby care within the three communities where the maternity centres are located.[111]

The Rankin Inlet Birthing Centre was established in Nunavut in 1996. Although the Centre initially had difficulty recruiting and maintaining midwifery services,[112] in 2005 it achieved stable staffing, which helped the centre expand.[113] The Rankin Inlet Birthing Centre integrates Western medicine with traditional methods, and both are funded by health services for the region[114] In developing government institutions, programs, and services (including health services), the Nunavut Government places priority on integrating *Inuit Quajimajatuqangit*, or Inuit knowledge.

However, competing midwifery legislation in Canada has numerous defects and impacts on birthing. The biggest defect is that traditional Aboriginal midwives are not recognized by all legislation. In the North, women have been routinely removed from their homes to give birth, usually transported to the south or Iqaluit. In Arviat, Nunavut, the total population is 2,100 and the birth rate is the highest in Canada (35 per 1000, as against the national average of 10.3 per 1000). Arviat has no permanent doctor, no hospital, no midwife, no public health nurse, and no one (except for seven overworked nurses at the health centre) to assist the estimated 70 women who get pregnant every year. Most women are flown 1,200 kilometres south to Winnipeg.[115]

In 1999, the Quebec provincial government legalized midwifery, but it recognized only one midwifery training program in the province. At present, Quebec's midwifery law recognizes Inuit midwives who are already trained, certified, and working in Nunavik, but it excludes those who are in training or who are traditionally trained. As it stands, all midwives must be registered with the *Ordre des sages-femmes du Québec* (OSFQ) to be permitted to practice.[116]

Most women in Canada now have nominal access to regulated and funded (paid for as part of the provincial health care system) midwifery care. They also have a choice of birth location (home, hospital, or birth centre). The Nunavut midwifery legislation is particularly problematic for Inuit women. It forces traditional Inuit midwives to be registered under the *Consolidation of Midwifery Profession Act*,[117] yet traditional midwifery is not recognized. The *Act* only goes so far as allowing traditional knowledge into the curriculum for teaching; it may criminalize women who act as midwives without formal training.[118]

On January 11, 2008, the Nunavut Tunngavik Inc. submitted their concerns about Bill 20, the *Midwifery Profession Act,* to the Nunavut Health and Education Standing Committee, on possible infringements on Aboriginal rights by way of extinguishing traditional birthing ways through the imposition of legislation that excluded traditional midwifery. They also expressed concerns that the Inuit were not consulted in any meaningful fashion. Their objections went unheeded. The Nunavut midwifery legislation passed, but it remains highly problematic for the same concerns that the Nunavut Tunngavik expressed.

In their submissions to the Standing Committee, the Nunavut Tunngavik Inc. used the example of British Columbia's *Midwifery Act*[119] and showed how it could be blended into legislation that would serve the needs of the Inuit. They stated that, "as an example of how Traditional Inuit Midwifery can adapt or evolve into the contemporary world, the province of British Columbia has defined aboriginal midwifery under the Midwives Regulations of the *Health Professions Act* (1995) as the following;

1. (a) traditional aboriginal midwifery practices such as the use and administration of traditional herbs and medicines and other cultural and spiritual practices,
   (b) contemporary aboriginal midwifery practices which are based on, or originate in, traditional aboriginal midwifery practices, or
   (c) a combination of traditional and contemporary aboriginal midwifery practices.[120]

The large Inuit population of Nunavut needs the support of legislation similar to British Columbia's model, so that those who wish to learn and practise Inuit traditional midwifery in Nunavut can do so.

To summarize, the examples in this section illustrate the legal foundation on which current Aboriginal health policies are built. Early government policies dispersed Aboriginal health care on an *ad hoc* basis, depending on the potential threat of those diseases affecting non-Aboriginal populations (i.e., smallpox, tuberculosis). In other words, health policies were geared toward protecting the good health of non-Aboriginal people. Aboriginal women have always faced social, economic, political, and cultural changes that have negatively affected health, cultural identity, and social and family structures. Years of assimilation have led to the medicalization of birthing and the decline of traditional midwifery practice. More recently, government legislation and political interest in the role of traditional Aboriginal midwives has begun to bring to the forefront the rebirth of a model that may blend ancient traditions with modern techniques, thus enabling Aboriginal women to bring childbirth back to their communities.

3.2.2   Residential Schools

The Canadian government sought to assimilate Aboriginal people by forcibly removing children from their homes, families, cultures, languages, and traditions, sending them far away to residential schools, teaching them English or French, and giving them a Christian education. Although residential schools had origins in the pre-Confederation times, it was in the 1880s that the federal government implemented the residential school model for Aboriginal education. At one time, Canada operated 88 schools. Although the Government of Canada officially withdrew in 1969, a few of the schools continued operating through the 1960s, 70s, and 80s. Akaitcho Hall in Yellowknife did not close until 1996.[121]

These schools were run through a partnership between the federal government, the churches, and Aboriginal people. The federal government paid for capital expenditures and salaries for the staff. The churches were responsible for school activities and daily operations. Aboriginal parents were forced to supply their children. An estimated 150,000 First Nations, Métis, and Inuit children attended residential schools. Thousands of former students have since come forward to claim that physical, emotional, and sexual abuse were rampant in the school system, and that little was done to stop it or to punish the abusers.[122]

Historical research and the *Report of the Royal Commission on Aboriginal Peoples*[123] document how the residential school system fostered the spread of disease. Inadequate health facilities contributed to the spread of European diseases, which seriously affect the health of Aboriginal people today. Although some former students have reported that life in residential schools was not that bad, the mere fact that attendance was mandatory and enforced by threats indicates that not all Aboriginal families shared this view. The many dimensions of abuse, including physical and sexual, inflicted by the residential school system forever damaged the souls of the children who were forced to attend. Given the cultural, social, and psychological damage, these schools have left a painful legacy that Aboriginal people must now face for generations.

The moment the children entered the schools, their physical and cultural markers (e.g., clothing, long hair) were removed.[124] Student activities were strictly regimented, and students who broke the rules were severely punished. Students were controlled military-style.[125] Many schools adopted harsh punishments, such as "food deprivation, strapping and solitary confinement."[126] Innocuous acts were also punishable by force. Students could be punished for bed-wetting, communicating with children of the opposite sex, speaking an Aboriginal language, stealing food, running away, talking back to staff, and being outside school grounds.[127]

The intention behind such excessive discipline and punishment of students was to cause pain and humiliation. Humiliation, such as that caused by public strapping, sought to diminish the student's sense of dignity and value of self and identity. Public humiliation has been reported by former students as one of the most devastating aspects of their experience while they attended residential school. At some schools, such as the Mohawk Institute and Mount Elgin, abuse was so frequent that students were classified based on the number of punishments they received and the reasons why they received them.[128]

Grant reports that inhumane treatment of sick children continued and was indeed the norm throughout the residential school years:

Winnipeg Free Press Nov. 10, 1990
Pam Sickles can never forget what happened to a sick friend:

She was sick and she threw up in her plate and she was forced to eat it all. I can see the nun pressing the spoon against her lips and she was pushing so hard there was blood on her lips. I can see it still so clearly after all these years. (St. Mary's, Kenora) [Ontario]

Winnipeg Free Press Aug. 6, 1991
Norman Whitford remembers a frail, eight-year old boy forced to sit for days on a pail inside a closet as punishment for having diarrhea:

It was extremely cruel because not only did they punish him for what I believe now was a medical problem, but the other children were expected to look at him and ridicule him. (Fort Resolution) [Northwest Territories]

Winnipeg Free Press Nov. 10, 1990
Phil Fontaine said one of his brothers is reluctant to talk about what happened to him when he broke his leg playing soccer and started crying:

Because he was crying he was kicked and forced to walk with a broken leg and he was kept in the school for I don't know how many days before they decided to do something.[129]

In most cases, the excessive disciplinary actions and punishments that students experienced went unreported. Even when it was reported, nothing was done to stop the behaviour.[130] A survivor remembers:

The nightmare began as soon as Emily [eight years old] and her sister Rose, then eleven years old, stepped on the small boat that would bear them away. "I clung to Rose until Father Jackson wrenched her out of my arms. . . . I searched all over the boat for Rose. Finally I climbed up to the wheelhouse and opened the door and there was Father Jackson, on top of my sister. My sister's dress was pulled up and his pants were down. I was too little to know about sex; but I know now he was raping her."[131]

Some have also described the residential school system as "institutionalized pedophilia"[132] at the hands of priests, nuns, staff, and other children. The stories are horrifying, and the legacy it has left is equally horrifying. Institutionalized violence, rapes, and ongoing sexual abuse permeate the history of the residential school system, and sexual violence and abuse lie at the root of many of the social ills that Aboriginal people face today. Parents lost the ability to parent, and children lost the ability to function in a family. The collective nature of the assault on Aboriginal identity and culture has been described as nothing less than cultural genocide.[133] To help address residential school issues, the Truth and Reconciliation Commission (TRC) was created in response to the Residential Schools Settlement Agreement. This Agreement was negotiated between former students, the churches, the government of Canada, the Assembly of First Nations, and other Aboriginal organizations. It was created as an independent body to provide former students a voice to share their individual experiences in a safe and culturally appropriate manner.

Research into the students who died or went missing while attending residential schools is currently being addressed through the Missing Children Project funded by the TRC. Relying primarily on incomplete federal government and church records, over 4,000 cases of Aboriginal children who died while attending residential schools have been identified. On June 8, 2012 the chief coroners and chief medical examiners of Canada unanimously passed a resolution committing each of them to enter into discussions with the TRC regarding the role that each office might play in advancing the project's aims.[134]

Despite the toll residential schools took, the resilience of former students, families, and their communities are incredible. In many cases, they did not go willingly or without resisting. Miller observes that, in the first six decades of the modern residential school system, resistance occurred at the level of the band, the family, and the student.[135] Considerable literature documents First Nations resistance to the residential school regime. Accounts of resistance can be found in the general histories of the schools, accounts of particular schools or peoples, or in individual memoirs, oral histories, and personal accounts. These stories must be told, too.

It is well documented that the Canadian residential school system has been overwhelmingly damaging for Aboriginal people, and has had destructive intergenerational effects on health as well.[136] The social problems that Aboriginal communities continue to face stem directly from residential school experiences and their impacts across generations.[137] These social problems, which are not limited to substance abuse, family dysfunction, and suicide, are inextricably linked to the health of Aboriginal people in Canada.

3.2.3   Forced Sterilization

The term "survival of the fittest" came to refer to human levels of intelligence and technological innovativeness, which were the Eurocentric, "scientific" criteria for determining if a person was fit for survival or not. A related notion of the time was that the most fit were facing depopulation, because the unfit were reproducing at a faster rate. The unfit included "mentally retarded persons, alcoholics, epileptics, schizophrenics, criminals, prostitutes, and others whose physical and behavioural characterizations were considered to be genetically determined and inherited."[138]

In Canada, both Alberta (1928) and British Columbia (1933) enacted eugenics legislation. Between 1929 and 1972, 2,800 people were sterilized under the authority of Alberta's *Sexual Sterilization Act*.[139] Although many provinces considered the idea of eugenics, British Columbia and Alberta were the only provinces that legislated in favour of it. Alberta sterilized far more people than did British Columbia, which sterilized 400 people under the BC law.[140]

Even though neither the Alberta nor the BC Sterilization Acts overtly discriminated against women and/or Aboriginal people, their implementation had devastating effects on both groups, since both provinces have always had high Aboriginal populations. Because of their social strata, a disproportionately high number of women[141] and Aboriginal people were referred and sterilized:

Although Indian and Métis constituted only 3.4% of the Alberta population, they constituted 25.7% of the total of all people sterilized. Between 1969 and 1972 more Indian and Métis persons were sterilized than British, which is particularly telling because Indian and Métis had the least population and the British had the highest population.[142]

The *Sexual Sterilization Act* was intended to stop "mental defectives" from having children. The Eugenics Board was comprised of four people who were mandated to authorize sterilization in Alberta.[143] The Act initially required the consent of patients unless they were "mentally incapable," in which case "the consent of the next of kin had to be obtained."[144] In 1937, however, the Act was amended: consent by patients or the next of kin was no longer required if the patient was considered "mentally defective."[145] The 1937 amendment also targeted "individuals incapable of intelligent parenthood."[146] Aboriginal peoples were easy targets for the new amendment, since the prevailing government view was that Aboriginal people were incapable of intelligent parenthood. In 1988, the Alberta government destroyed many of the 4,785 files created by the Eugenics Board. The government of Alberta maintained 861 of those files. Professor Jana Grekul reviewed them and commented:

[M]ost noticeably over-represented were Aboriginals (identified as "Indian," "Métis," "half breeds," "treaty" and "Eskimo"). While the province's Aboriginal population hovered between 2% and 3% of the total over the decades in question, Aboriginals made up 6% of all cases represented.[147]

Further:

[With] few exceptions particularly in the 1930's [8%] more women than men appeared before the Board. . . . We found that people were being referred to the board for reasons related to their social class, gender, and ethnicity, and there was no genetic condition for them to be considered for sterilization.[148]

[W]e conclude that Aboriginals were the most prominent victims of the Board's attention. They were over-represented among presented cases and among those diagnosed as "mentally defective." Thus they seldom had a chance to say "no" to being sterilized. As a result 74% of all Aboriginals presented to the Board were eventually sterilized (compared to 60% of all patients represented). In contrast, because patient consent was so often required, less than half (47%) of both Eastern and Western European patients were eventually sterilized.[149]

Inuit women in the North were sterilized without their consent in staggering numbers in the 1970s.[150] Missionary Father Robert Lechat reported that in 1976, "26% of women of Igloolik between 30 and 50 are sterilized thanks to the Canadian Government. . . . [151] If there is no precise policy for sterilization there is at least a very definite will to prevent the increase of Inuit in the Canadian North."[152]

A letter written to David Lewis from the Regional Director of the Alberta Region on October 21, 1970, states: "Congratulations for urgent intervention. Same butchery is exercised to Eskimo women elsewhere — under civilized blankets."[153] Father Lechat explains the effects of tubal ligation on Inuit women:

For the Inuk woman — and I speak again of the traditionally educated Inuk — there is no danger of upsetting the psychological equilibrium by too many births: on the contrary it would be easily upset by her not being able to bear children. She does not feel that she is a real woman unless she has a baby in her hood or a child to hold her hand: that is why you see women past the menopause and already grandmothers adopting children.[154]

Barry Gunn, former Regional Administrator in Frobisher, confirmed that "because of communication problems, many women agreed to operations and signed papers without realizing what they meant."[155] When the issue of sterilization of Inuit women was challenged in the House of Commons, the regulations were changed. The medical staff were required to clarify the permanence of the sterilization surgical procedure and to use consent forms that were translated into Inuktitut.[156]

A 1974 study of the Indian Health Services (IHS) by the Women of All Red Nations (WARN) revealed that "as many as 42 percent of all Indian women of childbearing age had by that point been sterilized without their consent."[157] These estimates were confirmed by a General Accounting Office (GAO) investigation of four IHS facilities that examined records only for 1973–76. The investigation that concluded that "during this three-year sample period, 3,406 involuntary sterilizations (the equivalent of over a half-million among the general population) had been performed in just these four hospitals."[158] Jane Lawrence recounts that Native Americans accused the Indian Health Service of sterilizing 25 per cent of Native American women between fifteen and forty-four years of age during the 1970s.[159]

In October 1989, Leilani Muir discovered that the Government of Alberta had sterilized her without her consent. She then brought "legal action against the Government of Alberta for wrongful confinement and for wrongful sterilization," and she won.[160] In Muir's case, "a single IQ test" had been enough to deem her mentally defective and therefore a candidate for sterilization.[161] Upon Muir's physical examination and the discovery that she had been sterilized, her doctor reported that her insides "looked like she had been through a slaughterhouse."[162]

When Leilani Muir won her case, the Government of Alberta responded with a proposition to override the *Charter of Rights and Freedoms* using s. 33 to limit the compensation to victims.[163] This proposition was met with a massive public outcry. The Government of Alberta finally apologized in 1999 and offered several individuals and groups the option to settle out of court. Many more victims of sterilization remain unnamed.

For Aboriginal women, the consequences of having been wrongfully institutionalized and sterilized are terrible. Their lives are changed irreversibly. Their hopes for having children and families are impaired, if not destroyed, and their ancestral lineage as a person, family, and people is, for many, brought to a brutal end. The debilitating harm left by forcible confinement and sterilization has harmed Aboriginal people today and certainly left a legacy that has added to the damage already encountered through the residential schools.

3.2.4   Experiments

At the Port Alberni Residential School children were denied basic dental treatment, and then "studied" as to the dental caries and gingivitis that would result. "No specialized, over-all type of dental service should be provided, such as the use of sodium fluoride, dental prophylaxis or even urea compounds," Dr. Brown, chief of the dental health division of the federal government, wrote in a one-page directive on October 3, 1949. Parental consent was not obtained.[164]

Maureen Lux recounts her studies on the use of the experimental BCG tuberculosis vaccine in the 1930s and 1940s on Indian children. The death rates revealed about 12 per cent of the patients actually died before their 5th birthday from other causes, vaccinated or not.[165]

Aboriginal women have been subjected to other long-standing forms of abuse as well. The Canadian government has used Aboriginal people to conduct experiments on humans without their consent in the corrections system as well as in other institutions.[166] In the 1960s, women imprisoned at the Kingston Prison for Women were subjected to lysergic acid diethylamide (LSD) and electro convulsive therapy (ECT) experiments. These experiments had devastating consequences and long-term effects on generations of Aboriginal women and their families. Evidence indicates that the government understood these dangers.

For instance, an Access to Information request to Health Canada in December 2007 revealed a December 21, 1962, letter to the Canadian Commissioner of Penitentiaries from the Department of National Health and Welfare. This 1962 letter was about regulating the use of LSD in one of Canada's prisons. He wrote to assure the Health Minister that he would have the authority to approve the drug for continued use at the Prison for Women in Kingston. He stated, "I have no hesitation at all in assuring you that the type of work which is going on in the prison at Kingston would be approved by my Minister for continuation." Concerning the drug's effects, he continued, "You will understand that all the evidence we have been able to gather from experts outside the Department, as well as inside, points to the fact that this is a potentially dangerous drug, especially if it were to get into the wrong hands."[167]

i) Dorothy Proctor

Dorothy Proctor was 18 years old and of Mi'kmaq heritage. She was incarcerated in the Prison for Women in Kingston from 1961 to 1963. She was one prisoner of at least 23 who were given LSD and electro convulsive therapy as research experiments. Proctor was told that if she took the treatments, she would not have to go back to segregation. In her words,

> I was taken to a room set aside for such treatments next to the prison infirmary. The prison nurse wordlessly strapped me to a hospital bed, both legs and arms, and a fifth strap held my head down. Sodium

pentothal was injected into my arm. "Begin counting backwards from one-hundred," said the nurse.

In walked a short man holding a little black box.

. . . I have no idea what happened to me while I was unconscious and helpless, but I do know that when I awakened back in my cell, my arms and legs twitched uncontrollably and I had a terrific headache. It felt like someone was inside my head with a jackhammers going at full trip. I do know I didn't want to see the man or his black box again. . . .

I screamed but no sound came out. . . .

I would faint all over the place. I went back to stuttering.[168]

In relation to the LSD experiments, she stated:

Dr. Mark Eveson was the doctor who administered the drug to me. The first time, he overdosed me by accident. Five days later, I was still on a trip without any luggage.[169]

I don't think it was fifteen or twenty minutes before Dante's Inferno. It was obvious. I am locked in. I can't get away. And the walls start to move in on me, and they melt. The bars turn to snakes, there was an awful physical vibration in my body. It was just awful, just awful, and of course, any mind that I had to think in reality, I just thought I had gone mad, that's it.[170]

When asked why she thought she was chosen for these experiments, she thought it was because she was an aggressive prisoner, young, and Aboriginal:

I believe I was targeted from the very beginning. I don't want to play the race card but I really can't help but think that perhaps I was targeted because first of all I was very, very young. I think I was the youngest inmate there. I didn't have any family support. I didn't come from a background of influence or power and plus I am Native and Black Canadian.[171]

Thirty-four years later, Proctor began a legal action against the perpetrators of the abuse she suffered in Prison for Women at Kingston. In October 1995, Dorothy Proctor contacted the Correctional Service of Canada (CSC) and stated her complaint. She was subjected to the experimental use of LSD 25, as well as to electro-convulsive therapy (ECT) without her informed consent, during her incarceration at the Prison for Women from March 22, 1960 to August 1, 1963. She considers that the Correctional Service of Canada did not properly protect her from such medical interventions. She further alleges that "being subjected to LSD 25 has had negative long term effects on her life: it precipitated her use of that and other drugs after her release; drew her into her role as an RCMP informant; prevented her from obtaining normal employment and reaching her potential and continues to have consequences for daily life."[172]

In response to Proctor's allegations, CSC requested that a Board of Investigation review the issues. CSC asked McGill Centre for Medicine, Ethics, and Law to review the allegations as well. Dr. Cameron had worked at the Allan Memorial Institute at McGill from 1957–64 to carry out potentially deadly experiments on non-US citizens. McGill subsequently produced *A Review on the use of LSD and ECT at the Prison for Women in the early 1960s*. The report, written by Professors Norbert Gilmore and Margaret Somerville, was to review the medical research and ethical context regarding the 23 female prisoners who were given LSD and electroconvulsive treatment (ECT) at the Kingston Prison. The report chronicled that the administration of LSD caused "substantial debilitating, long term negative effects."[173] They concluded:

> [T]he research itself was carried out in an unethical fashion: inmates returning alone to their cells, after being administered LSD, for instance, were heavily sedated "because there were no personnel available to provide overnight surveillance, support and, if needed, intervention," states the report. Also, LSD was administered, to at least one inmate, in quantities that were known to risk causing hallucinations.[174]

Compared to their proportion of the general population, Aboriginal people of both sexes in Canada are over-represented in federal, provincial, and territorial prisons. This fact has been well documented by inquiries and task forces. Aboriginal people comprise approximately three percent of the population in Canada, yet they represent roughly 17.5 percent of the federally sentenced prison population.[175] Given these inequities and the documented patterns of racist treatment of Aboriginal people by the government and the criminal justice system, it is likely that a large number of the prisoners who were subjected to the LSD and ECT experiments were Aboriginal.

These historical policies, laws, and practices have had devastating effects on Aboriginal health. This chapter has used historic examples to illustrate the foundation upon which current health policies for Aboriginal peoples are built. A somewhat grim but realistic picture has emerged. It is therefore not surprising that health services to Aboriginal people continue to fall far short of supporting full and robust health, or even strive to a status that is equal to non-Aboriginal Canadian health. Government policies dispersed health care to Aboriginal communities on an *ad hoc* basis according to the threat of contagion and the severity of diseases that might affect the non-Aboriginal population. In other words, health policies were geared toward protecting the good health of non-Aboriginal people. For government policies of abuse, negligence, or outright malevolence and criminality have had devastating effects for Aboriginal people and communities, and especially women.

PART TWO

The Law is a Determinant of Health

THE LAW PLAYS A MAJOR ROLE in shaping the social and structural factors that affect health. The law can also provide the teeth for enforcing public health standards and changing existing patterns that damage health. For instance, Canada-wide tobacco controls rely extensively on statute law and the enforcement of those laws through the courts. The criminal law power found in subsection 91(27) of the *Constitution Act, 1867* has great influence on health outcomes. The federal government has jurisdiction over "[t]he Criminal Law, except the Constitution of Courts of Criminal Jurisdiction, but including the Procedure in Criminal Matters"[1] In other words, the federal government holds tremendous power over health issues, because it can decide what is criminally harmful and what is permissible and good for human health.

It may seem harsh to invoke criminal law power in matters of public health. However, where public health regulations are concerned, this power can be either extremely useful or extremely harmful. It is extremely useful when it prohibits the sale of poisoned food or food that has been tampered with, advertising tobacco, and making false therapeutic claims for medicines. These are all important public health regulations that come under federal criminal law power.[2] However, this same federal power wields a heavy hand when it comes to regulating the use of traditional medicine. In this as in many other instances, Canadian laws may at times criminalize actions that are positive and normal in an Aboriginal context.

This chapter will review how law and health intersect and are interconnected. It will consider the effects of law on the health of Aboriginal people. It will also explore how the law has a role in shaping, recognizing, and addressing the determinants of Aboriginal health. To address these issues, this chapter will focus on two streams. First, it will consider how the constitutional division of powers and the ensuing conflicts over jurisdiction have contributed to the poor status of Aboriginal health. Associated laws and policies and the histories shed light on the present and can be instructive for creating a different and better legal framework for the future. Second, this chapter will review federal legislation designed to assimilate Aboriginal people into non-Aboriginal society and will show that ill health among Aboriginal people has resulted. Canada adopted an aggressive and brutal campaign to colonize and assimilate Aboriginal people into western, Euro-based society. In matters of health, the priority has been to protect the non-Aboriginal population from the ill health of the Aboriginal population. Yet, it was the non-Aboriginal population who not only brought disease but also destroyed the pre-existing Aboriginal lifestyles and medicine practices that had maintained good health over countless generations.

4.1   Why is the Constitution a Determinant of Health?

Canadian Confederation officially occurred on July 1, 1867, when Canada as a nation state was formed. Canadian constitutional governance was established, and powers were delineated between the federal and the provincial governments. At the time, the British Parliament omitted any mention of Canada's legislative power over health and health care. As a result, health does not expressly fall under the ambit of either the federal or the provincial governments.

Because the Constitution is silent on health, the courts have defined (and continue to define) how governmental powers should be distributed to meet health needs and concerns. As Professor Claude Emanuelli notes, health is the subject of ongoing federal–provincial negotiations and is subject to "jurisdictional currents"; "beginning with the adoption of the Constitutional Law of 1867, the evolution of Canadian constitutional law regarding health suffered the influence of different jurisprudential currents and of the political negotiations between the Federal Government and the provinces."[3]

Emanuelli explains that, in 1867, health was considered a private or local matter. The state intervened in health issues only during emergencies, such as epidemics. The *Constitution Act, 1867* stated that navy hospitals and the power to quarantine vessels fell within the federal sphere of power. Jurisdiction over hospitals, asylums, institutions, and orphanages, as well as "all Matters of a purely local or private Nature," fell within the provincial sphere.[4]

93

Although the Constitution's silence on matters of health and the provision of health care is problematic generally, it has been the cause of major concern for Aboriginal people. Without naming health specifically, several sections of the Constitution can nonetheless affect Aboriginal health. Health and health care issues obviously cut across federal, provincial, and territorial jurisdictions, and permeate constitutional law principles. Constitutional law prescribes how the federal and provincial governments exercise their powers (including any limitations) through the legislative, executive, and judicial function. A country's constitution has been described as reflecting the soul of the nation, because its job is to recognize and protect the nation's values.[5] The following section considers the federal constitutional powers as they apply to health.

4.1.1   Federal Powers Applicable to Aboriginal Health

The *Constitution Act, 1867* assigns Parliament a number of "heads of power" to legislate in areas that affect the practice of Aboriginal health and healing. Parliament's jurisdiction to regulate aspects of health products falls under two heads of power: first, criminal law and, second, peace, order, and good government and include:

Peace, Order, and Good Government

Parliament has a residual jurisdiction over "peace, order and good government" under section 91. This section permits Parliament to legislate where there may be "gaps" in jurisdiction under the Constitution, or where there is a national emergency or national concern. In order for there to be a "national concern," the matter must (a) have attained significant national importance, (b) be so single and distinct that giving jurisdiction to Parliament will be consistent with and not overly disturb the federal–provincial balance of power, and (c) be a matter which the provinces could not effectively regulate themselves. Examples of the exercise of this power include legislation regulating air and water pollution.[6]

Criminal Law

Under section 91(27) of the Constitution, Parliament has exclusive jurisdiction over criminal law. In addition to the *Criminal Code*, various criminal statutes have been enacted to protect public health and safety, such as: *Controlled Drugs and Substances Act,*[7] *Food and Drugs Act,*[8] and the *Hazardous Products Act.*[9] The implementation of these statutes may affect the use of traditional medicines.

Public debt and property

Section 91(1A) of the Constitution gives Parliament the power to make laws in respect of federally owned property.[10] This is one of the heads of power relied upon for legislation such as the *Canada Wildlife Act*[11] and the *Canada National Parks Act.*[12] These statutes may affect the Aboriginal and treaty right to hunt, gather and/or fish, which of course affects the quality of diet of Aboriginal peoples.

Intellectual Property Rights

Sections 91(22) and (23) of the *Constitution Act, 1867* give Parliament exclusive jurisdiction to legislate in the area of "patents of invention and discovery" and copyrights. These heads of power do not directly affect the practice of Aboriginal health and healing, but they may affect intellectual property rights associated with traditional Indigenous knowledge about health and medicine.

Spending

Perhaps the greatest means of influence that the federal government exercises in the area of health is through federal spending power.[13] This power has its source in a number of sections of the Constitution.[14] By imposing conditions on federal contributions to the provinces through the *Canada Health Act*, the federal government can exercise considerable control in areas of health, which may otherwise fall under provincial jurisdiction.

Indians and Lands Reserved for the Indians

Under s. 91(24), Parliament has constitutional jurisdiction over "Indians and Lands Reserved for the Indians." For the purpose of 91(24) and the determination of constitutional jurisdiction, Inuit are included within the term "Indians" in s. 91(24).[15] Pursuant to s. 91(24) and as the operative arm of s. 91(24), Parliament enacted the *Indian Act*.[16] The *Indian Act* is the key federal statute enacted pursuant to s. 91(24) of the *Constitution Act, 1867*, which authorizes the passage of laws regarding "Indians, and Lands reserved for the Indians" by the Parliament of Canada. The *Indian Act* effectively regulates much of the daily life of First Nations.

The Constitution was repatriated in 1982, and three distinct categories of Aboriginal peoples were recognized: Indian, Inuit, and Métis. Although the *Constitution Act, 1982* recognized the three Aboriginal groups equally, a vast cultural and linguistic diversity exists among them. They all, however, possess s. 35 Aboriginal rights. Some possess treaty rights as well. They all have common experiences resulting from how the federal and provincial governments have treated them historically and currently.

Under section 91(24) of the *Constitution Act, 1867*, the federal government has constitutional authority and responsibility for "Indians, and Lands reserved for the Indians." Judicial interpretation of the Constitution has determined that the Inuit are a federal responsibility.[17] The *Constitution Act, 1867* determined that health matters outside Indian jurisdiction in s. 91(24) may be found in several subsections of s. 92.

The provinces have primary responsibility for health care delivery for Métis and non-status Indians, which is no different from their responsibility to non-Aboriginal Canadians. Since the Yukon, Nunavut, and the Northwest Territories are under federal jurisdiction, each territory is responsible for delivering health care services to all their respective residents, including non-Aboriginal peoples living in their jurisdictions. Within this general framework, jurisdictional problems, conflicts, and ambiguities of enormous proportions have arisen and have had devastating effects on Aboriginal health. However, in January 2013, the Federal Court of Canada heard *Daniels* v. *Canada*[18] where it was held that Métis and non-status peoples are Indians within the meaning of s. 91(24) of the *Constitution Act, 1867*. The Federal government has subsequently appealed this decision to the Federal Court of Appeal. The Federal Court of Canada has laid the important distinction that may assist the Métis in a stronger political position in relation to federal jurisdiction when arguing for services and programs.

4.1.2 *Provincial Powers Applicable to Aboriginal Health*

The *Constitution Act, 1867* addressed health matters in general — outside Indian jurisdiction — found in s. 91(24) as well as in the following sections:

92. In each Province the Legislature may exclusively make Laws in relation to Matters coming within the Classes of Subjects next here-inafter enumerated; that is to say,

Health Institutions

Section 92(7) of the Constitution gives provincial legislatures authority over the "establishment, maintenance, and management of hospitals, asylums, charities, and eleemosynary institutions." The provinces thus have exclusive authority over the regulation of hospitals and other health institutions.

Property and Civil Rights

Section 92(13) of the Constitution provides jurisdiction over "property and civil rights in the province." This is the broadest head of power for the provincial legislatures. It gives the province the constitutional jurisdiction to, among other things, regulate medical and health care professionals, impose health and safety standards, and set requirements for valid consent to medical treatment. This head of provincial power is most likely to have an impact upon traditional healers, who are often caught between various definitions of health care professionals, health information custodians, and even physicians.

Natural Resources

As part of their powers over property and civil rights in s. 92(13), the management and sale of public lands in s. 92(5), and their control of forestry resources in s. 92A, the provinces also have jurisdiction generally over natural resources in the province. This includes the jurisdiction to regulate the collection of certain flora and fauna in the province. Regulations are generally established through legislation and are aimed at protecting endangered species. These federal and provincial powers have a close connection to Aboriginal practitioners and the collection of medicines.

Local or Private Matters

Section 92(16) of the Constitution contains a residual power for the provinces to deal "generally with matters of a merely local or private nature in the province." The Supreme Court of Canada has held that this head of power gives extensive authority over public health to the province.[19]

Taxation and Spending

In addition to these powers, provinces also have jurisdiction over direct taxation and spending.[20] This authority gives the province the power to implement health insurance schemes as well as to fund (or not fund) health programs and health institutions, etc.

Application of Provincial Laws to Indians

Generally, provincial laws apply unless they are prevented by one of the rules that exclude them. The Supreme Court has said that the provinces can legislate over Indians within their provincial powers, and such legislation is applicable to Indians both on and off reserve.

There is, however, a list of exclusionary rules: a) provincial laws cannot affect Indian rights; that is, the province cannot legislate on matters which go to the core of their "Indianness" (for instance, provincial authority cannot apply to practices, customs, and traditions that comprise Aboriginal rights); b) the application of provincial laws cannot impair the status or capacity of Indians, such as band membership or registration (this would be affecting their "Indianness"); c) provincial laws cannot single out Indians for special treatment (i.e., they cannot regulate Indians in the capacity of being an Indian — provincial laws may apply to Indians as long as they do not regulate in the federal sphere or risk being found outside their jurisdiction or *ultra vires*); d) provincial laws cannot affect Indian interest in lands; e) they cannot interfere with the paramountcy principle of federal legislation (i.e., provincial and federal powers can co-exist as long as they do not conflict — in which case the federal powers will prevail).[21] Indians are federal subjects under 91(24); but they still function under provincial powers as well, and these activities are non-distinguishable from their non-Indian counterparts. At times, Indians must function under both jurisdictions divisions (91 and 92).[22] Section 88 of the *Indian Act* also applies to provincial authority:

Subject to the terms of any treaty and any other Act of Parliament, all laws of general application from time to time in force in any province are applicable to and in respect of Indians in the province, except to the extent that those laws are inconsistent with this Act. . . .[23]

In the case of health and health practices, it may be argued that provincial laws do not apply to traditional healers because their work does go to the core of their Indianness. Similarly, provincial laws do not apply when the doctrine of federal paramountcy applies — that is, when a provincial law is inconsistent with a federal law. Section 91(24) of the *Constitution Act, 1867* could mean, therefore, that federal laws protecting Aboriginal rights trump any provincial laws dealing with or regulating traditional healers.

The relationships between the federal and provincial governments are complex and multifaceted. These relationships form a core element of decision making within the government as well as all policy making that affects Aboriginal people. Provincial regulation has had a major impact on many areas of traditional Aboriginal practices, but none have been as severely affected as traditional healers and practitioners.

4.1.3   *Provincial Regulation of Health Professions*

Provincial legislatures probably have the greatest power to affect the practice of traditional medicine, because they regulate health care professionals. No provincial legislation would attempt directly to regulate Aboriginal traditional healers. It would be *ultra vires*[24] for the provinces to do so, as it would single out First Nation (and arguably Inuit and Métis) healers.

However, in exercising their power to define activities that are subject to regulation, and to restrict the practice of certain health services to provincially licensed persons, the provinces have generally captured the activities of traditional healers. In some cases, they have made Aboriginal conduct illegal because of provincial licensing requirements. They have classified individuals as "practicing medicine" through a broad definition that would include the activities of traditional healers. The provincial acts have then prohibited Aboriginal healers from practising because they are not registered or licensed with the province.

The courts have struggled with how to define "practicing medicine." So far, provincial courts have relied on the 1907 Ontario Court of Appeal case of *R. v. Hill*[25] to claim that provincial medical licensing legislation applies to Indians. In that case, the defendant Hill was convicted of unlawfully practising medicine contrary to the Ontario *Medical Act.*[26] In the *Hill* case, the patient was non-Indian, and the services were provided on off-reserve territory. Would the same result have followed if the services had been provided on a reserve territory to an Aboriginal person?

Unfortunately, the case as reported lacks some important details. For example, was Hill charged for practising traditional Aboriginal medicine? This fact is probably absent because it did not matter for Hill's defence. The defence submitted that Hill was an Indian and, therefore, not legally considered a person. As a result, all provincial legislation was *ultra vires*, since only Parliament has jurisdiction over Indians. The court found that the law was *infra vires* the province, which meant that it did apply to Hill. Since Hill admitted that he was practising medicine, he was convicted, fined, and imprisoned.[27]

The *Hill* case was decided at a time when Indians were considered Crown wards and not eligible to vote, and before Aboriginal and treaty rights were recognized and affirmed in the *Constitution Act, 1982*. Owing to these factors and the absence of any evidence that Hill was practising traditional medicine, the decision in *Hill* must be limited to cases where an Aboriginal person is practising western medicine. In other words, *Hill* gives no guidance whatsoever that the provincial licensing legislation is within provincial authority, or *infra vires* the provinces, in cases involving Aboriginal traditional healers. Modern arguments for the legalization of the practice of medicine on reserve may be found in the *Indian Act*, s. 81(1(a)), where it allows band councils to pass bylaws that provide for health on reserve; recognizes that the practice of medicine goes to the core of Indianness; and that the practice of medicine is an Aboriginal right. The Court of Appeal in the *Delgamuukw* case suggested that "a person recognized as a Shaman according to Gitksan and Wet'suwet'en custom would not be qualified to practice as a medical doctor, nor would a medical doctor be qualified to practice as a Shaman." The Court called this an example of where the two laws might operate concurrently.[28]

The cases following *Hill* do clarify and confirm that provincial legislatures have the power to apply their laws on reserves, so long as the laws are connected to an issue that falls under a provincial head of power.[29] Similarly, in *R. v. Martin*[30] an Indian was convicted of unlawful possession of intoxicating liquor, which was contrary to a provincial temperance act. In *Four B Manufacturing* the application of provincial laws (in this case not medicine but labour issues) on reserve was confirmed and the *Paul* case (forestry) confirmed that "the division of powers does not preclude a validly constituted provincial administrative tribunal, legislatively empowered to do so, from determining questions of constitutional and federal law arising in the course of its work." Therefore, a tribunal could consider questions of Aboriginal rights arising incidentally to forestry matters (under provincial jurisdiction). Case authority clearly establishes that s. 88 of the *Indian Act* has the effect of making provincial laws of general application applicable to Indians that would not otherwise apply to them.[31] In 2008, *Quebec* v. *Rat* held that, generally, provincial laws apply to "native persons and on a reserve," as provincial legislatures have the power to apply their laws on reserves, provided the laws are connected to a subject matter that falls under a provincial head of power.[32] However, provincial legislatures cannot single out Aboriginal people for special treatment *because* they are Aboriginal. Based on this restriction, we can conclude that provinces have no jurisdiction to regulate, license, or register traditional healers. Yet, provincial legislation makes it illegal for anyone to practise medicine of any kind unless the province licenses him or her. Thus, provincial legislation claiming that traditional healers must be licensed by provinces conflicts with the *Constitution Act, 1867,* which states that the provinces have no jurisdiction to license traditional healers. In other words, conflicts between federal and provincial legislation over traditional healers can be examined in various ways, all leading to the same result.

All such conflicts may be resolved by a more precise interpretation of the statute. Given that provinces cannot license traditional healers, any legislation pertaining to the practice of medicine cannot be intended to apply to the activities of traditional healers under the meaning of "practicing medicine." Thus, there is no conflict. The statute does not apply to traditional healers because it was never intended to apply to them. However, from a practical perspective, such issues persist.

4.1.4   *Jurisdiction Conflicts*

The Health Council of Canada comments that many underlying factors negatively affect the health of Aboriginal people. These include poverty, the intergenerational effects of residential schools, and colonization itself. They note that "Aboriginal people are more likely than other Canadians to live with chronic conditions and infectious diseases, and to die prematurely."[33]

They also explained that the health of First Nations, Inuit, and Métis is well below the Canadian average.[34]

There are often difficulties in obtaining accurate health statistics, aggravated by the fact that federal and provincial/territorial governments are unclear about their responsibilities to Aboriginal people. The First Nations and Inuit Health Branch (FNIHB) strives to maintain partnerships among stakeholders. Yet, even with good intentions, health care services for Aboriginal people are in a transitory state, which can lead to fragmentation and gaps in delivery. For example, a gap may arise because of a recently completed self-government agreement or a modern treaty. Unclear divisions of power and responsibilities between Aboriginal communities and Canada's governments — federal, provincial, or territorial — may also cause gaps. Additional gaps occur for all residents living off reserve, including First Nations, Métis, and Inuit. In these cases, the provinces and territories are directly responsible for providing health care and public health programs and services, yet they often fail to do so.

The gaps created by jurisdictional conflicts between the federal and provincial governments have a severe impact on the health of Aboriginal people in Canada. They constitute a major determinant of ill health, disease, and death. For instance, provincial governments hold that the federal government is responsible for "Indians" under the *Indian Act*. Additionally, Aboriginal people have significant concerns with the federal government because of its system of classifying Indians as having or lacking status. The arguments between the federal and provincial/territorial governments over who has jurisdiction over whom has resulted in a complex and convoluted system of delivering — or not delivering — health care to First Nations and Inuit. It has also resulted in an assortment of provincial "hit or miss," under-funded programs for the Métis and non-status Indian populations. The problems we see today have a historical basis in how the government has delineated among First Nations, Métis, and Inuit.

Although services are delivered to the Inuit through FNIHB, the Inuit have unique jurisdiction issues distinct from Indian or Métis peoples. Under section 91(24) of the *Constitution Act, 1867*, the federal government has constitutional authority and responsibility for "Indians, and Lands reserved for the Indians." Judicial interpretation of the Constitution has determined that the Inuit are a federal responsibility. In 1912, for example, Quebec gained the northern territory that contained a large Inuit population. Quebec quickly categorized the Inuit as Indians under the *British*

North America Act, 1867 (now the Constitution Act, 1867) and therefore regarded them as a federal responsibility under subsection 91(24) of that Act. Law professor Kent McNeil notes that "confederation and the assignment to Parliament of legislative jurisdiction over 'Indians, and Lands reserved for the Indians' did not alter the nature of the Crown's fiduciary obligations to Aboriginal peoples. Those obligations continued, but primary responsibility for meeting them now rested on the Canadian government."[35] But the federal government did not agree, and regarded the Inuit as Quebec citizens. After much debate and confusion, the federal government assumed legal responsibility for the Inuit in 1924 through an amendment to the Indian Act that extended medical services to the Eastern Arctic.[36]

In 1932, the Indian Act was amended to delete the Inuit provision.[37] In the 1939 decision, Re: Eskimos,[38] the Supreme Court of Canada settled the issue and determined that the Inuit (at least in Quebec) were "Indians" under the British North America Act, 1867, and were therefore a federal responsibility. Eskimos were included within the definition of Indian under Section 91(24) of the BNA. In spite of this ruling, Canada continued the debate over whether the Inuit should be included under the Indian Act or if they should have an act of their own. Ultimately, an Inuit Act was not created, and the government department that managed northern affairs also managed Inuit affairs.[39]

In 1945, the responsibility for Inuit health was transferred to the Department of National Health and Welfare. For the first time, the federal government "publicly recognized the Eskimos as citizens of the Dominion by distributing among them family allowances to which a bill enacted a few months before had entitled all Canadian citizens." The 1951 Indian Act was amended to specifically exclude the Inuit, even though Inuit affairs continued to be administered federally.[40] In 1966, the Department of Indian Affairs and Northern Development was created. Quebec then negotiated a funding formula with the federal government based on the "recognition of the exclusive federally legislative authority"[41] that administered the Inuit. This arrangement remains in place today. Relying on Re: Eskimos, the Métis have argued that they should be included under subsection 91(24) of the BNA Act as well.[42] As noted in the 2013 Daniels v. Canada case, the Federal Court of Canada stated that, for the purpose of s. 91(24), Métis and non-status peoples are to be included in the definition of Indian. The federal government has subsequently appealed this decision.

Jurisdictional confusion leads to "Jordan's Principle"

Jordan River Anderson, a First Nations boy from Norway House Cree Nation in northern Manitoba, was born on October 22, 1999, with a rare neuromuscular disorder. He had complex medical needs that could not be managed on reserve near his home. Jordan was referred for treatment to Winnipeg, where, as his illness progressed, he became wheelchair bound, ventilator dependent, and unable to speak. He required a wide variety of medical services. Jordan was formally diagnosed with Carey-Fineman-Ziter syndrome.

By 2001, Jordan's medical team decided to discharge him to specialized foster home care near his home reserve where he could get the kind of health services that would substantially improve his quality of life. His medical team and his family agreed that this decision was best for Jordan, as he would have a nurturing environment in a loving home. However, the federal government and the Manitoba provincial government could not agree on who was financially responsible for Jordan's care. Squabbles over who would pay for every mediocre detail, including who would be responsible for Jordan's shower head, lasted for two years. Jordan died waiting for medical care. He was four years old.

Jurisdictional battles raged between Indian and Northern Affairs Canada and the First Nations and Inuit Health Branch, as well as inter-jurisdictionally between the federal government and the provinces. None of the parties in conflict had any hesitation about doling out much higher costs for institutional care instead of paying for family or community-based care, even to the detriment and death of the child. If Jordan had been living off reserve, the entire *per diem* cost would have been provided by the non-Aboriginal child welfare agency, with full reimbursement from the province. The child's needs would have been met first, and Jordan would not have been thrown into a jurisdictional tug of war. Jordan's case is not an anomaly.

The First Nations Child and Family Caring Society of Canada has asked the governments to immediately adopt a *child first* principle for resolving jurisdictional disputes that involve the care of First Nations children:

Under this principle, where a jurisdictional dispute arises between two government parties (provincial/territorial or federal) or between two departments or ministries of the same government, regarding payment for services for a Status Indian child which are otherwise available to other Canadian children, the government or ministry/department of first contact must pay for the services without delay or disruption. The paying government party can then refer the matter to jurisdictional dispute mechanisms. In this way, the needs of the child get met first while still allowing for the jurisdictional dispute to be resolved.[43]

On February 26, 2007, the Assembly of First Nations and the First Nations Child and Family Caring Society of Canada filed a human rights complaint about the lack of funding for home and community health care for First Nations children. At the time, more than 27,000 First Nations children were in institutional care. Three times more children had been removed from their families than were at the height of the residential schools system. Between 1995 and 2001, the number of registered Indian children entering care rose by 71.5 per cent nationally. The situation is dire in British Columbia, where over 50 per cent of the children in permanent institutional care are Aboriginal. In Saskatchewan and Manitoba, the situation is even worse: 80 per cent of the children in institutional care are Aboriginal.[44]

As the screening body for complaints, the Canadian Human Rights Commission sent the complaint to the Canadian Human Rights Tribunal, where it has met with various stalling, avoidance, and wrangling techniques by the federal government. On June 2 and 3, 2010, the Canadian Human Rights Tribunal heard Canada's motion to dismiss the First Nations child welfare complaint on the grounds that the *Canadian Human Rights Act* (*CHRA*) did not give the Tribunal jurisdiction to hear the case. The Crown argued that the *CHRA* only covers discrimination in cases of services, accommodations, or goods. The Crown argued that its funding program for First Nations child and family services is not a service. Therefore, Canada should not be held accountable for discrimination under the *CHRA*, no matter how inequitable its funding patterns have been. Opposing Canada are the Assembly of First Nations, the First Nations Child and Family Caring Society of Canada, the Chiefs of Ontario, Amnesty International Canada, and the Canadian Human Rights Commission.

The Tribunal rendered its ruling on Monday, March 14, 2011, and granted the motion of the Attorney General of Canada while dismissing the complaint of the Assembly of First Nations and First Nations Child and Family Caring Society of Canada against Indian and Northern Affairs

Canada. The most significant finding was that the *CHRA* does not recognize a valid comparator grouping between two different service providers (federal and provincial) with two different service recipients, therefore the complaint must be dismissed. The Canadian Human Rights Commission filed a Notice of Application on April 5, 2011, with the Federal Court of Canada, seeking judicial review. The Federal Court rejected the federal government's arguments, ordering a full hearing at the Canadian Human Rights Tribunal. The tribunal set aside several weeks of hearings on the issue in February and March. Beginning on February 25, 2013, the federal government has appeared before the Canadian Human Rights Tribunal to face allegations that it is racially discriminating against First Nations children by providing flawed and inequitable funding and policies for First Nations child and family services on reserves.

4.2 LEGISLATION

4.2.1 *The* Indian Act *as a Determinant of Health*

Broad definitions of the term "Indian" came into effect in 1850.[45] In 1876, section 3 specified the range of definition further: "[t]he term 'Indian' means 'any male person of Indian blood reputed to belong to a particular band,' 'any child of such person,' 'any woman who is or was lawfully married to such person.'"[46] In 1906, the *Indian Act* was amended to define a "person" as an individual *other* than an Indian.[47] Not until 1951 were amendments passed that redefined the terms, and the restrictions were lifted that affected women by defining them as legal "non-persons," thereby denying their entry into many professions.[48] For instance, "Indians were denied the right to vote, they did not sit on juries, and they were exempt from conscription in time of war (although the percentage of volunteers was higher among Indians than any other group). The attitude that others were the better judges of Indian interests turned the statute into a grab-bag of social engineering over the years."[49]

The following section deals with two aspects of the *Indian Act*: how it affected traditional healing practices, and how it caused discrimination and the legacy of devastating effects on the health and well-being of Aboriginal women and families.

Healing Practices

Chapter 2 details Aboriginal healing practices that maintained good health for generations. Canadian legislation has severely limited the use of these practices and, in some cases, criminalized them. Aboriginal healing practices were labeled "witchcraft and idolatry." They were ridiculed, denounced, prohibited, suppressed, and invalidated.[50] Western-based health care practices took over and suppressed Aboriginal healing practices.[51] The *Report of the Royal Commission on Aboriginal People* describes how this dominance began and then took form in legislation prohibiting Aboriginal health practices:

> Traditional healing methods were decried as witchcraft and idolatry by Christian missionaries and ridiculed by most others. Ceremonial activity was banned in an effort to turn hunters and trappers into agricultural labourers with a commitment to wage work. Eventually, the Indian Act prohibited those ceremonies that had survived most defiantly, the potlatch and the sundance. Many elders and healers were prosecuted.[52]

The Potlatch ceremony of coastal British Columbia peoples was forbidden. The 1884 *Indian Act* provision stated that a participant in the

> Indian dance known as the "Tamanawas" is guilty of a misdemeanor, and shall be liable to imprisonment for a term not more than six nor less than two months in any gaol or other place of confinement; and any Indian or other person who encourages, either directly or indirectly an Indian or Indians to get up such a festival or dance, or to celebrate the same, or who shall assist in the celebration of same is guilty of a like offence, and shall be liable to the same punishment.[53]

The Sundance ceremony of the Plains peoples was also outlawed by the 1895 *Indian Act*.[54] The 1914 *Indian Act* also prohibited Indians on reserve from dancing off reserve or from participating in "any show, exhibition, performance, stampede or pageant in aboriginal costume without the consent of the Superintendent general of Indian Affairs or his authorized Agent."[55]

The RCAP report states that many elders and healers were prosecuted under this law. As a result, Aboriginal peoples were stripped of "self-respect and respect for one another."[56] These discriminatory laws left a legacy that damaged the essence of Aboriginal communities. Declining health has been one of the inevitable outcomes.

Membership and *Indian Act* Status

Health and identity cannot be separated for Aboriginal women. The membership provisions in the *Indian Act* demonstrate this. In 1857, *An Act to Encourage the Gradual Civilization of Indian Tribes in the Province and to amend the Laws respecting Indians*[57] framed Indian enfranchisement as an "honour" and tied it to the acquisition of private property.[58] Private land holdings were granted to Indians who were enfranchised as Canadians and abandoned their Indian status. This included relinquishing their right to live on reserve, to receive health services, and to exercise hunting benefits. An Indian who had good moral character, who was free of debts, who could read and write English, and who could pass a three-year probationary period would receive a life estate allotment of up to 50 acres. He or she thus became a "Canadian citizen." Heirs could inherit interest in the life-estate allotment of Indian people in fee simple. These allotments, however, were taken from the reserve land base.[59]

For women in particular, the effects of forced enfranchisement have been devastating. Federal legislation from 1869 to 1985 determined a person's *Indian Act* status as well as band membership, and determined who would or would not live on reserve. When a woman married a man from another band, she automatically transferred to her husband's band.

Not only did the Act identify those who could live on reserves, it also defined an Indian as "a male Indian, the wife of a male Indian or the child of a male Indian." Indian women who married outside their band were stripped of their status and could not pass it on to their children. Indian men who married gave their status and band membership to their wives, children, and grandchildren. These patrilineal lines of status still have preference in the current *Indian Act*.

The *Report of the Royal Commission on Aboriginal Peoples* summarized the number of women who were "enfranchised" and removed from their home communities:

Between 1955 and 1975 (when forced enfranchisement of women stopped), 1,576 men became enfranchised (along with 1090 wives and children), while 8,537 women (as well as 1,974 of their children) were forcibly enfranchised and lost their status. From 1965 to 1975, only five percent of enfranchisements were voluntary; 96 per cent were involuntary and the great majority of these involved women.[60]

Since the 1960s, Indian women have been fighting for fairness to secure equal rights in the Indian registration provisions. Jeanette Corbiere Lavell[61] and Yvonne Bedard challenged section 12(1)(b) of the *Indian Act* as a breach of the 1960 *Canadian Bill of Rights* (sex equality),[62] but they lost their case before the Supreme Court of Canada. The Supreme Court rationalized that equal discrimination against all Indian women amounted to equality under the law. In 1981, Sandra Lovelace[63] successfully challenged Canada on section 12(1)(b) for being in violation of the *International Covenant on Civil and Political Rights*.[64] The United Nations Human Rights Committee found that First Nations women and their children were deprived of the fundamental right to enjoy culture in their communities.

Subsequently, in 1985, an amendment was made to the *Indian Act* through Bill C-31.[65] Bill C-31 sustained the Indian status of those already recognized, but relegated and reinstated women who had lost status because of sex discrimination to another class of Indian and second-class status category. As a result of Bill C-31, Indians who never lost status can pass their status to their children and grandchildren, while Indians who have a second class (and diminished) status can pass their status to their children, but not to their grandchildren.

Sharon McIvor has spent over 25 years arguing that the *Indian Act* violates the equality guarantees in section 15 of the *Canadian Charter of Rights and Freedoms*.[66] She challenged the continuing discrimination that gives preferred Indian status to men who married outside their band as well as to the descendants of male Indians. These provisions diminished the status of women who married outside their band as well as those descended from female Indians. Sharon McIvor was successful in arguing her case to the B.C. Supreme Court in 2007, as well as in the B.C. Court of Appeal in 2009. Both courts confirmed that the status provisions of the *Indian Act* violate the equality guarantees of the Charter.

Consequently, the federal government is in the process of amending the *Indian Act,* much like it did with Bill C-31 — that is, unilaterally and without input from the people whose lives the bill affects. On March 11, 2010, Bill C-3, the *Gender Equity in Indian Registration Act* was introduced to remedy the sex discrimination in the status registration provisions of the *Indian Act*. On May 18, 2010, Sharon McIvor wrote to the House of Commons, stating:

> Bill C-3 will not even confer equal registration status on those who will be newly eligible. The grandchildren of Indian women who married out will only receive section 6(2) status, and never section 6(1) status. So even those who will be newly entitled to status under Bill C-3 will be treated in a discriminatory way because their Aboriginal ancestor was a woman, not a man. The "second generation cut-off" will apply to the female line descendants a generation earlier than it does to their male line counterparts.[67]

Bill C-3 will not address all of the inequity in the *Indian Act* or solve all the discrimination problems that women and their families face. It will, however, positively affect the lives of an estimated 45,000 women. On December 15, 2010, Bill C-3, the *Gender Equity in Indian Registration Act,* received royal assent and was proclaimed in force January 31, 2011. AANDC currently has a process in place to receive applications for women who lost their status.[68]

Laws, legislation, and policies — including how they are enacted and enforced — have a direct impact on the health status of women in their communities, and the *Indian Act* is a prime example. The aggregate of Canadian laws have contributed to perpetuating the inequality of Aboriginal women, which translates into inequities in the area of health care and health services as well. Harmful health consequences for women negatively affect not only their own personal experiences but also the lives of their children, family, and community members.

4.2.2 The Criminal Code *of Canada*

Under subsection 91(27) of the *Constitution Act, 1867,* the federal government has jurisdiction over "[t]he Criminal Law, except the Constitution of Courts of Criminal Jurisdiction, but including the Procedure in Criminal Matters."[69] It may seem odd to rely on the criminal law to support public health, but where public health regulations are concerned, the criminal law power can be useful. The public needs protection against such things as tainted food, advertising tobacco to minors, and false therapeutic claims for medicines.[70]

However, Aboriginal healers could face serious problems in this area. Anyone who provides medical services to individuals in Canada could be exposed to some level of criminal liability for their actions. The legislation does not exempt Aboriginal traditional healers. In fact, because of the nature of Aboriginal traditional medicine — its unwritten traditions and the lack of visible internal or external regulation — traditional healers may find themselves vulnerable to criminal prosecution.

In addition to the liability outlined in existing legislation, such as the *Food and Drugs Act* and the *Natural Health Products Regulations*,[71] the Crown may use various sections of the *Criminal Code* to prosecute traditional healers.[72] Generally, prosecution occurs when a patient suffers injury during the course of treatment:

216. Every one who undertakes to administer surgical or medical treatment to another person or to do any other lawful act that may endanger the life of another person is, except in cases of necessity, under a legal duty to have and to use reasonable knowledge, skill and care in so doing.

217. Every one who undertakes to do an act is under a legal duty to do it if an omission to do the act is or may be dangerous to life.

219. (1) Every one is criminally negligent who
(a) in doing anything, or
(b) in omitting to do anything that it is his duty to do, shows wanton or reckless disregard for the lives or safety of other persons.

220. Every person who by criminal negligence causes death to another person is guilty of an indictable offence. . . .

221. Every one who by criminal negligence causes bodily harm to another person is guilty of an indictable offence and liable to imprisonment for a term not exceeding ten years.

245. Every one who administers or causes to be administered to any person or causes any person to take poison or any other destructive or noxious thing is guilty of an indictable offence and liable
(a) to imprisonment for a term not exceeding fourteen years, if he intends thereby to endanger the life of or to cause bodily harm to that person; or

(b) to imprisonment for a term not exceeding two years, if he intends thereby to aggrieve or annoy that person.

In addition to the *Criminal Code*, the *Controlled Drugs and Substances Act*[73] regulates a number of substances that may include those used by traditional healers. The legislation makes it illegal for anyone other than provincially licensed medical practitioners to dispense controlled substances. Provincial governments do not have constitutional jurisdiction to directly regulate Aboriginal traditional healers. Therefore, unless traditional healers also qualify as some other type of medical practitioner licensed provincially, traditional healers may not be subject.

The intersection of criminal law and Aboriginal healing practices raises the possibility that criminal charges could be laid against healers and/or communities. Charges that might arise include:

Criminal negligence: everyone is criminally negligent who in doing anything or in omitting to do anything that it is his or her duty to do shows wanton or reckless disregard for the lives or safety of other persons (*Criminal Code*, s. 219(1)(a)-(b)).

Homicide: a person commits culpable homicide when he causes the death of a human being, by criminal negligence (*Criminal Code*, subpara. 222(5) (a)).

Homicide: death from the treatment of an injury (*Criminal Code*, s. 225).

Murder: where a person who causes the death of another human being means to cause their death or means to cause him or her bodily harm that he or she knows is likely to cause his death and is reckless whether death occurs or not (*Criminal Code*, s. 229(a)(i)-(ii)).

Murder in the commission of offences — i.e., an "offender willfully stopping, by any means, the breath of a human being and death ensues therefrom" (*Criminal Code*, s. 230).

Accessory after the fact: everyone who is an accessory after the fact to murder is guilty of an indictable offence and liable to imprisonment for life (*Criminal Code*, s. 240).

Bodily harm and acts and omissions causing danger to the person: everyone who administers or causes to be administered to any person or causes any person to take poison or any other destructive or noxious thing is guilty of an indictable offence (*Criminal Code*, s. 245)

Kidnapping: forcible confinement (*Criminal Code*, s. 279(2)).

Break and enter with intent, committing offence or breaking out: (*Criminal Code*, s. 348(1)).

Assault: The application of force intentionally to another person, directly or indirectly (*Criminal Code* s. 265 (1)).

In addition to possible offences under the *Criminal Code of Canada*, Aboriginal healers may find themselves in conflict with various provisions of the *Controlled Drugs and Substances Act*, i.e., trafficking in substance (s. 5) and importing and exporting (s. 6). The basis for this conflict is that the medicine(s) used in traditional and ceremonial practices may fall within a list or lists of controlled drugs or substances. Traditional healers have reason to be concerned. Among reported cases, Aboriginal people have, in fact, been charged under the *Criminal Code* for a variety of offences that arose in connection with their healing work.

Some early criminal cases deal with consequences of denying Aboriginal healing. In the 1897 decision, *R. v. Machekequonabe*,[74] an Indian man killed another man because he believed his victim was a Wendigo.[75] The victim was actually Machekequonabe's foster father, and the accused was mistaken. The accused was subsequently convicted of manslaughter. The case contains a brief discussion of a Wendigo. On appeal, the defence argued:

> J. K. Kerr, Q.C., for the prisoner. The evidence shews the Indian tribe were pagans, and believed in an evil spirit clothed in human form which they called a Wendigo, and which attacked, killed and ate human beings. The man that was shot was thought to be a Wendigo, a spirit as distinguished from a human being. It is true there was a mistake, but there was no intention even to harm a human being much less to kill. The evidence shews the mistake was not unreasonable. At common law the following of a religious belief would be an excuse. The trial Judge wrongly directed the jury to find the prisoner guilty. There should be a new trial at least.[76]

The court refused to entertain the thought that Machekequonabe had a mistaken belief, and instead found sufficient evidence to convict him of manslaughter.

Conversely, nearly 100 years later, in *R. v. Jacko*,[77] Jacko used a self-defence argument during his murder trial. He successfully argued that he killed a man because the man was a bear walker and that he would have caused harm to Jacko. Jacko struck at least two blows to the victim's head with a walrus bone, which caused extensive damage to the left side of the skull behind the left ear. Jacko was small in stature, with a humble disposition. The victim, on the other hand, was a large man and violent and likely the instigator of the fight that caused his death. Counsel offered the following evidence:

> The first of the utterances made by the Accused at the Trudeau home were preceded 20 minutes earlier by a bellowing noise like bears fighting, a sound Ronald Roy had never heard from a human. They were followed by human voices cursing and yelling. One of the voices sounded like Tab's, according to Roy. The utterances made to Roy and other Native witnesses, included statements that "I am a warrior." "I got the Bearwalker." "I won the victory." "I cut my wrist by killing a Bearwalker — the bearwalker won't bother us anymore." The Native witnesses described the Accused as crying, dazed, looking like a cornered animal, emotional, and screaming as he uttered the words.
>
> . . .
>
> His description of himself as a warrior, who killed the Bearwalker, must be understood, not as an act of aggression but as an act of self defence, an act to protect others from an evil spirit.[78]

The court allowed Jacko's claim of self-defence as defined in s. 34(2) of the *Criminal Code*. The court did not say, one way or the other, whether the accused was an unsuspecting victim of a bear walker. It did, however, allow the self-defence argument because the evidence was not clear and convincing of murder. The Crown could not prove, by a reasonable-doubt standard, that Mr. Jacko struck the fatal blow with the intent to murder and not in self-defence under s. 34(2) of the *Criminal Code of Canada*.

The 2002 Ecuadorian Healers Case is particularly interesting for healers visiting from out of the country when something goes awry and the *Criminal Code* is invoked in accidental death. Two Ecuadorian healers, Juan and Edgar Uyunkar, were invited into Wikwemikong, Ontario, by the Naandwedidaa program of the Wikwemikong Health Services Department to perform healing ceremonies for community members.[79] Mrs. Jean (Jane) Maiangowi, a terminally ill woman, died during one of the healing ceremonies. Initial investigations into her death revealed that she had died due to natural causes. One month later, after further investigations and pressure from the elderly woman's family, the healers were charged with various criminal charges, including criminal negligence causing death, administering a noxious substance, and importing and trafficking in a controlled substance. The Crown alleged that the Uyunkars provided a mixture of water, nicotine, and harmaline known as natem to Mrs. Maiangowi. Mrs. Maiangowi's cause of death was the result of acute nicotine poisoning. Maria Ventura, the healers' interpreter, was also charged with administering a noxious substance and trafficking in a controlled substance.[80] The Uyunkars were released on bail but were forced to relinquish their passports and were unable to leave the Manitowaning area. They were ordered to report to the Ontario Provincial Police on a regular basis. As a bail condition, the healers were prohibited from possessing the medicines that they used in their healing ceremony.[81]

At the trial of the healers and their interpreter, the healers pled guilty to two of the charges: administering a noxious substance and trafficking in a controlled substance. The remaining charges — criminal negligence causing death, importing a controlled substance into Canada, and possession of a controlled substance — were dropped in a negotiated plea. The interpreter, Maria Ventura of Manitowaning, had all charges against her dropped. Juan Uyunkar received a 12-month conditional sentence and a 12-month probation. He was required to serve 150 hours of community service, reside in the area of Wikwemikong, observe a curfew, and not leave Ontario. Edgar Uyunkar received a 12-month conditional sentence and one day in jail. He was also ordered to return to Ecuador within 14 days of the trial.[82]

While the healers and their interpreter are Indigenous people from Ecuador, the Canadian charges laid against them are illustrative of the fact that traditional practitioners are vulnerable to criminal charges. Since it can be generalized that most traditional medicine people and healers have a helper to support them throughout the ceremony, the helper of a medicine person is also vulnerable. In the rare situation where death occurs and the medicine person is charged with murder, it follows that his or her helpers may face charges as accessories to murder. In the Ecuador healers case, the interpreter was charged. The Ecuadorian healers are not considered to fall within the scope of persons possessing existing Aboriginal and treaty rights and thus cannot avail themselves of the protection of section 35 of the *Constitution Act, 1982*. This reasoning is open to question in light of the global rights of the world's Indigenous peoples and the application of International laws.

As the Uyunkar situation suggests, specific provisions of the *Criminal Code* may be problematic for Aboriginal healers. In some instances, for example, traditional medicines may be deemed to be "noxious" substances.[83] A person charged and convicted of this offence faces the possibility of a term of imprisonment not to exceed fourteen years. Although it is unlikely that Aboriginal healers will force their practices on others, the issue of forcible confinement may arise. The facts in the *Thomas* v. *Norris* case suggest that criminal charges for forcible confinement or assault may be laid.

The 1992 decision of the court in *Thomas* v. *Norris*[84] is illustrative of the clash of two worldviews in the initiation of a spirit dancer in a First Nation healing ceremony of the Coast Salish peoples. Typically, a member of the family will ask that a participant be initiated because they need to learn some type of "lesson." David Thomas was creating difficulties for his family through his excessive alcohol consumption, so his future wife asked that he be initiated. This initiation was a common Coast Salish practice. Thomas was taken by the "spirit dancers" to participate in a sacred ceremony. The Spirit Dancing of the Coast Salish people was the traditional healing practice on trial in this case. Justice Hood described this ceremony:

> The initiation process is commenced by the initiate being "grabbed," by his or her initiators, and taken to a Long House and there detained for a number of days, presumably the time it takes to complete the initiation. It is completed when the initiate has his or her vision experience, which is evidenced by the initiate dancing and singing his or her song. While in the Long House, the initiate undergoes a process which includes being lifted horizontally to shoulder or head height, by eight or so initiators, who, among other things, blow on the body of the initiate to help the initiate "bring out" or sing his or her song. This ritual is repeated daily, four times each morning and four times each afternoon. The initiation is done under the guidance of elders who are in charge of the process, which takes a number of days. During the process the initiate participates in rituals including

a ceremonial bath, dressing in clean clothes, fasting and sleeping in a blanket tent set up in the House. The initiate is always accompanied by an attendant who is called his or her "babysitter."

The initiate is captured or grabbed either with or without his or her consent. The only consent required is that of a senior member of the initiate's family. Apparently, it is not uncommon for a wife to ask the elders to have her husband initiated by the house dancers. It is said that in the end the initiate sings his or her song while dancing, and the song is said to be proof of a supernatural vision experience.[85]

In the case, the complainant argued that he was taken against his will. Thomas sued for assault, battery, and wrongful confinement. At trial, the court found that Thomas satisfied the burden of proof with respect to these allegations, so he was awarded non-pecuniary and exemplary damages. The court stated that, on the facts of this case, there was insufficient evidence "to prove that spirit dancing is an aboriginal right, or that it was in existence and practiced at all the material times." In addition, the judge was not satisfied that the ancient activities involving force or confinement against the will can be said to be an Aboriginal right; the trial judge noted, "under the Criminal Code both assault and confinement of a person are criminal offences in certain circumstances."[86]

The *Thomas* v. *Norris* decision may be somewhat less important than it appeared initially, as it can be distinguished as having been decided prior to a number of significant Supreme Court of Canada decisions concerning Aboriginal rights, such as *Van der Peet*,[87] *Delgamuukw*,[88] *Marshall*,[89] *Sappier and Grey*,[90] and *Morris*.[91] However, in the case of *Moulton Contracting Ltd.* v. *British Columbia*, Hinkston J. commented, "The torts of conspiracy to commit unlawful conduct and unlawful interference with contractual relations, as well as the defences to them, have not been thoroughly fleshed out by Canadian courts."[92] He added:

However, in this case, I find that the treaty rights guaranteed by the s. 35 of the Constitution Act, 1982 do not provide for civil immunity for unlawful tortious conduct. Unlike in other cases where treaty rights have been alleged as defences to regulatory prosecutions (see for example, *R.* v. *Sappier,* 2006 SCC 54 and *R.* v. *Morris,* [2006] 2 S.C.R. 915) the defendants here are not alleging constitutional invalidity of the statutory provisions where the offence is set out. Instead, they are attempting to use treaty rights to justify tortious conduct.[93]

The court also held that even if the healing ceremony was an Aboriginal right and protected by sections 35 and 52 of the *Constitution Act, 1982*, it still would not justify tortious conduct.[94]

As seen in *Thomas* v. *Norris*[95] even though the defendants were sued for false imprisonment, assault, and battery that occurred in a traditional ceremony that they argued was protected under s. 35 of the *Constitution Act, 1982* Mr. Justice Hood surmised, "[p]lacing the Aboriginal right at its highest level it does not include civil immunity for coercion, force, assault, unlawful confinement or any unlawful tortious conduct on the part of the defendants. . . ."[96] However, unlike *R.* v. *Sappier* and *R.* v. *Morris,* where treaty rights had been infringed through a regulatory scheme, the use of Constitutional supremacy framework arguments in Moulton could have held that the contractual relations were an infringement of their Aboriginal and treaty rights as protected by the *Constitution Act, 1982.*

In the *R.* v. *Cummings* decision,[97] a case concerning adverse possession, the court considered the prior possession of land by an "Indian medicine man" named Klaw Chaw or Dr. Johnson. The court recognized the unique status of a medicine man and his existence on the land prior to the birth of the Canadian colony. The case, however, was reversed a year later.[98] In *R.* v. *Lafferty,*[99] the Crown brought an application for change of venue because the jurors might be influenced by the anticipated appearance of a local "medicine man" at the new trial. The court entertained competing affidavits concerning the powers of the medicine man, but Justice de Weerdt found that bias was unlikely and dismissed the Crown's application. The court accepted that community members understood that the powers of the medicine man were limited and not supernatural. This acceptance was based in large part on the supplementary affidavit sworn by the Grand Chief of the Dogrib Nation; Eddie Erasmus noted that "medicine men and women in our culture are authorized to deal only in matters of health and healing. These persons are not priests nor prophets. . . . The people in the Rae Edzo community know of the very limited powers of these said powers and specifically that they have no supernatural powers."[100]

Traditional healers may be liable for negligence or for other areas of tort law. Issues may arise with respect to tortious liability for malpractice. The law states that a medical practitioner does not guarantee the success of any treatments.[101] The medical practitioner is held to the standard of an average practitioner. Where an individual practises Aboriginal medicine, a problem arises with such uncertainty and ambiguity. Can this individual be employed by a medical doctor and be covered by the doctor's insurance, or would it be possible for the individual who practises Aboriginal medicine to be insured independently?

There are also problems with people claiming to be healers who are not, as in the 2000 case of *R. v. Mianskum*.[102] Jonathan Harold Mianskum was charged with sexual assault and sexual touching contrary to s. 271 and s. 153(1) of the *Criminal Code of Canada*. The young woman was 17 years old and went to Mianskum's home for the purpose of healing her abdominal pains, since she found no relief from her medical doctor. She had recently discovered that she had an Aboriginal heritage and had met Mianskum at the local friendship centre. While she was receiving her "healing," Mianskum touched various parts of her body, including her breasts, with a liquid, sucked out brown liquid from her abdominal area by placing his lips near her navel, and inserted a "medical bundle" into her vagina. He also forcibly kissed her. The court relied on the evidentiary procedure in *R v. Mohan*[103] and was able to discern from testimony from a credible and court-approved healer. Wanda Elizabeth Whitebird testified that Mianskum was not acting appropriately as an Aboriginal healer. Whitebird testified that she had never seen a ceremony like this. She testified that she had never heard of stripping naked at a healing ceremony and that if a man and woman were involved in a process like that, they would be totally clothed, and she had never heard of anything being placed in the vaginal area. Whitebird also testified that, if a woman approached her who was complaining of abdominal pain, she would initially take her history, then decide upon a healer and the next processes to take. There would always be another person present in the room, with all parties being fully clothed. If the pain was in the abdominal area, pants may be undone or loosened, but the underwear would never be removed. She testified that it would be important to know what nation the healer came from, and to learn of his or her credentials.[104] Mianskum was subsequently convicted on both counts of sexual assault and sexual touching.

Similarly, in the case of *R. v. H.G.*,[105] an uncle of the 12-year-old victim performed smudging ceremonies on his grandniece on three occasions. He claimed to be an elder and a medicine man. While he was performing two of his ceremonies, he made suggestive remarks to the young girl, and during the last "ceremony" he told her to take her shorts and underpants off and put his finger in her vagina. He received an eighteen month conditional sentence, which he unsuccessfully appealed.

The law can be a double-edged sword; some people claim to be healers and they clearly are not, but they use traditional healing practices as avenues for abuses and are thus prosecuted under the *Criminal Code*. On the other hand, the law may be used against genuine healers who are practising their inherent rights to medicine and healing but become involved in a clash of two worldviews between the Western world and the traditional one and the *Criminal Code* is used against them.

In the family law arena, Aboriginal spirituality has also played a role in the awarding of custody in cases involving Aboriginal children. In *Kudaka v. Kudaka*,[106] the court granted custody to the mother of a young boy because the child's stepfather was against Native spirituality and the teaching of it to the child. The child's birth father was a First Nations man and the child's mother wanted her son to know about his cultural heritage.

Generally, Aboriginal healing practices and traditional medicines are not recognized through legislation. The use of the Canadian legal system as a means of regulating traditional healing is generally considered unsatisfactory, as seen in the cases above. Healers, educators, and communities have resisted the regulation of traditional practices. This resistance is expected to continue, particularly given that the Canadian legal system has clashed with the systems and beliefs of Aboriginal peoples.

4.3 LEGAL ISSUES AFFECTING TRADITIONAL PRACTICES

In general, the various heads of provincial power give the provinces greater jurisdiction over health matters than the federal government. The exception is those areas of health practices that the *Indian Act* specifically suppresses. Each province exercises its own discretion about its own legislation; however, the provinces are generally uniform in their exercise of jurisdiction in a number of areas that have an impact on Aboriginal traditional health and healers. Without going into a province-by-province survey of legislation, this section will review the general nature of provincial legislation and how it might affect traditional medicine and the practice of traditional healers.

Tobacco Legislation

The provinces have enacted various statutes that control the use of tobacco in public places. Federal legislation may be seen as failing to accommodate the traditional use of tobacco by Aboriginal people by making it illegal to provide tobacco to a youth under any circumstances. However, many provinces accommodate traditional tobacco use specifically in their statutes or legislation by suspending the federal laws in cases of traditional use by Aboriginal people, and section 13 of the *Tobacco Control Act, 1994* establishes that provincial and municipal laws and regulations that prohibit smoking do not apply to the Aboriginal use of tobacco.[107]

Collection of Medicines

Just as the federal government can control the collection of medicines within federal jurisdiction, so, too, the provinces have authority to control the collection of flora and fauna within their regions. However, the jurisdictional limits placed on the provinces by the Constitution would affect whether a restriction on the collection of traditional medicines would apply to Aboriginal healers and their helpers. Thus, if provincial legislation infringed upon the Aboriginal right to harvest traditional medicine, the province would have the burden of proving that the infringement was justified according to the principles set out by the Supreme Court of Canada in *Sparrow* and subsequent decisions.[108]

Exercising its constitutional authority over federal lands and the residual "peace, order, and good government" head of power, Parliament has enacted a number of statutes that may restrict the ability of traditional healers to collect or harvest traditional medicines. Because of its authority over lands held by the federal government, Parliament is able to control the wildlife, including flora and fauna, in national parks. The *Canada National Parks Act*[109] regulates access to and use of all national parks. Amendments to the Act in 2001 now permit the Governor in Council to protect flora and fauna in national parks, which includes regulating the taking of specimens. Regulations such as the National Parks General Regulations[110] and the National Historic Parks General Regulations[111] restrict the removal of any flora or fauna from parks. At the same time, the *Canada National Parks Act* authorizes the Cabinet to permit Aboriginal traditional harvesting activities for the "use or removal of flora and other natural objects, by Aboriginal people for traditional spiritual and ceremonial purposes."[112]

Whereas the *Canada National Parks Act* regulates flora and fauna by virtue of their location in national parks, the *Species at Risk Act*[113] regulates flora and fauna by virtue of their designation as species at risk. Once designated, Parliament can prohibit the collection, possession, and trade of particular species of flora and fauna. Although it is not legally binding, the preamble to this statute states, "the traditional knowledge of the aboriginal peoples of Canada should be considered in the assessment of which species may be at risk and in developing and implementing recovery measures."

The legislation goes on to create two committees for providing "Aboriginal advice." First, the Minister is supposed to select six representatives of Aboriginal peoples to sit on the *National Aboriginal Council on Species at Risk* (NACOSAR) to provide advice on administering the Act (s. 7.1). Second, the Committee on the *Status of Endangered Wildlife in Canada* is to set up a sub-committee specializing in Aboriginal traditional knowledge (s.18(1)). The role of the NACOSAR is to advise the Minister of Environment on administering the Act and to provide advice and recommendations to the Canadian Endangered Species Conservation Council (CESCC) as set out in section 8(1) of the Act. NACOSAR is made up of six representatives of Aboriginal peoples who are appointed by the minister for two-year terms.[114]

The Courts have issued interlocutory injunctions in certain cases of plant harvesting. For example, in *Hunt* v. *Halcan Log Services Ltd.*,[115] a case concerning a land dispute, the right to harvest herbal medicines is mentioned in passing. The parties in this case each sought interlocutory injunctions to prevent the other party from interfering with proprietary and other rights to Deer Island. The Kwakiutl Indian Band (and one of its hereditary chiefs) sought to prevent Halcan Log Services from logging on Deer Island until the trial was over. This argument was advanced on both Aboriginal and treaty rights to the land. In the context of these rights, the Band and their Hereditary Chief asserted claims to, among other things, harvest medicines.

For its part, Halcan had recently purchased the land in issue and sought to prevent the band members from trespassing or obstructing Halcan's access to the land. The firm based its argument on its "ownership" of the land in fee simple as well as on a logging permit issued to the firm by the Ministry of Lands and Forests. Justice Trainor of the British Columbia Supreme Court granted the interlocutory injunction that restrained the company's logging activities.

In *MacMillan Bloedel Ltd.* v. *Mullin*,[116] the court issued an interlocutory injunction that prohibited MacMillan Bloedel from clear-cutting an area of Meares Island claimed by the Clayoquot Island Band. The Court found that the area to be clear-cut would be wholly logged and permanently destroyed as a result. The Court considered the symbolic and cultural importance of the island to the Band, which included harvesting plants.

In British Columbia, the Wet'suwet'en asked for a continuance of a stay to prevent herbicide use on their traditional territories. The Wet'suwet'en submitted that if their lands were subjected to chemical treatment, the land would suffer harm that "is clearly harm of the type that cannot be quantified in monetary terms or otherwise cured." Specifically, the herbicides would destroy traditional foods, medicines, and cultural resources. They also claimed that the Wet'suwet'en frequently visited the areas proposed for chemical application for the purposes of harvesting food, medicine, and cultural resources. They used approximately 90 per cent of the plants gathered there. The Wet'suwet'en claimed that applying the chemical would cause not only the loss of the plants themselves but also the loss of the animals who rely on the plants as well as fish and wildlife.[117] In this case, the Wet'suwet'en were unsuccessful, and the court did not grant a stay.

In *McCrady* v. *Ontario*,[118] Theron McCrady, the chief of Poplar Point Ojibway Nation, asked the court for an injunction to stop the construction of a hydroelectric power dam at High Falls on the Namewaminikan River near Beardmore in the District of Thunder Bay. McCrady claimed that an environmental assessment should be completed, because of the repercussions on "the potential impacts of the project on our Aboriginal food and medicine harvesting rights and on our sacred sites."[119]

The courts have seen a myriad of applications and motions and injunctions among First Nations and others who seek to exploit property in First Nation territories. There have been difficult proceedings in such cases as *Frontenac*[120] and *Platinex*[121] as well as the Haudenosaunee claims[122] at Caledonia and Brantford, Ontario. These conflicts raise complex legal, cultural, and spiritual issues. In the cases of *Frontenac* and *Platinex,* Algonquin community protestors were charged with contempt for ignoring injunctions in favour of the mineral exploration companies. In both cases, elders and community representatives were jailed and fined for protecting their lands. The process of consultation in these cases was minimal and somewhat unrealistic; the results for the lands are that traditional territories are exploited and medicines are forever destroyed.

4.3.1 Codex Alimentarius

Codex Alimentarius is a subcommittee of the United Nations that is mandated to establish guidelines on food trade issues. Although these guidelines themselves are not legally binding, countries that are part of the World Trade Organization (WTO) may be severely penalized for not following the Codex.

The Codex Alimentarius Commission, formally established in 1963, is a subsidiary of a joint program of the Food and Agriculture Organization of the United Nations and the World Health Organization's Food Standards Program. The Commission, composed of member governments, including Canada, is mandated to set international reference standards for trade in all kinds of food products. In the early 1990s, Codex began harmonizing standards for food supplements. By 2005, the guidelines prevented the sale of all vitamins, minerals, enzymes, and other essential nutrients as food supplements and treated them as pharmaceutical drugs. This meant that only pharmacists could dispense them. The materials were to be only manufactured by pharmaceutical companies and only made from synthetic materials, including genetically engineered substances.[123]

Most of the information available regarding Codex Alimentarius refers to its role in the USA, but it is not a US-specific body. Codex is involved in every national or international body concerned with public health. It is noted that in 2012, the United States is the North American representative on the Codex Executive Committee (2011–2013); Canada is the host country for the Codex Committee on Food Labelling (CCFL); the Codex Committee on Vegetable Proteins is adjourned *sine die*. Canada hosts the Codex Regional Co-ordinating Committee for North America and the Southwest Pacific on a rotational basis, sharing the hosting responsibilities with Australia, New Zealand, and the United States.[124]

The Codex program in Canada is managed by an Interdepartmental Committee for Codex consisting of senior officials from Health Canada, the Canadian Food Inspection Agency, the Department of Foreign Affairs and International Trade, Industry Canada, and Agriculture and Agri-Food Canada. The designated Codex Contact Point for Canada is located in the Food Directorate of Health Canada's Health Protection Branch. The key issue is that the Codex will move all natural products into the drug category. In Canada, this could have been be accomplished through Bill C-51, which would have moved natural products into the drug category. Bill C-51 did not pass into law due to the timing of the election; however, the intent of the Bill may be converted into another, similar Bill. If Canada defined natural products as food by law, then the Codex would have no jurisdiction in the country. With natural medicines being categorized as drugs, it may prove difficult for Aboriginal healers to practise medicine without being criminalized, since drugs may only be dispensed by pharmacists.

CONCLUSION

This chapter has reviewed the law as a determinant of health by reviewing two large intersecting bodies of Canadian law: the Constitution and legislation. The law has a direct link to many social and societal factors that affect Aboriginal health, not just in the public health context but in many areas where the heads of power are delineated that affect Aboriginal health and traditional healers, such as the criminal law; peace, order, and good government; and Indians and lands reserved for the Indians. The Constitution does not specifically address health, but through these heads of power it does affect the health of Aboriginal people, not directly but inadvertently. The courts and legislatures continues to define what this means.

Jurisdiction is a large and looming problem for First Nations, Métis, and Inuit peoples; it has caused internal strife among the federal and provincial governments and has resulted in a jumble of programs and inequities for on reserve residents, Inuit in the north, and the Métis. The *Daniels* case may assist in clarifying Métis rights as far as federal jurisdiction goes; however, this case will probably be entangled in the courts for a few more years.[125]

The second category of law as a determinant of health is legislation. The prohibitive laws found in the *Indian Act* from 1850 on have been reviewed as to their potential harmful effects on the health of Aboriginal people. The impacts of provincial laws applicable to health have also been reviewed and categorized as to their impacts on traditional healers, patients, and the *Indian Act*. Finally, an examination of the *Criminal Code* and its application on traditional healers and people who claim to be traditional healers provides a critical analysis of the dangers of not only practising traditional medicine but accessing traditional medicine from someone who is not qualified.

The following chapter delves further into the Constitution and Aboriginal and treaty rights, and provides an analysis that solidifies Aboriginal and treaty rights to health within the structure of the *Constitution Act, 1982*.

CHAPTER FIVE

Aboriginal and Treaty Rights to Health

IN CHAPTER ONE THE CURRENT STATE OF ABORIGINAL HEALTH was presented, showing a large disparity between Aboriginal and non-Aboriginal health in general. Health determinants and historical health influences were also introduced that were shown to have an effect on the general health of Aboriginal people today. Included in these influences were the applications of government policies and laws whose effects have also contributed to the poor state of Aboriginal health. Health practices have shown that Aboriginal people enjoyed a relatively disease-free society and practiced medical and health ceremonies with a detailed and self-sustaining pharmacopeia of medicines and treatments for prevention of disease and treatment of medical conditions. Beginning at European contact, a degradation of the state of health began.

It is important to discuss what is meant by "health." When discussing the treaty right to health, we are looking at the oral and written clauses of the treaties which are closely aligned with medicine and medical care as well as the provision of services and access to those services, so the term "health" refers to these terms. In addition to defining the term "health," it may be helpful to define the application of Western law in relation to those rights. Jurisdiction over health and health matters for First Nations, Métis, and Inuit may be seen as law-making powers that affect Aboriginal health — that is, the provision of medical care by the federal government (that is intertwined with jurisdiction); the ability to practise and maintain traditional health care free from Canadian interferences (meaning legal sanctions); and the ability to seek and maintain good health. The objective of this chapter is to consider how the law can be used to bring Aboriginal and non-Aboriginal health status closer together — to help close the gap by discovering the reasons there are gaps and to identify if any constitutional legal breaches are the cause. To achieve this objective, the rights that

Aboriginal people possess are examined to highlight any breaches of the government's constitutional obligations that may have contributed to poor health outcomes. This involves first establishing that health is an Aboriginal and/or treaty right (that has constitutional protection) and determining if there have been breaches (through a comparison of Aboriginal and non-Aboriginal health determinants) that are justified in law. If no justification can be found, then the government may be held accountable for the result of a health system that has resulted in a two- or three-tiered health system, with Aboriginal people on the lowest rung.

Aboriginal and treaty rights are entrenched in Canadian law through s. 35 of the *Constitution Act, 1982*: "existing aboriginal and treaty rights of the aboriginal peoples of Canada are hereby recognized and affirmed."[1] These existing rights are affirmed without definition, or providing a reference to the sources of the rights. Section 25 further enforces that the *Charter* must not "derogate from any, treaty or other rights or freedoms that pertain to the aboriginal peoples of Canada."[2]

The constitutional entrenchment is important because even though not all people who possess Aboriginal rights also possess treaty rights, the *Constitution Act, 1982* confirms that anyone who possesses treaty rights also possesses Aboriginal rights (if these rights were not extinguished or modified by treaties). Aboriginal rights are inherent to all Aboriginal people in Canada and are passed down from generation to generation. They are derived from Aboriginal knowledge, heritage, and law.[3] Traditional healing and health practices, medicines, and medical applications for the prevention and promotion of good health are ways through which Aboriginal people manifest or express an inherent right to health. The term "health" is defined in this broad manner when referring to Aboriginal rights.

The evidence produced through recordings and historical documents of elders, historians, early explorers, traders, and Jesuit priests show that early measures were in place that exemplified how Aboriginal people treated disease and maintained good health in their respective societies. They developed highly evolved pharmacopeias and formularies and plant and food sources to prevent disease and maintain good health. It may then be said that the practice of medicine, healing, and preventative health measures comprised an integral part of a distinctive culture, of central significance to Aboriginal society, which has passed from generation to generation in various forms and is still in existence today in modified forms. Because these are core underpinnings of Aboriginal society that manifested into

Aboriginal and treaty rights that have evolved into the modern equivalent of traditional health and health care, they thus fulfill the requirements of the common law tests that the courts have set out to prove an Aboriginal right.

In addition to Aboriginal rights, some Aboriginal peoples also possess treaty rights. A treaty is an agreement and an exchange of promises between two sovereign nations.[4] In this case, the promises were between the Crown and the Indian nations who signed the treaties. Treaties are legal instruments of Canadian law and international law, and also the law of the Indian signatories. The purpose of the treaties was to ensure peaceful relations, military alliances, and trade, and mandated the British sovereign and Canadian government to provide protection and services for treaty signatories.[5] Some treaties supplement the Aboriginal right to health care, such as the medicine chest clause and the pestilence and famine clause of Treaty 6. Other treaties contain references to medicine, health care, and protection. These protections continue to exist today, as First Nations did not relinquish their sovereignty to the Crown, nor did they relinquish their health care systems to the Crown when signing the treaties. Evidence does not exist to support relinquishment. There is, however, a presumption that if the Crown did intend to limit any Aboriginal rights to health care it would violate the Crown's promises of protection found in the treaties and the *Royal Proclamation, 1763*. Thus, it may be said that treaty rights have evolved and manifested themselves into the modern existence of the provision of health care. The purpose of this chapter is to illustrate that First Nations, Métis, and Inuit do have Aboriginal rights — and in addition some have treaty rights — to health and meet the tests that the Supreme Court has deemed to prove these rights.

5.1   ABORIGINAL RIGHTS TO HEALTH

The existence of Aboriginal rights originates from two important understandings. The first is that before European contact, Aboriginal societies were self-sustaining nations. The Supreme Court is clear:

> In my view, the doctrine of aboriginal rights exists, and is recognized and affirmed by s. 35(1), because of one simple fact: when Europeans arrived in North America, aboriginal peoples were already here, living in communities on the land, and participating in distinctive cultures,

as they had done for centuries. It is this fact, and this fact above all others, which separates aboriginal peoples from all other minority groups in Canadian society and which mandates their special legal, and now constitutional, status.[6]

The Supreme Court further clarified that Aboriginal societies consisted of practices, traditions, and cultures which were manifestly comprised of evolved institutions such as health, policing, education, law, and "the aboriginal rights recognized and affirmed by s. 35(1) must be directed towards the reconciliation of the pre-existence of aboriginal societies with the sovereignty of the Crown."[7]

This chapter deals with the existence of Aboriginal rights that protect essential aspects of Aboriginal health. The common law view of Aboriginal rights is based on pre-contact views and practices of Aboriginal knowledge and heritage, culture, and traditions of health care (sectors of Aboriginal law) but also exists in contemporary forms through practices that currently guide the lives of Aboriginal people in their individual and collective health. This will be examined through the analysis of common law tests as applied to Aboriginal health.

The Supreme Court of Canada has dealt extensively with the meaning of Aboriginal rights in s. 35 of the *Constitution Act, 1982* through case law addressing various matters before the Court. In 1990, the Supreme Court of Canada decided *R. v. Sparrow*,[8] and then followed with a 1996 trilogy of *Van der Peet, Gladstone,* and *NTC Smokehouse*.[9] The Court continues to refine the meaning through more recent decisions such as *Sappier and Gray,* and *Bernard* and *Marshall*.[10] The following section will review the tests and approaches that the Court has used and will assess its applicability to Aboriginal health.

In *R. v. Sparrow*, the Supreme Court of Canada addressed the meaning of "existing" Aboriginal rights:

The word "existing" makes it clear that the rights to which s. 35(1) applies are those that were in existence when the Constitution Act, 1982 came into effect. This means that extinguished rights are not revived by the Constitution Act, 1982 . . . . The phrase "existing aboriginal rights" must be interpreted flexibly so as to permit their evolution over time.[11]

The Court also held that only imperial statutes can extinguish Aboriginal rights, and these rights cannot be altered or extinguished by federal policy or law. They, however, may be infringed by federal law or policy as per the justification test that was developed in *Sparrow*. The Crown must prove that the infringing measures serve a "valid legislative objective;" that they are in keeping with the special trust relationship and responsibility of the government; that the infringement has been minimal; whether fair compensation has been available in a context of expropriation; and whether the affected Aboriginal group has been consulted.

In 1996, the Supreme Court of Canada articulated and added the concept of distinctive cultures in *R. v. Van der Peet*: "when Europeans arrived in North America, aboriginal peoples were already here, living in communities on the land, and participating in *distinctive cultures*, as they had done for centuries."[12] The Court then developed another test to be used to further identify an existing Aboriginal right. The activity must not only be integral to the distinctive culture, it must have been of "central significance" to the society in issue and must be a "defining characteristic" and "one of the things that made the culture of the society distinctive."[13] The activity that is claimed to be an Aboriginal right must have developed before "contact."[14] Practices that developed "solely as a response to European influences" do not qualify as an Aboriginal right:[15] *Van der Peet* and subsequent cases have held that the test for the existence of an Aboriginal right is specific to a definable Aboriginal group, and that the right at issue must be distinctive to that society. This is important in order to prove an Aboriginal right to health.

In regard to Métis rights, the Supreme Court of Canada wrestled with citizenship issues in the *Powley* decision. The Court said Métis do have constitutionally protected rights, but the test is different than for First Nations and the Inuit:

> [T]he inclusion of the Métis in s. 35 is not traceable to their pre-contact occupation. . . . s.35 as it relates to the Métis is therefore different from . . . Indians or the Inuit. The constitutionally significant feature of the Métis is their special status as peoples that emerged between first contact and the effective imposition of European control.[16]

The Court noted that they developed a pre-contact test in *Van der Peet* for First Nations based on the constitutional premise that Aboriginal communities are entitled to continue those practices, customs, and traditions that are integral to their distinctive existence or relationship to the land. Comparing the core purpose of this test for Métis practices should focus on identifying those practices, customs, and traditions that are integral to the Métis community's distinctive existence. It is important to note what the court stated in this case to apply the analysis to Métis health:

> This unique history can most appropriately be accommodated by a post contact but pre-control test that identifies the time when Europeans effectively established political and legal control in a particular area. The focus should be on the period after a particular Métis community arose and before it came under the effective control of European laws and customs. This pre-control test enables us to identify those practices, customs and traditions that predate the imposition of European laws and customs on the Métis.[17]

In addition to defining when the rights arose, the Supreme Court continued to expand their approach to Aboriginal rights for First Nations through *Sappier* and *Gray*,[18] which were log harvesting cases. Although most of the case law deals with resources, these cases are important and useful to provide an analogous argument for proving an Aboriginal right to health.

In *Sappier* and *Gray*, the Court focused on seeking the significance of a resource to the Aboriginal lifestyle, thus creating a restriction on the exercise of these rights. They recognized the Aboriginal right to harvest for domestic uses but rejected any "commercial dimension" to it. The Court held that the Aboriginal right must be protected to preserve Aboriginal society. While the Court accepted the evidence of a Mi'kmaq historian, they also recognized the importance of recognizing harvesting as an Aboriginal right — although in this case there was no evidence of it being a pre-contact practice. In *Bernard*, the Supreme Court held that logging for sale or trade was not a traditional practice but actually interfered with the traditional practice of fishing.[19]

The *Sappier* and *Gray* decision also addressed some of the problems that have arisen since the 1996 "integral to a distinctive culture" test found in *Van der Peet*. The problems encountered were such that there was some thought that the distinctness had to be different from other cultures (that is, not practised by other people). Because many societies historically harvested wood, the central issue is whether or not the harvesting of wood for survival purposes (to provide shelter) is central to the Mi'kmaq's distinctive culture. If it is central, then it is an Aboriginal right. The Court notes the difference in the terms "distinctive" versus "distinct."[20] To be considered *distinct*, harvesting timber would have to be seen as unique to that Aboriginal community (as compared to other communities) whereas *distinctive* would mean that harvesting wood must be of "central significance" to the community culture (regardless of whether other communities do the same). The Mi'kmaq "culture" focuses on the pre-contact way of life which includes their "means of survival, their socialization methods, their legal systems and, potentially, their trading habits."[21] The Court also confirmed the *Sparrow* requirement that the right (as in not commercial) may be carried out in a modern form and not frozen in time. The historical fact that wood was used in pre-contact days to create temporary structures "must be allowed to evolve into one to harvest wood by modern means to be used in the construction of a modern dwelling."[22]

The Court also reviewed the site-specific requirement of this Aboriginal right and acknowledged that the evidence showed that the harvesting of wood was within the traditional territories of the Mi'kmaq and Maliseet peoples, and found that the site-specific test did not apply, but did say that harvesting should be within traditional territory. The majority of the Court in *Sappier* held that the right had no commercial aspects to it. They held that the harvested wood could not be sold or traded for any reason, even if it was to construct a new home.

Applying the tests found in *Sappier* and *Gray* to Aboriginal health, one might first characterize the practice of preventative care, healing, and the maintenance of good health in relation to the tests found in *Van der Peet*.

In *Sappier* and *Gray*, the court sought to understand how the logs were harvested, extracted, and utilized, as they were the practices that are integral to their culture — these are considered the "Aboriginal component." Although the court found that it was not necessary to recognize harvesting as a pre-contact practice, they still found the Aboriginal component in the fact that ancestors of *Sappier* and *Gray* historically had harvested logs, which thereby created an Aboriginal right. In either version — pre-contact or not — Aboriginal people clearly practised good health care, or they would not have survived as thriving peoples and societies. Aboriginal health passes the first leg of the *Van der Peet* test as the court could clearly identify the specific *practices* of Aboriginal health that help to define a distinctive way of life as an Aboriginal community. The court in *Sappier* and

Gray stated that "the importance of leading evidence about the pre-contact practice upon which the right is claimed should not be understated. In the absence of such evidence, courts will find it difficult to relate the claimed right to the pre-contact way of life of the specific aboriginal people, so as to trigger s. 35 protection."[23]

Health practices are varied and distinctive to each culture, depending on where they were located geographically in North America; they ranged from sweat lodges to the Grand Medicine Society. Arguably, this more than satisfies the evidentiary burden of proving the pre- and post-contact practices of Aboriginal health and healing. The second arm of the test is to identify the pre-contact practices that have evolved into present day form. In earlier chapters it was shown that health and healing were practised since time immemorial and continued, albeit often underground, because Canadian policies and laws attempted to destroy ceremonies, languages, and healing practices. The mere fact that healing practices evolved through the underground may be achievement enough to satisfy this test. Akin to harvesting wood for a communal purpose, the right to practise Aboriginal health and healing assists the society in maintaining its distinctive character. It also should be noted that the Supreme Court has referenced the principle that an interruption in the continuity of the use will not prejudice the claimants.[24] This means that the practice does not have to be a unique practice, done only by the group claiming the right. In the context of Aboriginal health this is useful, as all Aboriginal societies practised some form of health care and provided protection for the survival of the Aboriginal community, thus garnering s. 35 protection.

Additionally, in relation to the distinctive culture test, Henderson and Barsh argue that culture has been taken to mean a "fixed inventory of traits or characteristics," which is inappropriate because culture is a moving process, not an actual thing that can be permanently described. The Supreme Court in *Sappier* explained what is meant by culture in relation to *Van der Peet*: it is really "an inquiry into the pre-contact way of life of a particular Aboriginal community, including their means of survival, their socialization methods, their legal systems, and, potentially, their trading habits."[25]

When the Courts looked at the term "distinctive," they qualified that it did not mean distinct, and the notions of being Aboriginal cannot be reduced to racialized stereotypes of Aboriginal people. Earlier chapters of this book provided a variety of documented evidence from elders, historians, Jesuits, traders, explorers, and fur traders that showed the colourful and diverse healing and health practices from various Aboriginal communities across Canada in different time spans and geographical regions, thereby showing that the practices of Aboriginal health and healing were integral to pre- and post-contact distinctive cultures of Aboriginal people in Canada.

The nature of the right must be considered in the context of the pre-contact distinctive culture of the particular Aboriginal community, and must be determined in light of present-day circumstances.[26] There are many instances of the modernization of Aboriginal healing practices. For instance, among many others, the Wabano Centre of Aboriginal Health in Ottawa, Sioux Lookout Meno-Ya-Win Health Centre, the Nisga'a Valley Health Board and Weeneebayko Health Ahtushkaywin, Muskeg Lake Cree Nation, and Sturgeon Lake Cree Nation all practise modern forms of ancient Aboriginal health practices.[27] Although the Health Council of Canada notes that many Aboriginal people integrate a holistic approach to health care, these values are often undervalued in mainstream health care systems. For many Aboriginal people, holistic care is based on ceremonies and spirituality; although many mainstream health care organizations accommodate ceremonies, many Aboriginal people feel that traditional practices are not welcome and understood.[28]

However, many First Nations, Métis, and Inuit communities persevere and are successfully involved in delivering health services to their communities by combining Western medicine with their own traditional knowledge and medicine as their core foundation. For instance, the White Horse General Hospital (WHGH) negotiated agreements with local First Nations to meet the ongoing needs of Aboriginal people within the communities it serves. The seven programs implemented at WHGH to address First Nations needs are: First Nations Health and Social Liaison Workers, Child Life Workers, Traditional Diet, Traditional Medicine, Interpretation Services, In-Service Training/Education, and Community Liaison Health Promotion.[29] Patients at this hospital can "choose to receive the services of a traditional healer, including traditional medicines."[30]

In Treaty 4 territory, the All Nations' Healing Hospital was built in 2004 and replaced the old Fort Qu'Appelle Indian Hospital. The All Nations' Healing Hospital has an approach to health care that recognizes the relationship between mind, spirit, body, and community. It has 13 acute care beds, including one palliative care bed, outpatients, diagnostics, and support services. It provides health services to a population base of

10,000 (20,000 in the summer), of which 4,500 people live on reserve. The Women's Health Centre at the hospital opened in 2007:

> [It] is staffed by nurse practitioners and midwives and provides care for all women, from premenstrual through to post-menopausal, and in the spirit of the First Nations culture and philosophy that healthy women give life to healthy children which give life to healthy communities.[31]

The All Nations' Healing Hospital in Fort Qu'Appelle, Saskatchewan, provides a comprehensive range of integrated acute, preventative, health promotion, and cultural health services. It brings together a holistic vision of addressing all the needs of a patient by providing services across the entire continuum of care. The facility consists of the hospital itself as well as the First Nations Health Services area, which administers health care to on-reserve residents. There are approximately 80 acute care staff and an additional 40 First Nations Health Services staff. Emergency services are provided 24/7 and diagnostic services are also offered. Various health care professionals work in collaboration in the facility in a unique multidisciplinary team environment.[32]

The White Raven Healing Centre operates as a partner with the hospital and provides culturally appropriate mental health services and programs:

> The philosophy of "Traditional Healing" is to use culture as healing. This encompasses the concept that the human body is an organism with self-healing and strong recuperative capabilities, which when maintained properly is capable of on-going health and longevity. Where disease does exist, a Traditional Healer aims to correct both the internal and external imbalances between the four aspects of human beings. In First Nations cultures healing is the process of bringing one's body, mind, spirit to a deeper level of inner knowing that leads toward integration and balance. Where Euro-Canadians physicians seek to cure disease, First Nations Traditional Healers do not claim to cure the disease but work to facilitate the body's own recuperative power. Our traditional and contemporary healing methods strive to assist individuals in restoring balance in a holistic manner and a spiritual cultural program.[33]

It appears that the practice of health and healing has evolved over time, and that the continuity of the Aboriginal right to health and healing may be confirmed as a modern form of a distinctive ancient practice.

The next requirement is the "site specific" requirement. In *Sappier* and *Gray*, this issue was not required to be addressed. However in *Marshall* and *Bernard* there was a site-specific requirement and "[o]ccasional forays for hunting, fishing and gathering are not sufficient to establish Aboriginal title in the land."[34] In relation to Aboriginal health, a site-specific requirement would not be applicable, as Aboriginal health was practised throughout Canada and North America.

5.1.1 Aboriginal and Treaty Rights Tests as Applied to Aboriginal Health

When the principles emanating from the Supreme Court of Canada in *Sparrow*, *Van der Peet*, and *Sappier* and *Gray* are applied to health and healing of Aboriginal people, it appears that there may be an Aboriginal right to practise Aboriginal health. However, the tests the Supreme Court of Canada has laid out are stringent. Under the *Sparrow* test, the activity had to be a practice that was never properly extinguished. *Van der Peet* added that the activity had to be central to the pre-colonial Aboriginal culture, thereby creating another hurdle, in that it had to be compatible with Canadian law as a whole. The Court in *Sappier* and *Gray* modified the tests somewhat by holding that a practice can be an Aboriginal right even if it is related to survival or a practice that is engaged in by other Aboriginal people.

To assist in this analysis, law professors Barsh and Henderson question the logic of the Supreme Court in *Van der Peet* of the requirement to tie certain activities to a culture in order for it to be recognized as an Aboriginal right.[35] The Court reasons that the purpose of referring to Aboriginal rights in the *Constitution* was to reconcile pre-existing Aboriginal societies with the sovereignty of the Crown. To qualify for s. 35 protection the practice must be "a central and significant part of society's distinctive culture;" must not have existed in the past "simply as an incident" to other cultural elements or as a response to European influences. The Court proposed a two-stage decision-making process involving the concept of "reconciliation" which "takes into account the Aboriginal perspective while at the same time taking into account the perspective of the common law," and that "true reconciliation will, equally, place weight on each." These Aboriginal perspectives must then be rendered "cognizable to the non-Aboriginal legal system" through a process of judicial adaptation.[36] Even the Court in *Sappier* and *Gray* determined that in order for a practice to receive s. 35 protection, it must pass the *Van der Peet* test:

- Examination of the historical roots of the practice to determine its centrality to the pre-colonial Aboriginal culture.
- If it passes, the practice then should be adapted to make it recognizable to the Western legal system.

Barsh and Henderson argue that the requirement to view the centrality of a practice or a custom as an object is problematic, as the practice may be overlooked or regarded as incidental to either accept cultural testimony or reject it. The determination of centrality is left to the judges who wrongly apply centrality to all the rights of Aboriginal people. This process also cannot distinguish between cultural elements that exist independently, so the loss of one element does not compromise the perpetuation of the others. The presumption of independence is incompatible with Aboriginal thought (all human activity is interdependent). Barsh and Henderson dismiss this notion of centrality in human society as absurd as "arguing that an ecosystem remains the same after the removal of a few incidental species," calling it a "judicial fiction." They argue that the term "culture" in *Van der Peet* means a fixed inventory of traits or characteristics which leads judges to presume they understand what a certain Aboriginal society once believed or valued at a certain point in time.[37] This subjective viewpoint solidifies European paternalism (and the implementation of the "guardian and ward" theory that underpins laws, legislation, and policies today) when determining if a practice is an Aboriginal right. An excellent example of evolving Aboriginal culture is found in the Haudenosaunee concept of "adding to the rafters," which allows for new laws to be added to the Great Law of Peace, just as new rafters would be added to the longhouses in which they lived. Future generations would be able to adapt to the natural changes in their lives and society through this concept.[38]

The fact that the Supreme Court of Canada assessed Aboriginal practices in *Marshall* and *Bernard* and insisted on the "translation" of the practice into a modern legal right is problematic, and is akin to saying that if it isn't compatible with Canadian law then it may be deemed to be extinguished at law or at least unprotected by s. 35 and unenforceable. Although the Court in *Sappier* and *Gray* somewhat modified this requirement when they held that a practice can be an Aboriginal right even if it is related to survival or a practice that is engaged in by other Aboriginal people, the most stringent tests from *Van der Peet* must still be met.

The question arises whether the specific nature test (or centrality) developed by the Supreme Court of Canada in *Van der Peet* is appropriate in relation to Aboriginal people in the context of health and health-related activities. The practice of healing in accordance with their own customs would apply to all traditional societies everywhere, for example, and was not unique to a specific group of Aboriginal people; rather, practices will vary but remain integral to all Aboriginal people as part of collective societies. This regime established persistent and connected traditions. In *Sappier* the Court found that a practice can be an Aboriginal right if it is related to survival even if practised by others. Thus, a general rather than a specific type of test appears more applicable.

These tests, however, are not appropriate for the Métis. The court in *Powley* found that the pre-contact test might not be so useful to prove the varied range of "Métis customs, practices or traditions that are entitled to protection, since Métis cultures by definition post-date European contact."[39] In *Sappier* and *Gray,* the Court supported the notion that Aboriginal rights did not have to be proven pre-contact but could assume this when it is obvious for survival (for instance, Mi'kmaq would not have to prove they were "loggers" pre-contact and, similarly, Inuit would not have to prove their proficiency in snow hut building or using the sled dog for healing). The practice can be then seen as an Aboriginal right even if it is related to survival or a practice that is engaged in by other Aboriginal people, thereby fulfilling the requirements for classification as a generic right (which may be in direct contradiction to *Sparrow,* which said the activity had to be a practice that was never properly extinguished). Accordingly, in general, when Aboriginal people came under the sovereignty of the Crown, a standard array of generic rights was recognized by virtue of the common law Doctrine of Aboriginal Rights. Some examples of generic rights are:

- The right of self-government;[40]
- The right to conclude treaties;[41]
- The right to an autonomous legal system;[42]
- The right to Aboriginal title;[43]
- The right of sustenance;[44]
- The right to cultural integrity.[45]

Although the Aboriginal right to health may fall into every category, it particularly falls in closely with a set of generic rights in cultural integrity (and may be seen to stand on its own as a generic cultural Aboriginal right to health) and "gives rise to a range of distinct specific rights to engage in particular activities, whose nature and scope are established by reference to the practices, customs and traditions of the group at time of contact."[46]

When generic status is applied to the Aboriginal right that includes health and healing, at the abstract level, the rights are uniform. As discussed, all Aboriginal groups were practising some type of health-based practices or ceremonies to maintain good health and to prevent ill health at the time of Crown sovereignty and pre-contact. However, at the concrete level, this generic right assumed a variety of particular forms that were distinctive to each Aboriginal group. For instance, the methods used were designed specifically to suit local needs (culturally, linguistically, geographically, environmentally; i.e.: what medicines are available and otherwise). The different forms of health practices are specific rights. In health matters, the practice of health generally (generic rights) may be broken down into sub-rights by putting into practice the application of health measures (specific rights).

Using a generic rights analysis while interpreting *Van der Peet,* in that the existence of an Aboriginal right must be specific to a definable group and the right must be distinct to that group, is not useful when recognizing a general or generic right to health. Rather, analyzing *Van der Peet* as being reflective of a generic right with distinctive specific rights may be more appropriate to establish Aboriginal health (which traditionally consisted of methods [specific rights] to create a good state of health).

Certainly, *Sappier* and *Gray* illustrate that a practice can be an Aboriginal right even if it is related to survival, into which category health clearly falls. Additional case law illustrates that an Aboriginal right to health has been accepted as a generic right. The courts have stepped out of the *Van der Peet* framework and recognized rights (specific rights) outside the basic (generic) Aboriginal rights and recognized "incidental" rights as the ability to pass the accompanying knowledge of the use of the Aboriginal right to a succeeding generation.[47]

While the Courts recognize incidental rights to Aboriginal rights, it is reasonable to assume that Aboriginal rights then are not static but generic to a genus of rights that can change with cultures and environments, and specific rights are integral and a sub category of Aboriginal rights. Cultural elements are interdependent, and the courts struggle with the concepts of recognizing these rights as being in a constant state of change. The centrality of cultural elements cannot be tied to a specific culture (knowledge, heritage, and traditions of health care). Therefore, it may said that the right to health and the practice of these rights are integral to all human beings, but for Aboriginal people the specialized practices (as illustrated earlier) were/are integral to their distinctive cultures pre-contact and pre-sovereignty by Aboriginal nations in general.

5.2 Treaty Rights to Health and Healing

The treaties entrenched legally binding relationships between the Crown and Indian nations with the intent to create obligations:

> The three purposes for entering into treaties or "covenant" with the British sovereign was to ensure that future generations would continue to govern themselves and their territories according to Aboriginal teachings and law; (2) would make a living (pimachihowin), providing for both spiritual and material needs; (3) would live harmoniously (witaskewin) and respectfully with treaty settlers.[48]

A treaty is an exchange of solemn promises from formal negotiations between two sovereign nations — the Crown and Indian nations — whose nature is sacred. Obligations between the parties are derived from the intent and context of the treaty negotiations.

A critical purpose of the treaties was to ensure that the British sovereign and Canadian governments would provide protection for Aboriginal people. Some First Nations, through conveying territory to the sovereign, understood that the sovereign could use the lands to generate revenue for government services — services that would include Aboriginal people. The government stance that no one deserves to benefit from "free" medical services certainly rings true for Aboriginal people — as within the treaties and within inherent Aboriginal rights, the costs of these services have been dear and were paid for through the exchange of land for government services.[49]

First Nations have retained their treaty rights regarding matters relating to jurisdiction over internal health matters, unless specific treaties contained terms to the contrary that were clearly understood by both parties as diminishing the sovereign authority of the First Nation concerned. This is clearly not the case.

The treaty provisions carry verbal and written promises of medicines and protection and a new way of life. For the purposes of reviewing health and healing, we are focusing primarily on the post-confederation treaties and the settlement in the western provinces where promises and undertakings were made specifically in relation to health with no relinquishment of First Nation jurisdiction in this area.

Treaties are not simple business contracts. The English words in the treaties encompass British legal traditions, but they do not encompass ways of knowing through Aboriginal legal traditions. The traditions inform the parties' respective historical lineages; however, these are found behind the text and function within the treaty text. For Aboriginal people, the best sources of information from an Aboriginal perspective are the oral traditions of those who were present at the signing of the treaties or accounts transmitted orally or by legal traditions. Thus, while being sensitive to the unique cultural and linguistic differences between the parties, construing the English words generously, and resolving all doubts in favor of the Indians, Courts cannot alter the terms of the treaty by exceeding what "is possible on the language" or realistic in the Court's terms.[50]

Outside the written text of Treaty 6 which refers to the medicine chest, there is documentary evidence that health was discussed in the negotiations of other treaties. Historian René Fumoleau provided considerable information on the actual negotiation of the treaties and their terms (as distinguished from the written versions) such as details on epidemic diseases and failure to provide medical care as promised in the treaties. Fumoleau presented a great number of quotations from archival, published, and interview material regarding the history of the treaties from the varied perspectives of the Aboriginal people, traders, police, commissioners and government employees, Métis and other observers, translators, and missionaries. In brief, this material provided considerable support for the view that the treaties are not accurately represented by the written documents. For instance, in 1887, Thomas White, Superintendent of Indian Affairs, recorded that the Indians of the Peace River district were very sick and that they had little food and were suffering from the croup and measles. White reported that the Hudson's Bay Company stated that the government should be responsible for the sick and destitute as their protectors and the Hudson's Bay Company should not be responsible. Fumoleau also reported that an article described "Starving Indians" where it was suggested that the destitute Indians needed a treaty to alleviate their poor conditions.[51]

Fumoleau also reported that the negotiations of Treaty 8 included medicines and medical care and relied on a report by J. D. McLean, Assistant Deputy of Indian Affairs, in 1919, that the Indians were "assured . . . the Government would always be ready to avail itself of any opportunity of affording medical service."[52] The report of the treaty commissioners also stated that Indian-requested assistance in seasons of distress and the "old and indigent who were no longer able to hunt and trap and who were consequently often in distress should be cared for by the government." The treaty commissioners promised that supplies of medicines would be put at various points by the government and distributed free of charge to those who require them. They also explained that it was impossible for the government to arrange regular medical care to all Indians as they were so spread out, but they did say that the government would avail itself of every opportunity to provide medical services by way of the physician who traveled with the commissioners.[53] As for Treaty 11, the stories are similar, as the destitute and sick Indians asked to be in the treaty to alleviate their suffering.[54] Treaty 5 Indians were angry in 1915 when a physician did not pay his annual visit as they had expected him to.[55] A Treaty 7 elder commented that the "only two promises they kept were with regard to medicine and education."[56] The provision of medicines and medical care were linked to the treaties themselves because the medical doctor accompanied the treaty parties after the treaties were signed and on all subsequent treaty annuity days. The link between treaty and medicines and medical care was clear as well, as oral terms of the negotiations formed the whole of the treaty.[57] Under the interpretative principles of treaties,[58] these oral and written statements of the treaty commissioners would create a treaty right to Aboriginal health (meaning full health services on par with other Canadians in a modern context). The following sections review specific health promises made.

5.2.1 Protection and Non-interference

In 1871, Treaty Commissioner Archibald opened the negotiation of the numbered treaties by stating that the "Great Mother" Queen Victoria wished the Indian people to be "happy and content and live in comfort . . . to make them safer from famine and distress . . . to live and prosper."[59] The Great Mother "has no idea of compelling you to do so," but left the lifestyle decision to their own "choice" and "free will."[60]

In the 1874 Treaty 4, the Qu'Appelle Treaty, Commissioner Archibald reaffirmed the Queen's wishes:

[t]he Queen cares for you and for your children, and she cares for the children that are yet to be born. . . . The Queen has to think of what will come long after today. Therefore the promises we have to make to you are not for today only but for tomorrow, not only for you but for your children born and unborn, and the promises we make will be carried out as long as the sun shines above and water flows in the ocean.[61]

In 1876, during the Treaty 6 negotiations, the Treaty Commissioner "fully explained" to the Cree that they (the treaty makers) "would not interfere with their present mode of living,"[62] and that what was being offered by the Treaty Commissioner "does not take away your living, you will have it then as you have now, and what I offer you is put on top of it." Additionally, "we have not come here to take away anything that belongs to you."[63] In Treaty 7 in 1872, the treaty commissioner told the Blackfoot that the purpose of the treaty was so that the Great Mother "would hold them in the palm of her hand and protect them and look after them just like a child, as long as the sun, rivers and mountains last. . . . [The Queen] will take the best care of you. Whatever you ask for will be given to you."[64]

Again in 1899, the Treaty 8 chiefs and headmen stressed the importance of maintaining their way of life and livelihood during the negotiations. The treaty negotiations also contain many references to the protection and non-interference with Aboriginal ways of life and non-interference with their traditional ways. As being vital to life, these references naturally apply to Aboriginal people's health and wellbeing. From 1837 to 1901, under the treaties, for example, the "Great Mother" was obliged to "create an enriched way of life for treaty beneficiaries and their ancestors."[65] In Treaties 6, 8, 9, and 10 there is explicit reference to medicine in either the wording of the treaties or in records of the oral negotiations surrounding the Treaties. Treaty 7 elders confirm the treaty right to medicines, medical care, and indeed health was negotiated. In none of the numbered treaties is there any reference to the relinquishment of jurisdiction over health by any First Nation; logically, then, the First Nation retained this jurisdiction as it had before the treaties were negotiated.

5.2.2 Medicine and Medical Care

Treaty 6 specifically included a medicine chest clause in the written text of the treaty. It states, "a medicine chest shall be kept at the house of each Indian Agent for the use and benefit of the Indians at the direction of such agent."[66] The Indian people told Treaty Commissioner Alexander Morris that they required "provisions for the poor, unfortunate, blind and the lame," "the exclusion of fire water in the whole Saskatchewan [district], and a free supply of medicines."[67] Morris's report did not include a reply to the medicine request.[68] However, the records of Dr. A. G. Jackes, MD, acting as the Secretary of the Treaty Commission, provide insight into the issue of medical services. Jackes recorded the Indians' request that medicine be provided free of charge and Morris's response as: "[a] medicine chest will be kept at the house of each Indian agent, in case of sickness amongst you."[69]

Numerous promises were made by the Treaty 7 commissioners during negotiations of Treaty 7. There is a unanimous opinion by the Treaty 7 elders that there were prominent and repeated promises of medical assistance. The five Treaty 7 nations were to give commitments to peace and access to land in exchange for the government's many "sweet promises." The elders recalled that what they had agreed to was virtually unrecorded and what emerged was far different than what was agreed to. They all agreed that they were supposed to be taken care of by the government of Canada, and this included the treaty right to health care.[70]

Treaty 8 of the First Nations of Alberta state that, among other guarantees, there is a definite guarantee to health care for the signatory nations:

> We promised that supplies of medicines would be put in the charge of persons selected by the Government at different points, and would be distributed free to those of the Indians who might require them. We explained that it would be practically impossible for the Government to arrange for regular medical attendance upon Indians so widely scattered over such an extensive territory. We assured them, however, that the Government would always be ready to avail itself of any opportunity of affording medical service just as it provided that the physician attached to the Commission should give free attendance to all Indians whom he might find in need of treatment as he passed through the country.[71]

In Treaty 9, the commissioners report that medical care was provided during negotiations for the treaty. For instance, "Dr. Goldie had been giving the Indians free medical attendance as far as the medicine he had with him permitted, and he also offered his services in association with Dr. Meindl during our stay at the post."[72] Additional promises were made in Treaty 10:

I promised that medicines would be placed at different points in the charge of persons to be selected by the government, and would be distributed to those of the Indians who might require them. I showed them that it would be practically impossible for the government to arrange for a resident doctor owing to the Indians being so widely scattered over such an extensive territory; but I assured them that the government would always be ready to avail itself of any opportunity of affording medical service just as it provided that the physician attached to the commission should give free attendance to all Indians whom he might find in need of treatment.[73]

According to historians Coates and Morrison:

This meant that the federal government would move very slowly in extending its obligations to the Native Peoples covered by Treaty Ten. Most essential demands were met: assistance was forthcoming in times of severe hardship, financial support was offered for mission schools, medical aid was provided when illness or disease struck, and efforts were made to protect the Natives' special rights to hunt and trap, subject to conservation regulations.[74]

Fumoleau cites a 1919 report by Assistant Deputy Minister and Secretary of Indian Affairs J. D. McLean, stating that Indians were "assured that the government would always be ready to avail itself of any opportunity of affording medical service."[75] Considering the oral and documentary evidence, and under the legal treaty interpretive principles, it is proposed then that treaty rights to medicines and medical care exist in at least Treaties 6, 7, 8, 10 and 11.

5.2.3 Pestilence and Famine, Sickness and Disease

It was noted in Treaty 3 by Treaty Commissioner Simpson that due to an outbreak of disease and the worry that scarletina would spread, the Indians dispersed during the negotiations.[76] There is ample evidence that sickness and diseases brought to North America played an important role in the decision-making to enter into treaties, and this was recognized in the treaty text. For instance, Treaty 6 contains a pestilence or famine clause:

> In the event hereafter of the Indians comprised within this treaty being overtaken by any pestilence, or by a general famine, the Queen, on being satisfied and certified thereof by Her Indian Agent or Agents, will grant to the Indians assistance of such a character and to such extent as Her Chief Superintendent of Indian Affairs shall deem necessary and sufficient to relieve the Indians from the calamity that shall have befallen them.[77]

When Treaty Commissioner Morris negotiated Treaty 6, he wrote in the official texts that "[t]he Indians were apprehensive about their future. . . . Small pox had destroyed them by hundreds a few years before, and they dreaded pestilence and famine."[78]

In 1887, Thomas White, Superintendent of Indian Affairs, described repeated verbal and written requests by the Indians for protection and linked diseases with famine:

> [Q]uite recently the Hudson's Bay company has renewed its solicitations in the same behalf, alleging that serious sickness is now prevalent among the Indians of the Peace River District and there is apprehension of there being an insufficiency of food during the winter. . . . The diseases they are stated to be suffering from are measles and the croup.[79]

According to Superintendent White, the Hudson's Bay Company took the position that "the expense of providing and caring for the sick and destitute Indians should be the government's responsibility as their natural protectors." Fumoleau cited an 1887 *Calgary Tribune* article where it was suggested that Indians needed a treaty in order to alleviate their suffering.[80]

Treaty 11 documents a similar story in that the Dene were suffering from sickness and starvation. Tuberculosis, dysentery, whooping cough, measles, and Spanish influenza were taking their toll. The intent of the Dene in making the treaty was to lessen their suffering.[81]

As noted earlier, medical doctors generally accompanied treaty parties dispensing medicine and providing medical care. This demonstration of medical care was important to the First Nations people, since their knowledge system is built on demonstrations and words. The providing of medicine and medical care at this critical time created a reasonable expectation of medical care among the First Nation parties. The promises and the provision of medical services should be linked to the justification of chiefs and headmen entering the treaties to help ameliorate the suffering of their people. The treaty commissioners indicated to the Indians that medicine and the provision of medical services would be available at subsequent treaty annuity ceremonies. Physicians attended these ceremonies, examining and treating patients at no cost. It is possible that the demonstration of providing medical care influenced the chiefs to enter in to the treaty; a connection and an expectation was thereby created between the two — medical care and treaty.

5.2.4 *Judicial Interpretations of the Treaty Right to Medicine and Health Care*

In 1935, the federal Court in *Dreaver* established that the medicine chest clause meant that all medicines, drugs, or medical supplies were to be supplied free of charge to treaty Indians.[82] Dreaver, Chief of the Mistawasis Band in Saskatchewan, had been present at the signing of Treaty 6. Dreaver launched a lawsuit against the federal government to recover money he had spent on medical supplies between 1919 and 1935, arguing that all medicines were guaranteed at no cost to Indians under the medicine chest clause in Treaty 6. He further supplied evidence that medicines had been provided free of charge from the time of the treaty in 1876 to 1919. The trial judge agreed. To date, *Dreaver* has not been overruled.

With the creation of provincial medical care, the Court has dealt with the issue of payment of health taxes. In 1965 in *R. v. Johnston*, an off-reserve Treaty 6 Indian was charged with failing to pay tax under the *Saskatchewan Hospitalization Act* R.S.S. 1953, c. 232.[83] Johnson claimed that the provisions of Treaty 6 gave him tax-exempt status under the Regulation 23(1)(v) of the

Act. The trial judge followed the *Dreaver* decision and found:

> Referring to the medicine chest clause of Treaty No. 6, it is common
> knowledge that the provisions for caring for the sick and injured in
> areas inhabited by the Indians in 1876 were somewhat primitive com-
> pared to present day standards. It can be safely assumed that the In-
> dians had limited knowledge of what provisions were available and it
> is obvious that they were concerned that their people be adequately
> cared for. With that in view, and possibly carrying the opinion of An-
> gers, J., a step farther, I can only conclude that the "medicine chest"
> clause and the "pestilence" clause in Treaty No. 6 should be properly
> interpreted to mean that the Indians are entitled to receive all medic-
> al services, including medicine, drugs, medical supplies and hospital
> care free of charge.[84]

The 1965 decision was ultimately overturned by the Saskatchewan Court of
Appeal, which relied on a literal interpretation of the treaty and, as such,
held that only a "first aid" kit was required to be provided. The Court further ruled that the provincial government did not have to provide comprehensive and free medical services to Indians. It was held that the provision
of medicine was at the discretion of the Indian agent on the reserve. Similar literal interpretation methodology was used by the courts in the 1969
Klein[85] decision and again by the Appellant Court in the 1970 *Swimmer*
decision.[86]

In *Klein and Spence*,[87] a member of Peguis band was involved in a mo-
tor vehicle accident. Spence recovered her expenses from the Unsatisfied
Judgment Fund and the Manitoba Hospital Commission acted to recover
their expenses from Mrs. Spence. Spence claimed that as a treaty Indian
she was entitled to free medical care and the Commission's claim was void.
The court ruled in favour of the Commission and stated that Treaty 1 and
2 had no provisions for medical care, and although Treaty 6 had the medicine chest clause it was not valid in Manitoba for two reasons: Alexander Morris signed Treaty 6 in his capacity as Lieutenant Governor of the
Northwest Territories and not in his capacity as Lieutenant Governor of
Manitoba; second, the Court decided to follow the plain reading of the
medicine chest clause found in *Johnson*.

In 1969, the trial judge found that Andrew Swimmer,[88] another Treaty
6 Indian, who also did not reside on a reserve, was wrongfully charged

for not paying a tax under the *Hospital Services Insurance Act*[89] and *Saskatchewan Medical Care Insurance Act.*[90] The federal government had an arrangement with the Saskatchewan government to pay hospitalization tax for reserve Indians, and Indians residing outside a reserve for less than 12 months. Mr. Swimmer had not lived on a reserve since 1957.

The justice of the Magistrate's Court accepted that the medicine clause entitled Indians to free medical care, and that Swimmer was exempt from the tax. The Crown appealed and the Court of Appeal interpreted the medicine chest clause to not entitle off-reserve treaty Indians to free medical services under the *Hospital Services Insurance Act* and *Saskatchewan Medical Care Insurance Act.* As in *Klein and Spence,* the Court of Appeal also overruled an affirmative ruling from the trial court. The Court of Appeal interpretation of the treaty rights is inconsistent with current interpretive principles. The refusal of the court to give a fair and liberal interpretation in favour of the Indians to the concept of the medicine chest clause at the time of the treaty cannot be relied upon in modern interpretative principles of *sui generis* treaty rights.

Dreaver was correctly decided. However, the decisions in *Klein, Swimmer,* and *Johnston* likely would not be upheld in the courts today. All three cases following *Dreaver* were decided before 1982 and prior to Supreme Court of Canada decisions setting out the principles of treaty interpretation. These decisions predate the coming into force of ss. 35 and 52 of the *Constitution Act, 1982,* as well as the *Canadian Charter of Rights and Freedoms* and the constitutional entrenchment of Aboriginal and treaty rights.

In 1999, *Wuskwi Sipihk Cree Nation* v. *Canada (Minister of National Health and Welfare)* was heard in the Federal Court on the interpretation of the medicine chest clause in Treaty 6. Prothonotary Hargrave briefly addressed the issue of "jurisdiction over health care to First Nations":

> Mr. Justice Angers took a proper approach in his 1935 decision Dreaver, reading the Treaty No. 6 medicine chest clause in a contemporary manner to mean a supply of all medicines, drugs and medical supplies. Certainly, it is clear that the Saskatchewan Court of Appeal took what is now a wrong approach in its literal and restrictive reading of the medicine chest clause in the 1966 decision in Johnston. In a current context, the clause may well require a full range of contemporary medical services.[91]

Prothonotary Hargrave referred to the Supreme Court of Canada decision in *Nowegijick* v. *The Queen* as authority for treaties (and statutes) being "liberally construed and doubtful expressions resolved in favour of the Indians." He also referred to the Supreme Court of Canada's decision in *Sparrow* as authority for interpreting rights in a flexible manner "in order to permit their evolution" as opposed to adopting a "frozen rights" approach where the right in issue is interpreted rigidly within the confines of that concept at the time the treaty was signed. [92]

In *Duke* v. *Puts*, the Court referred to the medicine chest clause and observed that appellate courts in Saskatchewan had been critical of lower courts that gave a broad interpretation to the medicine chest clause. Mr. Justice Kyle observed that following the introduction of the *Canadian Charter of Rights and Freedoms* in 1982, government policy had favoured "the generous provision of . . . medicines, drugs and medical supplies free of charge."[93] These comments reflect the interpretive principles for treaty interpretation, in particular the medicine chest clause and the observations in the *Wuskwi Cree Nation* case. The 1935 decision of Justice Angers in *Dreaver* appears to be the precedent on the federal obligation to provide Treaty Indians with medicine.

5.2.5   Interpretation of Treaties

Health Canada

The Government of Canada has always maintained that the provision of health services to First Nations and Inuit peoples is done as a matter of policy and not through any legal obligation. In 1957, the government insisted that a treaty obligation existed only under Treaty 6.[94] Canada, however, did not implement any special programs for the beneficiaries of Treaty 6 so its beneficiaries were caught in a quagmire of bickering and buck-passing among government departments. For instance, the Medical Services Branch of the National Health and Welfare Department claimed that the responsibility for discussing treaties on behalf of Canada resided with the Department of Indian Affairs. Although the Medical Services Branch maintained that it was prepared to participate in discussions of a treaty matter involving health, the Department of Indian Affairs adopted the position that discussion of a treaty right to health was not their responsibility as the Medical Services Branch was responsible for health. As a result, no one took responsibility.[95]

In 1964, the government announced that it had "never accepted the position that Indians are entitled to free medical services by treaty rights."[96] This position was reiterated again in 1968,[97] 1969,[98] and 1971 in that "despite popular misconceptions of the situation and vigorous assertions to the contrary, neither the federal nor any other government has any formal obligations to Indians or anyone else, with free medical services."[99]

In 1974, the Minister of National Health and Welfare tabled the *Policy of the Federal Government concerning Indian Health Services* which reiterated that no statutory or treaty obligations exist to provide health services to Indians. However, the federal government wanted to ensure "the availability of services by providing it directly where normal provincial services (were) not available, and giving financial assistance to indigent Indians to pay for necessary services when the assistance (was) not otherwise provided."[100]

In 1995, the government reported in an internal document that "undertakings" for health care were made in relation to other treaties besides Treaty 6:

> For example, Treaty 6 (1876) contains a medicine chest clause which stipulates that ". . . a medicine chest shall be kept at the house of each Indian Agent for the use and benefit of the Indians at the discretion of such agent." Similar verbal undertakings were made by treaty commissioners when negotiating Treaties 7, 8, 10 and 11.[101]

In 1999, the federal government participated in an Exploratory Treaty Table discussion with First Nations in Saskatchewan, where they reiterated their social policy perspective on the treaties as being "the Government of Canada, as a matter of public policy, seeks to provide a basic level of health care, access to education, economic opportunities, and the like to all citizens, regardless of treaty status."[102]

The government has remained steadfast in its position that there is no treaty obligation to provide health care. The 2002 Romanow report on *The Future of Health Care in Canada* notes that "[a]ccording to the federal government, however, there is no constitutional obligation or treaty that requires the Canadian government to offer health programs or services to Aboriginal Peoples."[103] In 2012, Health Canada reiterated, "[i]t is the Government of Canada's position that current health programs and services including Non-Insured Health Benefits are provided to First Nations and

Inuit on the basis of national policy and not due to any constitutional or other legal obligations."[104]

Although the government has denied a treaty right to medical care, medicine, and health services, some common understandings between the government and First Nations have been measured through the Saskatchewan Office of the Treaty Commissioner where both the federal government and Saskatchewan First Nations recognized that the treaties are a foundation for future relations through ongoing treaty discussions.

First Nation Organizations

The Federation of Saskatchewan Indian Nations expressed their views on the importance of the treaties:

> [T]hey granted some of their powers to the Crown in exchange for certain benefits and rights. . . . Indian people entered into a political arrangement with the Crown so that they could live as Indian people forever. . . . By signing the treaties, the Indian nations created an ongoing relationship with the Crown in Indian social and economic development in exchange for lands surrendered.[105]

In 2007, the Federation of Saskatchewan Indian Nations passed a resolution to accept a set of important Treaty Implementation Principles. This document outlines the responsibilities of the Crown in implementing treaty promises in, among other areas, health and through the medicine chest clause in Treaty 6:

> Our Elders also tell us that we did not agree to give up the land. The written text contains the words "cede, release, surrender and yield up . . . all their rights, titles and privileges, whatsoever to the lands. . . ." These words are contrary to what actually took place in the negotiations. First Nations intended to share the land. The word *witaskiwin* was used in the negotiations when describing the accord relating to land. *Witaskiwin* means sharing or living together on the land. More particularly, First Nations only intended to share the topsoil to the depth of a plough. According to our Elders, this was because the white man asked us if they could use this soil for farming and we agreed.
> In return the Crown undertook to provide assistance in a num-

ber of areas including: education, *health* and medicine, economic independence, hunting, fishing, trapping, gathering, annuities, agriculture, prohibition of liquor, exemption from taxes and conscription.[106]

Further, "the *spirit and intent* of the Treaty also means that the written terms must be interpreted to reflect changes with the progression of time. The medicine chest clause means a comprehensive type of health and medical coverage to supplement First Nations health and medicine." Additionally, "the pestilence and famine clause in the modern day context would mean assistance in times of extraordinary circumstances such as diseases, pandemic and floods."[107]

In 2008, Treaty 6 Nations across Alberta, Saskatchewan, and Manitoba met at the Thunderchild First Nation to propose a health system that is autonomous from the federal government. They proposed First Nation run hospitals where patients can access western and First Nation medicine based on treaty promises for full health care coverage.[108]

In the view of the Assembly of First Nations, the Assembly of First Nations Chiefs Committee on Health have approved the Treaty Right to Health as a part of their overall strategic plan as a means of ensuring and improving health services:

> Elder Helen Gladue, who spoke on the second day of the meeting, reminded the Chiefs that they should concentrate on the Treaty Right to Health. "Being a direct descendant of a signatory of Treaty Six, it goes without saying that the Treaty right is a sacred belief," she said. "We have had equal rights right from the beginning. We have a bundle of rights. And those are sacred rights."[109]

The Health and Social Secretariat of the Assembly of First Nations has a mandate and a role to ensure that all First Nations citizens, regardless of residence, have access to quality health services funded by the First Nations and Inuit Health Branch (FNIHB) of Health Canada. The AFN further asserts that health benefits are

> an Inherent Aboriginal and Treaty Right and are constitutionally protected. Health services are to be comprehensive, accessible, fully portable, and provided as needed on a timely basis without regard to a person's financial status, residence, or the cost of benefit.[110]

There are obvious differences in how First Nations and the Federal Government view treaties. A core disagreement has been the reading of the medicine chest clause in Treaty 6. First Nations interpret it as a promise for health care and medicines. The federal government has interpreted it more along the lines of a literal box for medicines. This policy disagreement has never been fully resolved, either by court rulings or by substantive realignment in federal and provincial health policies so a treaty right to health is given a new, modern meaning in keeping with the original intent. The Government of Canada, the Province of Saskatchewan, and the Federation of Saskatchewan Indian Nations were able to make some progress on this issue, through the Office of the Treaty Commissioner (OTC) located in Saskatoon, that assisted to outline the respective parties' understanding of treaty rights to health in the modern context and understanding of the treaties.

Although it seems as if the Government of Canada and First Nation organizations are miles apart with their views on treaty obligations, in 1997 and 1998, the Office of the Treaty Commissioner brought the parties together and created some common understandings of the treaties as a foundational key for future relations and discussions on treaty obligations. The federal government entered into exploratory discussions for the first time in over 100 years. The Federation of Saskatchewan Indian Nations, as leaders in this area, stated:

> Treaties provided us with a shared future, treaties prevented war and guaranteed peace, treaties defined and shaped relations between nations through enduring relations of mutual respect, and treaties guaranteed the shared economic bounty of one of the planet's richest and most productive lands.[111]

The federal government expressed similar views:

> The federal government understands that the treaties between Canada and First Nations were intended by the parties to endure into the future. It recognizes that treaties define fundamental aspects of the continuing relationship between Canada and Treaty First Nations and that they are important instruments guiding the way to a shared future for First Nations and other Canadians. The federal government recognizes that, by doing justice to the treaties, it may honour the past and enrich the future.[112]

It has been well over 10 years since the Exploratory Treaty Table was initiated in Saskatchewan; the Office of the Treaty Commissioner has worked tirelessly to advance treaty issues in schools, the public forum for broad-based outreach, research, and facilitating discussions. The Treaty Table functions as a neutral meeting ground where elders are listened to and the treaty parties openly explore treaty issues. The mandate of the Office of the Treaty Commissioner is to advocate on behalf of the treaty relationship, and not on behalf of either party.

Treaties must be considered within the context of the historical ceremonies and the assurances of friendship and brotherhood, and the Queen's concern for her Indian subjects, which were such a prominent feature of the historical treaty negotiations. The treaties must be interpreted not only in cultural and historical terms, but within the context of a modern and ever-changing Canada.

The *Report of the Royal Commission on Aboriginal People* stated that it is "indisputable, however, those existing treaties have been honoured by governments more in the breach than in the observance."[113] The Report concluded that the treaty relationship between the Treaty Nations and Canadian government are "mired in ignorance, mistrust and prejudice. Indeed, this has been the case for generations."[114] The dishonoured treaties are part of the negative "ghosts" of Canadian history.[115] Although small steps have occurred, Treaty obligations and rights of Aboriginal people remain unfulfilled while Aboriginal health continues to suffer.

CONCLUSION

This chapter has considered Aboriginal and treaty rights and how they may lay the groundwork for how the law can be used to bring Aboriginal and non-Aboriginal health status closer together. The chapter has provided an analysis that health is an Aboriginal and/or treaty right (that has constitutional protection) through descriptions of historical facts and documentation that Aboriginal health has been practised pre-contact and has evolved through time into a modern Aboriginal right. The practice of medicine, healing, and preventative health measures comprised a vital facet or integral part of a distinctive culture, or of central significance to Aboriginal society, which has passed from generation to generation in various forms and is still in existence today in modified forms. These are core underpinnings of Aboriginal society that manifested into Aboriginal and treaty rights that have evolved into the modern equivalent of traditional health and health care, and thus fulfill the requirements of the common law tests that the courts have set out to prove an Aboriginal right. In addition to Aboriginal rights, some Aboriginal peoples also possess treaty rights. Some treaties supplement the Aboriginal right to health care, such as the medicine chest clause and the pestilence and famine clause of Treaty 6. Other treaties contain references to medicine, health care, and protection. These protections also continue to exist today in modern forms and have evolved and manifested themselves into the modern existence of the provision of health care. The purpose of this chapter was to illustrate that First Nations, Métis, and Inuit do have Aboriginal, and in addition some have treaty rights, to health and meet the tests that the Supreme Court has deemed to prove these rights. When laws, legislation, and policies are based on these correct legal underpinnings, then the outcomes in health may be more equalized.

CHAPTER 6

Reconciliation of Aboriginal Health and Healing Practices

PROFESSOR JAMES SA'KE'J YOUNGBLOOD HENDERSON describes the "Aboriginal renaissance" as rising from Aboriginal students and faculty from various departments within university settings (such as law, humanities, sciences, and education) creating new and holistic types of study that breed the development of new research and knowledge formation, development, and implementation:

> Aboriginal renaissance has shifted the agenda from recrimination to rebirth, from conflict to collaboration, from perceived deficiency to capacity. It has also shifted university thinking from a defensive/assimilative narrative to a receptive/transformative narrative that accepts that benefits to Aboriginal peoples is a benefit to the whole academic community and the multiple publics who look to elite institutions to lead and to listen. As such, innovation from diverse sources can lead to beneficial change for all.[1]

The Aboriginal renaissance sets a perfect stage for applying a combination of knowledge identified in this book: from health to law to science and humanities, new theories can be crafted which bring new perspectives and new solutions in a receptive/transformative setting. This chapter attempts to utilize and provide this combined narrative approach to addressing issues outlined thus far.

Coupled with Henderson's Aboriginal renaissance tools, an approach may be crafted that gives meaning to the recommendations provided at the conclusion that meshes law with health and science. Recommendations are gleaned from throughout the book and in particular the ideas that have flowed from the concepts of reconciliation.

6.1 Influencing Policy Development

New government health policies must address the causes of ill health and be based on a revamped, fair, and rational economic and social order, and on an analysis that implements constitutionally protected rights. This must be outside the realm and structure of other parties (i.e., the federal government) directing what is best for Aboriginal people.

The legal background for the practice of the government "knowing" what is best for Aboriginal people stems from the basic legal premise of the guardian-and-ward theory. This is the premise on which health policies were developed. It is outdated and incorrect. To initiate new government health policies, certain principles must be acknowledged and discussed. National linkages must be created that bridge the divide between policy makers, the government, and Aboriginal people. A good example may be found in the workshops provided by the partnership between the Johnson Shoyama Graduate School of Public Policy and the Indigenous People's Health Research Centre in Regina. These workshops have proven popular among interdisciplinary and diverse groups of policy makers in government in Saskatchewan — from municipal to provincial and federal. The goal is to move Aboriginal and treaty rights law into action through education and direction on how to recognize incorrect and damaging existing policy and make changes through various avenues, such as the development of briefing notes to Ministers or changing the language of the existing policies so that it reflects the correct legal underpinnings that equalizes rather than separates policies and peoples.

Another effective method may be through implementation of the principles found in the *Blueprint on Aboriginal Health*[2] that was created in 2005. The purpose was to improve access and quality of health services for all Aboriginal people through a collaborative approach that included the Canadian government and the national Aboriginal organizations (representing their constituents). The key principles noted were:

- Health is holistic in nature;

- Recognition of the distinctiveness of the constitutionally recog-

. nized Aboriginal groups with partnerships built on inclusion;

- Recognition that a funding source is required and that the blueprint must be reviewed in a timely manner to ensure accountability and goal attainment.

Integral to the framework are several approaches that were fundamental to the *Blueprint*, such as building on Indigenous knowledge, women's participation, determinants of health, engagement and inclusivity, sustainability and accountability, and description of current mandates. To put the frameworks into action, a distinction-based approach was implemented that addressed the specific needs of First Nations, Métis, and Inuit, respectively. The 2005 *Blueprint* called for a 10-year transformative plan (the federal self-government agreements were cognizant of the timelines) and for the recognition of the constitutionally protected rights of Aboriginal peoples in Canada. The *Blueprint* did not confine itself to health necessities but looked at policy developments from a collaborative, holistic perspective, confirming that there are no "quick fixes."

6.2   The "Whole Approach"

Using the whole of Aboriginal and non-Aboriginal government approach, a collaborative effort is critical and must address the needs of both Aboriginal people and government in order to move forward. In addition, certain key principles must be reflected and adhered to while developing, changing, and influencing policy:

- Every Aboriginal person born in Canada has a powerful set of constitutionally protected rights through Section 35 of the *Constitution Act, 1982*.

- Health care policies must reflect the constitutional rights as expressed in s. 35.

- These constitutional rights include (among others) the inherent right to self-determination, self-government, to control one's own living circumstances and quality of life.

- Root causes of ill health (colonization, historical policies, legislative policies, guardian and ward theories, etc.) must be addressed, rejected, and replaced with policies that reflect the fiduciary relationship between the federal and provincial and territorial governments and Aboriginal people.

- A collaborative approach must be utilized which includes: i) the whole of government, federal, provincial, municipal, and/or Aboriginal governments; ii) all three constitutionally recognized Aboriginal groups and a recognition of the distinctions within each group. This approach is required to establish the political will to effect change and implement policy reform and constitutionalized Aboriginal health care.

- A holistic approach must be engaged that considers all determinants of health and all aspects of health that connects every person to their family, community, and nation through a cycle of interdependence, and that is cognizant of the requirement that self-determination includes the ability to determine timelines. Self-determination also recognizes the fact that some First Nations, Métis, and Inuit do not want to have the courts define their rights and may choose alternative methods to implement their inherent rights.

- An evidence-based approach must be utilized to advance Aboriginal health.

6.3   GATHERING EVIDENCE

In 2005, the First Nations and Inuit Health Branch of Health Canada (FNIHB) produced a manual for the Aboriginal Head Start Program that addressed the needs of children with disabilities. The manual for government use was produced based on treaty rights, fiduciary obligations, constitutional rights, The *United Nations Convention on the Rights of the Child* via "Canada's Fit for Children," Canada's current and past initiatives via "Canada's Fit for Children," and federal government programs and initiatives.[3]

To accomplish FNIHB's goal of understanding the rights of an Aboriginal child with special needs, an implementation table was created that compared Aboriginal and treaty rights to health with selected articles from the *United Nations Convention on the Rights of the Child*. The table also includes past and current initiatives that Canada has undertaken to respect these Aboriginal and treaty rights. This project is interesting in that the constitutional obligations of the federal government are listed and implemented in relation to children's rights. It is a starting point for the correct development of policies relating to Aboriginal health and the constitutionalization of Aboriginal health care. It would therefore be useful to use the federal government document *Aboriginal Child's Rights Special Needs Focus,* to expand and develop these ideas for future implementation in all Health Canada's policies that affect Aboriginal peoples.

6.4   HEALTH IMPACT ASSESSMENT SYSTEM APPLICATION

Health impact assessments are important tools to safeguard health. For instance, there is a succinct spiritual and cultural connection between the land and First Nations, Métis, and Inuit people. Environmental and human health is inextricably interlinked and therefore, a health impact assessment (HIA) must be an integral part of an environmental impact assessment (EIA). A cornerstone of HIA is the recognition of the need for public participation in the definition and scoping of human health concerns, and in decision-making. Environmental assessments have been in existence since the 1970s:

> EA involves determining any changes or impacts that a project or action will have on our surroundings be it positive or negative effects — before that project is carried out in order to prevent irrevocable damage from occurring.

> A set of criteria is used to determine possible impacts on human and environmental health and it is graded according to its significance and degree of impact. . . . The final step in an EA is to decide whether or not the project should be allowed to proceed, and if so, what conditions should be attached to the approval.[4]

Government-led policies, laws, and legislation have had enormous negative impacts on Aboriginal peoples. First Nations, Métis, and Inuit have questioned the government-led processes and have called for more community-driven and culturally relevant health models specifically in relation to environmental issues. In response, the Human Environmental Health Impact Assessment was created to assess the potential risks and benefits of proposed developments and natural resource management within Aboriginal communities.[5] The World Health Organization (WHO) describes the Health Impact Assessment as

> a practical approach used to judge the potential health effects of a policy, programme or project on a population, particularly on vulnerable or disadvantaged groups. Recommendations are produced for decision-makers and stakeholders, with the aim of maximizing the proposal's positive health effects and minimizing its negative health effects.[6]

A positive example of measuring health impacts can be seen at Baker Lake. The Inuit women of Baker Lake are researching the impacts of the mining industry on women in their area. The Baker Lake women are learning how to conduct research and interviews. Assisted by Frank Tester of the University of British Columbia, the women turn their data collection into a report that will be made public.

Like the Baker Lake study, a health impact assessment is based on values that link it to the policy environment in which it is being undertaken. For instance, democracy allows "people to participate in the development and implementation of policies, programmes or projects that may impact on their lives. . . ." Equity "assesses the distribution of impacts from a proposal on the whole population, with a particular reference to how the proposal will affect vulnerable people (in terms of age, gender, ethnic background, and socio-economic status)."[7]

One of the reasons WHO uses HIA is that it has actually proven to improve health and reduce inequalities:

> Addressing inequalities and improving health is a goal for many organisations and all governments. One way of contributing to the health and inequalities agenda is through the use of HIA. At the very least, HIA ensures that proposals do not inadvertently damage health or reinforce inequalities. HIA uses a wide model of health and works across sectors to provide a systematic approach for assessing how the proposal affects a population, with particular emphasis on the distribution of effects between different subgroups within the population. Recommendations can specifically target the improvement of health for vulnerable groups.[8]

It is possible to apply these same principles to programs, policies, laws, legislation, and projects that affect Aboriginal health. At the very least, there is great value to be gained through its application within the most dire health circumstances. For example, a screening could occur with a checklist on how far-ranging the impacts are, what Aboriginal and treaty rights are affected, and what the long-term impacts could be. This may include the Haudenosaunee principles of "the effect of their decision on peace; the effect on the natural world; and the effect on seven generations in the future."[9]

6.5 IMPLEMENTING THE UNITED NATIONS DECLARATION ON THE RIGHTS OF INDIGENOUS PEOPLES

In its Fact Sheet, the Office of the High Commissioner for Human Rights has noted that the *United Nations Declaration on the Rights of Indigenous Peoples* (*UNDRIP*) "provides the foundation — along with other human rights standards — for the development of policies and laws to protect the collective human rights of Indigenous peoples."[10] The *UNDRIP* affirms the "minimum standards for the survival, dignity and well-being of the indigenous people of the world."[11] These promote a human-rights-based approach to addressing issues faced by Indigenous peoples and provide a just legal framework for "achieving reconciliation, redress and respect."[12]

On September 13, 2007, 370 million Indigenous people in 70 countries applauded the adoption of the *UNDRIP* as a huge step in addressing human rights violations against them.[13] The vote was 144 states in favour and four opposed: Canada, the United States, New Zealand, and Australia. Canada did not sign the *UNDRIP*; even though Canada was involved in the 22-year drafting process, Canada stated that the UNDRIP "might not fully accord with the norms and precedents that have been established through judicial decisions and negotiations on land claims and self-government,"[14] also noting that its decision to oppose it was the "right one"[15] and it had "principled and well-publicized concerns" while dealing with Indigenous issues "openly, honestly and with respect."[16] Contrary to international legal precedent, Canada claims that "*UNDRIP* is a non-legally binding aspirational document."[17] However, on March 3, 2010, the Speech from the Throne stated that the Government of Canada would now endorse the *UNDRIP* in a manner consistent with Canada's Constitution and laws.

On November 12, 2010, Prime Minister Stephen Harper issued a statement for Canada's support for the *UNDRIP*. Canada stated:

> After careful and thoughtful consideration, Canada has concluded that it is better to endorse the UNDRIP while explaining its concerns, rather than simply rejecting the overall document. Although the UNDRIP does not reflect customary international law or change Canadian laws, Canada believes that the UNDRIP has the potential to contribute positively to the promotion and respect of the rights of Indigenous peoples around the world. [18]

The *UNDRIP* sets out minimum standards of the collective and individual rights of Indigenous people. On the day *UNDRIP* became a part of international law, it was celebrated as a major victory. It became a valuable tool to protect Indigenous rights. Canada has stated that the *UNDRIP* is not representative of customary international law. Legal scholars argue that while it is true that a Declaration alone does not create binding legal obligations, other assessments have found that the key provisions of *UNDRIP* can be regarded as equivalent to already established principles of international law. This fact alone implies the existence of equivalent and parallel international obligations that states are legally bound to comply with. The scope of *UNDRIP* is broad and covers almost all aspects of Indigenous lives. In relation to health matters, Article 23 states:

> Indigenous peoples have the right to determine and develop priorities and strategies for exercising their right to development. In particular, indigenous peoples have the right to be actively involved in developing and determining health, housing and other economic and social programmes affecting them and, as far as possible, to administer such programmes through their own institutions.

UNDRIP alone is not enough to protect or promote Aboriginal and treaty rights to health. With the implementation of *UNDRIP,* a dovetailing must occur within the Canadian legal framework of Aboriginal and treaty rights. It is critical that there should be a reliance on *UNDRIP* standards during negotiations of agreements, contracts, and any implementation of Indigenous laws/processes that deals with Aboriginal health. Relying on the standards in human rights cases, conventions, and judicial decisions should all be put before the decision makers in domestic Canadian court cases to guide an interpretation of Aboriginal and treaty rights in relation to health.

Conclusion

DISPARITIES IN HEALTH STATUS typically arise from social, political, cultural, and economic determinants, which lie largely outside the health realm. Certain disparities inevitably have an impact on individuals, their communities, and their nations. These determinants also have an impact across generations. Determinants affect the health of both the individual and the communities in which they live. Many underlying health determinants for Aboriginal people include poverty, homelessness, inadequate or substandard housing, unemployment, violence, lack of access to health services, lack of cultural awareness within the existing health system, lack of education, and high rates of unemployment indicating that "social inequality, whether measured at the population or individual level, is the single leading condition for poor health."[1] Social and economic disadvantages increase the risk to the health and well-being of Aboriginal people. The negative impact of these socioeconomic factors extends further. They damage the biological development of Aboriginal children and youth, reducing their immunity to disease. The consequences of weakened health accumulate across individual life spans as well as through succeeding generations.

Although the poor health of Aboriginal people is directly linked to "the corrosive effects of poverty and economic marginalization,"[2] the determinants of health are themselves both direct and indirect consequences of historic policies of colonization. It follows, then, that the damages caused by colonization are directly related to the risks to health caused by colonial socio-economic disadvantage.

The social conditions of many Aboriginal communities show the results of colonization in the form of addictive behaviours and violence. Alcohol and drug abuse are the most prevalent types of addictive behaviours, and they are associated with a range of serious physical and mental health problems. Aboriginal women face additional problems unique to their gender and place in Canadian society.

As noted throughout, Indigenous populations have a lower life expectancy than non-Indigenous populations, a higher incidence of most diseases (diabetes, cardiovascular diseases, cancers, etc.), and commonly experience high rates of communicable Third-World-type diseases such as tuberculosis. It is difficult to make completely accurate comparisons when variable methods of enumeration and statistics for Aboriginal populations are used. It is, however, clear that inequalities in health status are an important measure of the quality of the health system.

In spite of their health and societal status, Aboriginal people hold special constitutionally entrenched rights. Aboriginal and treaty rights are recognized and affirmed in the *Constitution Act, 1982*. These rights are in addition to the rights that all Canadians are entitled to through the *Canada Health Act*.[3] While the *Canada Health Act* is geared to distributing health care to all Canadians equally, Aboriginal peoples argue that their constitutional difference is relevant to the just distribution of health rights and entitlements. Treatment of Aboriginal people as merely "other peoples" ignores their constitutional rights and creates inequality of services. The Supreme Court recognizes the constitutional supremacy of these rights and has provided guiding principles for the legislature, governments, and courts. Aboriginal and treaty rights are remarkable sets of rights that recognize Aboriginal people as distinct rights-bearing holders of unique customs, practices, and traditions. Moreover, these rights are constitutionally entrenched in the Supreme law of Canada. However, 30 years have elapsed since the Constitution of Canada was amended. In light of these incredible rights, Aboriginal people still suffer disproportionately. It is clear that Aboriginal health and health practices have been compromised. The evidence lies in the statistics noted earlier in the stark discrepancies of Aboriginal health and non-Aboriginal health: the infringement continues. It would be untenable to assume that this right was extinguished by treaty, statute, or any laws, as there has never been any clear intention to do so, nor has it been implicitly extinguished. Additionally, through the examination of the legal history of health care in Canada, as applied to Aboriginal people, one is able to conclude that Aboriginal rights and treaty rights have been largely ignored by the federal government when passing laws and implementing health policies.

A broad spectrum of sources has been identified that has led to the poor health of Aboriginal people today — it has also identified a broad spectrum of interventions to improve the health of Aboriginal people in Canada. Within that spectrum, politicians, legislative drafters, policy makers, academics, Aboriginal communities (locally, regionally, and nationally), lawyers, health professionals, and scientists can have a major role in contributing to equalizing Aboriginal health in Canada. Together, these groups can produce dramatic reductions in mortality and morbidity through a) high-quality primary health care services for proactive detection, prevention, and early treatment, b) changes to the legislative schemes that affect Aboriginal and treaty rights to health, c) implementation of health policies that reflect a holistic approach, and d) implementation of Health Impact Assessments before Aboriginal and treaty rights to health are affected.

In terms of health institutions, capacity building, research, cultural education for health professionals, funding and resources for Aboriginal health are critical to improve health. It is also important to cultivate an Aboriginal work force with Aboriginal health and cultural perspectives. The knowledge must be utilized that is already available to effectively diagnose and treat the conditions that cause illness and death. The critical health service issue is one of adequate primary healthcare services for prevention and early diagnosis and treatment of the high levels of illness and illness precursors that are already present in much of the Aboriginal population. This could be achieved through nation-wide initiatives to further develop Aboriginal community controlled primary health care services at an adequate needs-based funding level.

Change in the culture of Aboriginal health care itself is critical. Tertiary institutions, universities, and colleges must acknowledge their inherent responsibilities to recruit and retain culturally relevant and competent, responsive clinicians and health care professionals. All governments, Aboriginal, and non-Aboriginal agencies and funding bodies must support the access and delivery of appropriate services.

The acceptance of continuing disparities in health for Aboriginal people is not appropriate when the root causes of those disparities and the solutions/remedies are well understood. Politicians, legislators, and policy makers must be educated not only in the process that created the poor health status but the one that will improve health outcomes. The process must include the recognition and implementation of Aboriginal and treaty rights to health and the implementation of constitutional health care for all Aboriginal people in Canada. If all governments are truly to contribute to positive change, they must commit to transcending political agendas and election cycles and recognize and halt the colonization that was implemented with the early health policies and legislation and that remain a barrier to progress in the health of Aboriginal people today.

Notes

NOTES TO INTRODUCTION

1   The term "Aboriginal People" refers to the original inhabitants of Canada who are First Nations (Indian), Inuit, and Métis peoples. Aboriginal people are recognized in section 35(2) of the *Constitution Act, 1982: (Constitution Act, 1867* (U.K.), 30 & 31 Vict., c.3, reprinted in R.S.C. 1985, App. II, No. 5. S. 35 (2)) In this Act, "aboriginal peoples of Canada" includes the Indian, Inuit, and Métis peoples of Canada.

2   Canada, Health Canada, *First Nations, Inuit and Aboriginal Health* (Ottawa: Health Canada, 2012), online: http://www.hc-sc.gc.ca/fniah-spnia/pubs/index-eng.php (accessed January 5, 2014). See also The Indigenous People's Health Research Centre, 2013, online: http://iphrc.ca/index (accessed January 5, 2014).

3   Health Council of Canada, "Rekindling Reform, 2003–2008, online: http://health-councilcanada.ca./tree/2.46-HCC_5YRPLAN_WEB_FA.pdf at 31 (accessed October 29, 2012).

4   M. Battiste & J. Y. Henderson, *Protecting Indigenous Knowledge and Heritage: A Global Challenge* (Saskatoon: Purich, 2000) at 212 – 215.

5   *Ibid.*

6   *Ibid.* at 205. See also *R.* v. *Van der Peet*, [1996] 2 S.C.R. 507, [1996] 4 C.N.L.R. 146; *Delgamuukw* v. *British Columbia*, [1997] 3 S.C.R. 1010, [1998] 1 C.N.L.R. 14, reversing in part (1993), 10 D.L.R. (4th) 470, [1993] 5 C.N.L.R. 1 (B.C.C.A.), varying in part [1991] 3 W.W.R. 97, [1991] 5 C.N.L.R. 1 (B.C.S.C.).

7   G. Graham-Cumming, "Northern Health Services," *Canadian Medical Association Journal*, 100 (March 15, 1969) 526–531 at 526. [Graham-Cumming]

8   *Ibid.*

9   Canada: *Report of the Royal Commission on Aboriginal Peoples: Gathering Strength*, vol. 3 (Ottawa: The Commission, 1996), ch. 3, "Health and Healing," [RCAP] quoting Nicholas Denys (1672), quoted in Cornelius J. Jaenen, *Friend and Foe: Aspects of French-Amerindian Cultural Contact in the Sixteenth and Seventeenth Centuries* (Toronto: McClelland and Stewart, 1976) at fn 6.

10   RCAP, *ibid.,* citing Virgil J. Vogel, *American Indian Medicine* (Norman, Okla.: University of Oklahoma Press, 1970) at 159.

11   J. Waldram, D. A. Herring, & T. K. Young, *Aboriginal Health in Canada. Historical, Cultural and Epidemiological Perspectives* (Toronto: University of Toronto Press, 1995) at 23. [Waldram]

12   William Canniff, *The Medical Profession in Upper Canada, 1783-1850: An Historical Narrative with Original Documents Relating to the Profession, Including some brief Biographies* (Toronto: W. Briggs, 1894) at 19.

13   John McLean, 1799–1890, *Notes of a Twenty-five years' Service in the Hudson Bay Territories* (Toronto: The Champlain Society, 1932) at 315.

14   *Ibid.*

15   Waldram, *supra* note 11 at 101.

16   *Ibid.* at 23.

17   See Gerald V. Mohatt, "Healing and Spirituality: Implication for Training and Practice of Psychologists," Education, Resources Information Center, 1991, online: http://www.eric.ed.gov/ERICWebPortal/custom/portlets/recordDetails/detailmini.jsp?_nfpb=true&_&ERICExtSearch_SearchValue_0=ED343739&ERICExtSearch_SearchType_0=no&accno=ED343739 (January 5, 2014).

18   World Health Organization, "Traditional Medicine, Key Facts," ohttp://www.who.int/topics/traditional_medicine/en/ (accessed January 5, 2014).

19   RCAP, *supra* note 9.

Notes to Chapter One

1   Preamble of the Constitution of the World Health Organization as adopted by the International Health Conference, New York, 19–22 June 1946; signed on 22 July 1946 by the representatives of 61 States (Official Records of the World Health Organization, no. 2, at 100) and entered into force on 7 April 1948. [WHO]

2   Enrique González (2000), "Circle of Rights, Economic, Social & Cultural Rights Activism: A Training Resource, Module 14 the Right to Health," at para. 6, online: University of Minnesota Human Rights Resource Center, http://www1.umn.edu/humanrts/edumat/IHRIP/circle/modules/module14.htm (accessed January 5, 2014).

3   E. Geyorfi-Dyke (2008), Poverty and Chronic Disease: Recommendations for Action. In Chronic Disease Prevention Alliance of Canada (Ed.): CDPAC.

4   J. Reading, *The Crisis of Chronic Disease among Aboriginal Peoples: A Challenge for Public Health, Population Health and Social Policy* (University of Victoria Centre for Aboriginal Health Research: 2009), online: http://cahr.uvic.ca/docs/ChronicDisease%20Final.pdf (accessed January 5, 2014) at 10. [Chronic]

5   See National Native Addictions Partnership Foundation 2012, online: www.nnapf.ca (accessed October 5, 2012).

6   Janet C. Currie, *Best Practices: Treatment and Rehabilitation for Women with Substance Abuse Problems,* Ottawa: Minister of Public Works and Government Services Canada, 2001.

7   See Women's College Hospital, 2012, at Women's College Research Institute, Toronto, online: http://www.wchospital.ca/ (accessed January 5, 2014).

8   World Health Organization, 2008c, "The Urgent Need for Action. Chapter Two. Chronic Diseases and Poverty, Chronic Diseases and Health Promotion," online: http://www.who.int/chp/chronic_disease_report/part2_ch2/en/index.html (accessed August 30, 2012).

9   *Ibid.*

10   Public Health Agency of Canada, *Actions Taken and Future Directions, 2011. Curbing Childhood Obesity: A Federal, Provincial and Territorial Framework for Action to Promote Healthy Weights, 2012,* online: http://www.phac-aspc.gc.ca/hp-ps/hl-mvs/framework-cadre/2011/hw-os-2011-eng.php (accessed January 5, 2014).

11   Street Health, online: http://www.streethealth.ca/home.htm (accessed January 5, 2014).

12   S. W. Hwang, (2001), "Homelessness and Health," *Canadian Medical Association Journal,* 164(2), 229–233; S. W. Hwang & A. L. Bugeja (2000), "Barriers to appropriate diabetes management among homeless people in Toronto," *Canadian Medical Association Journal,* 163(2), 161–165.

13   National Aboriginal Health Organization, Report for Participants, "Homelessness and Housing Realities for Inuit," (Ottawa: 2008), online: http://www.naho.ca/documents/it/2011_Homelessness-Housing-Realities-Inuit-Workshop-Report.pdf (accessed January 5, 2014).

14   *Ibid.*

15   Ajunnginiq Centre, National Aboriginal Health Organization, "Homelessness and Housing Realities for Inuit: Background for Discussion" March 18, 2008, online: http://www.naho.ca/documents/it/2011_Homelessness-Housing-Realities-Inuit-Workshop.pdf (accessed January 5, 2014).

16   First Nations Information Governance Centre, (2013), "RHS Phase 2 (2008/10): National Report on Adults, Youth and Children Living in First Nations Communities." Ottawa: online: http://www.fnigc.ca/ (accessed January 5, 2014). [RHS]

17   Canada, Health Canada, First Nations Inuit and Aboriginal Health, "Tuberculosis 2009," online: http://www.hc-sc.gc.ca/fniah-spnia/diseases-maladies/tuberculos/index-eng.php (accessed January 5, 2014).

18   RHS, *supra* note 16 at 55.

19   *Ibid.* at 344.

20   *Ibid.* at 59.

21   Canada, Health Canada, First Nations, Inuit and Aboriginal Health, "Drinking Water and Wastewater," online: http://www.hc-sc.gc.ca/fniah-spnia/promotion/public-publique/water-eau-eng.php#how_many (accessed December 3, 2013).

22   Canada, Health Canada, First Nations, Inuit and Aboriginal Health, "Backgrounder: Priority List of First Nation Communities with High Risk Water Systems and Drinking Water Advisories," online: http://www.ainc-inac.gc.ca/ai/mr/nr/j-a2006/02757bk-eng.asp (accessed December 3, 2013).

23   Canada, Aboriginal and Northern Affairs Canada, December 19, 2012, "Water," on-line: http://www.aadnc-aandc.gc.ca/eng/1100100034879/1100100034883 (accessed December 3, 2013). [Water]

24   In June 2011, the government of Canada changed the name of the department of Indian Affairs and Northern Development Canada (INAC or IAND) to Aboriginal Affairs and Northern Development Canada (AANDC).

25   Water, *supra* note 23.

26   Canada, Human Resources and Skills Development Canada, 2011, "Canadians in Context: Aboriginal Population," online: http://www4.hrsdc.gc.ca/.3ndic.1t.4r@-eng. jsp?iid=36 (accessed January 5, 2014).

27   RHS, *supra* note 16.

28   National Aboriginal Health Organization, Ajunnginiq Centre, Health Sectoral Roundtable: Background Documents on Inuit Health Issues. Ottawa. 2004, online: http://www.naho.ca/documents/naho/english/health_sectoral_AC.pdf   (accessed January 5, 2014).

29   World Wildlife Fund, "Contamination: The Result of WWF Biomonitoring Survey," online: http://www.wwf.org.uk/filelibrary/pdf/biomonitoringresults.pdf (accessed October 22, 2012).

30   Office of the Auditor General, 2009 Fall Report of the Auditor General of Canada, Chapter 6: Land Management and Environmental Protection on Reserves, online: http://www.oag-bvg.gc.ca/internet/docs/parl_oag_200911_06_e.pdf (accessed January 5, 2014).

31   *Ibid.* at 6.40.

32   Christina Spencer, Parliamentary Bureau; *Toronto Sun*, "Feds fund 'quit smoking' programs for Inuit," May 31, 2010, online: http://www.torontosun.com/news/canada/2010/05/31/14200866.html (January 5, 2014).

33   David Ljunggren, "Every G20 nation wants to be Canada, insists PM," Reuters, September 25, 2009, online: http://www.reuters.com/article/idUSTRE58P05Z20090926 (accessed January 5, 2014).

34   J. Sa'ke'j Henderson, "Postcolonial Ghost Dancing: Diagnosing European Colonialism," in Marie Battiste (Ed.), *Reclaiming Indigenous Voice and Vision* (Vancouver: University of British Columbia Press, 2000) at 58.

35   S. H. Razack, *Looking White People in the Eye: Gender, Race and Culture in Courtrooms and Classrooms* (Toronto: University of Toronto Press, 1998).

36   See, on the Doctrine of Discovery, Robert A. Williams, *The American Indian in Western Legal Thought: The Discourses of Conquest* (Oxford: Oxford University Press, 1990); Robert A. Williams, "Columbus's Legacy: Law as an Instrument of Racial Discrimination against Indigenous Peoples' Right to Self-Determination" (1991), *American Journal of International and Comparative Law*, Vol. 8 issue 2; Robert J. Miller, Jacinta Ruru, Larissa Behrendt, & Tracey Lindberg, *Discovering Indigenous Lands: The Doctrine of Discovery in the English Colonies* (Oxford Scholarship Online: September 2010).

37   International Network for Indigenous Health Knowledge and Development, *A Discussion Document: Knowledge Translation to improve the health of Indigenous Peoples* (Townsville: 2003), online: http://www.inihkd.org/INIHKD_Discussion_Document per cent20_March_2003.pdf (accessed October 22, 2012).

38   Taiaiake Alfred & Jeff Corntassel, "Being Indigenous: Resurgences Against Contemporary Colonialism." *Government and Opposition*, 2005, online: http://web.uvic.ca/igov/uploads/pdf/Being%20Indigenous%20GOOP.pdf (accessed January 5, 2014).

39   RHS, *supra* note 16.

40   *Ibid.* This issue is also important as disabilities restrict access to health services. Michael Oliver discusses the theory of people with disabilities being marginalized; for Aboriginal people, this marginalization is doubled by being disabled and being Aboriginal. See Michael Oliver, *The Politics of Disablement* (London: MacMillan, 1990.)

41   Statistics Canada, Aboriginal Peoples Survey, 2006, "An Overview of the Health of the Métis Population: Fact Sheet," Ottawa: Minister of Public Works and Government Services Canada, online: http://www.statcan.gc.ca/pub/89-637-x/89-637-x2009006-eng.pdf (accessed January 5, 2014).

42   National Aboriginal Health Organization, "Overview of Inuit Health," online: http://www.naho.ca/inuit/e/overview/ (accessed January 5, 2014). [NAHO]

43   Statistics Canada, *The Daily Monday*, September 27, 2004, "Ajunnginiq Centre" at the National Aboriginal Health Organization, 2004.

44   NAHO, *supra* note 42.

45   *Ibid.*

46   Native Women's Association of Canada, *Aboriginal Women: Statistics and Demographics*, (Ottawa: 2009). [NWAC]

47   Canada, Statistics Canada, *Women in Canada, 5th Edition*. Statistics Canada, 2006.

48   NWAC, *supra* note 46.

49   Laurence J. Kirmayer, Gregory M. Brass, & Tara Holton, *Suicide Among Aboriginal People in Canada,* Aboriginal Healing Foundation, 2007, online: http://www.ahf.ca/publications/research-series_at 1 (accessed January 5, 2014). [Suicide]

50   *Ibid.* at 34.

51   *Ibid.*

52   Canada, Public Health Agency of Canada, "Diabetes in Canada: Facts and figures from a public health perspective," Chapter 6, December 15, 2011, online: http://www.phac-aspc.gc.ca/cd-mc/publications/diabetes-diabete/facts-figures-faits-chiffres-2011/chap6-eng.php#endnote1 (accessed October 23, 2012). For an excellent study in diabetes in youth and physical activity correlations see, Mark Lemstra et al, "Physical activity in youth: Prevalence, risk indicators, and solutions," *Can. Fam. Physician.* 2012 January; 58(1): e54–e61. [Lemstra]

53   Canadian Diabetes Association, 2012, online: http://www.diabetes.ca/diabetes-and-you/what/prevalence/ (accessed January 5, 2014).

54   Lemstra, *supra* note 52.

55   Sharon G. Bruce, Erich V. Kliewer, T. Kue Young et al, "Diabetes Among the Métis of Canada: Defining the Population, Estimating the Disease," *Canadian Journal of Diabetes*, 2003; 27(4):442–448.

56   L. F. Lavallée & H. A. Howard, *Urban Aboriginal Diabetes Research Project Report.* (Anishnawbe Health Toronto, 2011).

57   Ann C. Macaulay et al, "Primary Prevention of Type 2 Diabetes: Experiences of Two Aboriginal Communities in Canada," online: http://www.diabetes.ca/Files/T2DM-PreventionMacaulayDec03.pdf (accessed January 5, 2014).

58   Centre for Disease Control and Prevention, "HIV and TB, Facts," 2011, online: http://www.cdc.gov/hiv/resources/factsheets/hivtb.htm (accessed January 5, 2014).

59   Canadian Aboriginal Aids Network, "Canadian Aboriginal HIV and AIDS Statistics," 2012, online: http://www.caan.ca/regional-fact-sheets/ (accessed January 5, 2014).

60   Pauktuutit, "Sexual Health, HIV, AIDS, Hep C," 2012, online: http://www.pauktuutit.ca/index.php/health/sexual-health/hepatitis-c-hivaids/ (accessed October 22, 2012).

61   Canadian HIV/AIDS Network, News Release, "HIV and Hepatitis C Crisis in Federal Prisons, according to New CSC Report," April 21, 2010, online: http://www.aidslaw.ca/publications/interfaces/downloadDocumentFile.php?ref=1036 (accessed January 5, 2014).

62   Canada, Health Canada, "Hepatitis C," 2012, online: http://www.hc-sc.gc.ca/hl-vs/iyh-vsv/diseases-maladies/hepc-eng.php (accessed January 5, 2014).

NOTES TO CHAPTER TWO

1   J. Waldram, D. A. Herring, & T. K. Young, *Aboriginal Health in Canada. Historical, Cultural and Epidemiological Perspectives* (Toronto: University of Toronto Press, 1995) at 103. [Waldram]

2   Gerald Robert Vizenor, *The People Named the Chippewa: Narrative Histories* (Minneapolis: University of Minnesota Press, 1984) at 146.

3   Waldram, *supra* note 1 at 104.

4   Marie Battiste & James Youngblood Henderson, *Protecting Indigenous Knowledge and Heritage: A Global Challenge* (Saskatoon: Purich Publishing, 2000) at 43.

5   Robert Bell, "The 'medicine-man' or, Indian and Eskimo notions of medicine: a paper read before the Bathhurst and Rideau Medical Association, 20th January 1886," (Montreal, 1886) at 1–2. [Bell]

6   Waldram, *supra* note 1 at 110.

7   George Henry Loskiel, *The History of the Moravian mission among the Indians of North America: from its commencement to the present time, with a preliminary account of the Indians* (London: T. Allman, 1838) at 37.

8   *The Jesuit Relations and Allied Documents*, "Travels and Explorations of the Jesuit Missionaries in New France 1610–1791," Vol. VIII at 71, online: http://puffin.creighton.edu/jesuit/relations/relations_68.html (accessed January 5, 2014). [*The Jesuit Relations*]

9   Gail Guthrie Valaskakis, *Indian Country: Essays on Contemporary Native Culture*, (Waterloo: Wilfrid Laurier Press, 2005) at 19. [Indian Country]

10   *The Jesuit Relations, supra* note 8, Vol. III, chapter VII.

11   Waldram, *supra* note 1 at 104.

12   G. Williams, *Andrew Graham's Observations on Hudson's Bay 1767–1791* (London: Hudson's Bay Historical Society, 1969) in Waldram, *supra* note 1 at 105.

13   R. Glover, *A Journey from Prince of Wales's Fort in Hudson's Bay to the Northern Ocean, 1769, 1770, 1771, 1772, by Samuel Hearne* (Toronto: McMillan, 1958) in Waldram, *supra* note 1 at 106.

14   James Edward Colhoun, William H. Keating, & Stephen Harriman Long, *Narrative of an expedition to the source of St. Peter's River, Lake Winnepeek, Lake of the Woods, &c. &c.: performed in the year 1823 by order of the Hon. J.C. Calhoun, secretary of war, under the command of Stephen H. Long, major U.S. T.E.* (Philadelphia: H.C. Carey and I. Lea, 1824) at 417. [Colhoun]

15   Baron Lahontan [Footnote 3: New Voyages to North America, London, 1703, vol. 2, pp. 47, 48.] in Walter J. Hoffman, *The Midewiwin or Grand Medicine Society of the Ojibway: Seventh Annual Report of the Bureau of Ethnology, 1885–1886.* (Washington, D.C.: Government Printing Office, 1891). [Hoffman]

16   Waldram *supra* note 1 at 107.

17   *Ibid.*

18   Alexander Henry, 1976, *Travels and Adventures in Canada and the Indian Territories between the years 1760 and 1776* (New York: Garland [Original Publication, 1809]).

19   *The Jesuit Relations, supra* note 8, Vol. LVIX at 149.

20   Bell, *supra* note 5 at 6.

21   Olive Patricia Dickason, *Canada's First Nations: A History of Founding Peoples from Earliest Times* (Toronto: McClelland and Stewart, 1992), at 43–44.

22   Waldram, *supra* note 1 at 104, 105.

23   Edward Talbot, *Five Year's Residence in the Canadas: including a tour through a part of the United States of America in 1823* (London: Printed for Longman, Hurst, Rees, Orme, Brown and Green, 1824) at 314–316.

24 Henry Youle Hind, *Explorations in the interior of the Labrador peninsula: the country of the Montagnais and the Nasquapee Indians,* (London: Longman, Green, Longman, Roberts & Green, 1863) at 191. [Hind]

25 Peter Jones, *History of the Ojebway Indians: with especial reference to their conversion to Christianity* (London: A. W. Bennett, 1861) at 153. [Jones]

26 Hind, *supra* note 24 at 190.

27 *Ibid.* at 191.

28 *Ibid.*

29 *Ibid.* at 189.

30 *Ibid.* at 190.

31 *Ibid.* at 189.

32 Bell, *supra* note 5 at 6. In relation to "bad medicine" Dr. Bell noted that "some of their poisons, they pretend, are very dangerous to handle." Considering the following, caution would be advised: "One of the most curious preparations in use amongst them is the 'black Poison,' the effects of which are well known around the lakes of the Winnipeg basin and in the Swan River district. Sometime after administration, it changes the color of an Indian's skin from brownish-yellow or copper-color to a sooty black, at the same time causing hair to grow on unusual parts, especially in an Indian, as on the cheek bones, etc. Its first effects are sickness, headache, and pains in the back and limbs. Afterwards, ulcerative sores break out in various parts of the body, chiefly over the joints, more particularly the knuckles. I have tried in vain to ascertain the composition of the 'black poison,' or to obtain a specimen of it. I have been told by a person who professed to have seen it, that it is brown snuff-like powder, with a slight and rather sickening smell. A small quantity administered in food appears sufficient to produce the above effects." Bell, *supra* note 5 at 7, 8.

33 *Ibid.*

34 Colhoun, *supra* note 14 at 128.

35 *Ibid.* at 129.

36 Jones, *supra* note 25 in Hoffman, *supra* note 15.

37 Frank G. Speck, *Reptile Lore of the Northern Indians. Journ. Amer. Folklore* 36: 273–280 in L. G. K. Carr, "Interesting animal foods, medicines and omens of the eastern Indians with comparison to ancient European practices," July 1951 *J. Wash. Acad. Sci.* 41 229–235 at 229. [Carr]

38 John Josselyn, *New England rarities discovered,* London 1672 in Carr, *ibid.* at 229–230.

39 Bell, *supra* note 5 at 9.

40 James A. Jones, *Traditions of the North American Indians: being a second and revised edition of Tales of an Indian camp* (London: H. Colburn and R. Bentley, 1830) at 72. [J. Jones]

41 Waldram, *supra* note 1 at 108–109.

42   *Ibid.* at 109.

43   *Ibid.* at 98, 99.

44   Roxanne Struthers & Valerie S. Eschiti, "Being healed by an indigenous traditional healer: sacred healing stories of Native Americans," Part II, *Complementary Therapies in Clinical Practice*, Volume 11, Issue 2, 78–86 (May 2005).

45   Indian Country, *supra* note 9 at 192.

46   Ruth Holmes Whitehead, *The Old Man Told Us: Excerpts from Micmac History, 1500–1950* (Halifax: Nimbus Publishing, 1991) at 91. [Whitehead]

47   F. W. Hodge (Ed.), 1910, "Handbook of American Indians, North Mexico," *Bulletin of the US Bureau of American Ethnology* 11, Washington, DC: Smithsonian Institution in Indian Country, *supra* note 9 at 162.

48   Jones, *supra* note 25 at 143–144 in Hoffman, *supra* note 15.

49   Mark St. Pierre, *Walking in the Sacred Manner: Healers, Dreamers, and Pipe Carriers: Medicine Women of the Plains* (New York: Simon & Schuster, 1995).

50   Reuben Thwaites (Ed.), *The Jesuit Relations and Allied Documents*, 72 volumes (New York: Pageant Book Co., 1959).

51   E. B. O'Callaghan (Ed.), *Documents Relative to the Colonial History of New York, 1853–1887*, Vols. 9 and 10 (Albany: Weed Parsons, 1887).

52   P. F. X. Charlevoix, *History and General Description of New France*, John G. Shea (Ed.) (New York: Francis P. Harper, 1900).

53   See, for example, Elizabeth Tooker, "The League of the Iroquois: Its History, Politics and Ritual" in Bruce Trigger (Ed.), *Handbook of North American Indians*, Vol. 15 (Washington: Smithsonian Institute, 1978).

54   Dena Carroll & Cecilia Benoit, "Aboriginal Midwifery in Canada: Blending Traditional and Modern Forms," (2000) 4 *Canadian Women's Health Network Magazine* 3, s.n. based on the Chapter "Aboriginal Midwifery in Canada: Ancient Traditions/ Emerging Forms" in *Reconceiving Midwifery: New Canadian Model of Care* (University of Michigan Press, 2001).

55   Gillian Morantz-Ornstein & Louis-Patrick Haraoui, "Emerging Patterns in the Resistance to the Medicalization of Birth In North America," *McGill Journal of Medicine*, Vol. 7, No. 1, 2003, online: http://www.medicine.mcgill.ca/mjm/issues/v07n01/ commentaries/commentaries.htm#comment3 (accessed   January 5, 2014). [Ornstein]

56   Pauktuutit Inuit Women's Association, "Special Report on Traditional Midwifery," (1995) 10 *Suvaguug* 8.

57   Ornstein, *supra* note 55.

58   Colhoun, *supra* note 14 at 417.

59   *Ibid.* at 131.

60   *Ibid.* at 132.

61   The author makes a reference to Indians but is apparently referring to Cree or "Outchipwai," referring to Ojibway. Bell, *supra* note 5 at 1–2.

62   Oral history of Jeremiah Bartlett Alexis (Jerry Lonecloud), himself an Indian doctor, to Harry Piers, 22 July 1927, cited in Whitehead, *supra* note 46 at 91, at 275.

63   *Ibid.*

64   Christien Le Clercq, *New relation of Gaspesia, with the customs and religion of the Gaspesian Indians* (Toronto: Champlain Society, 1910) at 90.

65   J. Jones, *supra* note 40 at 72.

66   Jessica A. D. Bailey, *The Experiences and Education of Midwives in Three Canadian Provinces: Saskatchewan, Ontario and Nova Scotia* (unpublished MA thesis: Joint Women's Studies Programme, Mount St. Vincent University, Dalhousie University and St. Mary's University, 2002) at 11.

67   F. W. Beechey, *Narrative of a voyage to the Pacific and Bering's Strait, to co-operate with the polar expeditions performed in His Majesty's Ship Blossom, under the command of Captain F. W. Beechey, R.N., F.R.S. &c. in the years 1825, 26, 27, 28* (London: H. Colburn and R. Bentley, 1831) at 129.

68   Gilbert Malcolm Sproat, *Scenes and studies of savage life* (London: Smith, Elder, 1868) at 94.

69   Franz Boas & Horatio Hale, *Fifth Report of the committee: appointed for the purpose of investigating and publishing reports on the physical characters, languages and industrial condition of the north-western tribes of the Dominion of Canada* (London: The British Association for the Advancement of Science, 1888) at 40. [Boas & Hale]

70   Franz Boas & Sir Daniel Wilson, "Customs regarding Birth, Puberty, Marriage and Death, Committee on North-Western Tribes of the Dominion of Canada," *Seventh Report on the North-western tribes of Canada* (London : British Association for the Advancement of Science 1891) at 11–12. [Boas & Wilson]

71   *Ibid.*

72   Boas & Hale, *supra* note 69 at 41.

73   Boas & Wilson, *supra* note 70 at 12.

74   Cecilia Benoit & Dena Carroll, *Historical Trajectories in Canadian Midwifery: Blending Traditional and Modern Practices.* Report prepared for the Museum of Civilization, Ottawa (2004).

75   Leon Gerin, Charles Hill-Tout, and Benjamin Sulte, *Report on the Ethnological Survey of Canada*, British Association for the Advancement of Science (Ethnological Survey of Canada, 1900) at 479.

76   Colhoun, *supra* note 14 at 129.

77   *Ibid.* at 416.

78   Nicolas Denys, 1598–1688, *The description and natural history of the coasts of North America (Acadia)* (Toronto: the Champlain Society, 1908) at 382–383.

79   A. G. Morice, *Notes archaeological, industrial and sociological, on the western Denes, with an ethnographical sketch of the same* (Canadian Institute, 1893) at 132.

80   Colhoun, *supra* note 14 at 132.

81   *The Mide'wiwin or "Grand Medicine Society" of the Ojibwa*, Seventh Annual Report of the Bureau of Ethnology to the Secretary of the Smithsonian Institution, 1885-1886, Government Printing Office, Washington, 1891, pages 143–300; The Project Gutenberg EBook of The Mide'wiwin or "Grand Medicine Society of the Ojibwa," by Walter James Hoffman, online: http://www.gutenberg.org/files/19368/19368.txt (accessed January 5, 2014).

82   Indian Country, *supra* note 9 at 187.

83   *Ibid.*

84   *Ibid.*

85   *Ibid.* at 10:

86   Also known as Nanabush, Nanabozo, Winabozho, or Wenabozho — the "trickster."

87   Walter J. Hoffman, "The Midewiwin or 'Grand Medicine Society' of the Ojibway," *Annual Report of the Bureau of Ethnology*, Vol. VII (1886), in Gail Frances Guthrie, "A Study of the Theatrical Elements in the Grand Medicine Society (Midewiwin) Religious Cult as Practiced by the Northern United States Chippewa Indians," MA thesis, Cornell University, 1964 at 14.

88   The Métis National Council (MNC) anchors the constitutionally protected Métis peoples within the Métis homeland in western Canada. Métis peoples have a shared history, common culture (song, dance, dress, national symbols, etc.), a unique language (Michif with various regional dialects), extensive kinship connections from Ontario westward, a distinct way of life, a traditional territory, and a collective consciousness. Métis National Council, "Who are the Métis?" online: http://www.metisnation.ca (accessed January 5, 2014).

89   George McDermot, *In the Words of Our Ancestors: Métis Healing and Health*, National Aboriginal Health Organization, Métis Centre (Ottawa: NAHO, 2008) at 24.

90   Portions of the research materials for this section were collected by Contentworks Inc. for the Qikiqtani Truth Commission (2007–2010), an independent inquiry set up by the Qikiqtani Inuit Association to investigate and understand the history of Inuit–government relations in the 1950–1975 period and for the preparation of Y. M. Boyer, & W. D. McCaslin, "Fiduciary Responsibilities between the Federal/Territorial Governments and Inuit Peoples 1950–1980," prepared for the Qikiqtani Truth Commission (April 2010).

91   John D. O'Neil, "Self-Determination, Medical Ideology and Health Services in Inuit Communities," in Gurston Dacks & Ken Coates (Eds.), *Northern Communities: The Prospects for Empowerment*, 33–50 (Edmonton: Boreal Institute for Northern Studies, 1988) at 37.

92   I. Ootoova, Q. T. Atagutsiak, T. Ijjangiaq, J. Pitseolak, Aa. Joamie, Ak. Joamie, & M. Papatsie, 2001, Interviewing Inuit Elders, Vol. 5: Perspectives on traditional health. Nunavut Arctic College, Iqaluit, Nunavut, in Paleah L. Black, John T. Arnason, & Alain Cuerrier, "Medicinal plants used by the Inuit of Qikiqtaaluk" (Baffin Island, Nunavut) *Botany* 86: 157–163 (2008) at 157. [Black Study]

93   L. Borre, "Seal Blood, Inuit Blood, and diet: A biocultural model of physiology and cultural identity," *Medical Anthropology Quarterly* 5(1), 48–62 in Vasiliki Douglas, "Inuit healing and Southern Health Care: Conflicting Paradigms or Nested Epistemologies?" in Breaking the Ice: Proceedings of the 7th ACUNS Student Conference (2003) at 59. [Douglas]

94   *Ibid.* at 60.

95   M. Therrien, *Corps sain, corps malade chez les Inuit: Une tension entre l'interieur*. In *researches Amerindians au Quebec*. Vol. XXV(1) pp. 71–84 in Douglas at 60. [Therrien]

96   *Ibid.* at 60.

97   *Ibid.* at 60–61.

98   See Nunavut Arctic College, *Interviewing Inuit Elders*, Tununirmiut Elders (North Baffin), Sick Body: Diagnoses and Treatments, 2001, Vol. 5 Ch. 1 at 2, online: http://www.nac.nu.ca/OnlineBookSite/vol5/chapters.html (accessed October 22, 2012). [Interviewing Inuit Elders]

99   *Ibid.*

100   *Ibid.*

101   Therrien, *supra* note 95 at 60.

102   Bell, *supra* note 5 at 10.

103   *Ibid.* at 10, 11.

104   Black Study, *supra* note 92 at 157.

105   *Ibid.* at 161.

106   Medicinal plants with antioxidant properties as a dietary supplement for people relying on animal-based diets has been documented for boreal and Arctic plants. See, L. M. McCune, & T. Johns, 2002, "Antioxidant activity in medicinal plants associated with the symptoms of diabetes mellitus used by the Indigenous Peoples of the North American boreal forest," *J. Ethnopharmacol.* 82: 197–205; M.-H. Fraser, A. Cuerrier, P. S. Haddad, J. T. Arnason, P. Owen, & T. Johns, 2007, "Medicinal plants of Cree communities (Québec, Canada): Antioxidant activity of plants used to treat Type 2 Diabetes symptoms," *Can. J. Physiol. Pharmacol.* 85: 1200–1214.

107   K. Müller, 2001. "Pharmaceutically relevant metabolites from lichens," *Appl. Microbiol. Biotechnol.* 56: 9–16.

108   J. B. Lee, K. Hayashi, M. Hashimoto, T. Nakano, & T. Hayashi, 2004. "Novel antiviral fucoidan from sporophyll of *Undaria pinnatifida* (Mekabu)." *Chem. Pharm. Bull.* (Tokyo), 52: 1091–1094.

109   Francis Lévesque, "The Inuit, Their Dogs and the Northern Administration, from 1950 to 2007" (footnotes omitted). *Anthropology of a Contemporary Inuit Claim*, (2008) at 31. [Lévesque] This fulfills the Supreme Court requirement that the use of the *quimmiq* was in existence before the Europeans landed in North America and not as a result or response of the Europeans landing in North America (*R. v. Van der Peet* [1996] 2 S.C.R. 507, [1996] 4 C.N.L.R. 146, at para. 73). The activity that is claimed to be an Aboriginal right must have developed before "contact." Practices that developed "solely as a response to European influences" do not qualify as an Aboriginal right (paras. 60–62).

110   Elder interview in Kerrie Ann Shannon, "The Unique Role of Sled Dogs in Inuit Culture: An Examination of the Relationship between Inuit and Sled Dogs in the Changing North." (MA thesis. Edmonton: University of Alberta, 1997) at 92. [Shannon]

111   *Ibid.* at 49.

112   Lévesque, *supra* note 109 at 36–42.

113   Shannon, *supra* note 110 at 46.

114   Frédéric Laugrand & Jarich Oosten, 2002, "Canicide and Healing: The Position of the Dog in the Inuit Cultures of the Canadian Arctic," *Anthropos (St-Augustin)* 97(1): 89–105. [Laugrand & Oosten]

115   Shannon, *supra* note 110 at 1.

116   *Ibid.*

117   Lévesque, *supra* note 109 at 58.

118   *Ibid.* at 56, emphasis added.

119   *Ibid.*

120   It is then easy to understand why the killing of Inuit dogs in the 1950s and 1960s caused great social harm. See the Qikqitani Truth Commission, online: http://www.qtcommission.com/ (accessed October 22, 2012).

121   Lévesque, *supra* note 109 at 60.

122   Laugrand & Oosten, *supra* note 114 at 94.

123   Milton M . R. Freeman, 1967, "An Ecological Study of Mobility and Settlement Patterns Among the Belcher Island Eskimo," *Arctic* 20(3): 154–175; 1969, "Adaptive Innovation Among Recent Eskimo Immigrants in the Eastern Canadian Arctic," *Polar Record*, 14 (93): 769–781; J. G. Taylor (1993). "Canicide in Labrador: Function and Meaning of an Inuit Killing Ritual." *Études/Inuit/Studies* 17 (1) pp. 3–14.

124   Bent Jensen (1961), "The Folkways of Greenland Dog-Keeping," *Folk*, Vol. 3, 43–66.

125   *Ibid.*

126 Agiaq interview in Lévesque, *supra* note 109 at 66, citing Laugrand & Oosten, *supra* note 114.

127 Lévesque, *supra* note 109 at 66, citing interviewee M-020.

128 Laugrand & Oosten, *supra* note 114 at 97.

129 *Ibid.* at 102. ·

130 *Ibid.*

131 Lévesque, *supra* note 109, commenting on and citing Laugrand & Oosten, *ibid. at* 67.

132 ANC/GSA/Peck Papers M56-1, XXXV no. 19 in Laugrand & Oosten, *supra* note 114 at 97.

133 *Ibid.* at 100.

134 *Ibid.*

135 Salami Ka&&ak Qalasiq & Felix Pisuk. Interviews with H. Kablalik & F. Laugrand, December 1999. In South Baffin Island, elders state that if you throw your tooth to a dog, you would have strong and excellent teeth. M. Therrien & F. Laugrand, *Perspectives on Traditional Health* (Iqaluit: Nunavut Arctic College, Nortext, 2001) in Interviewing Inuit Elders, *supra* note 98 at 210.

136 Laugrand & Oosten, *supra* note 114 at 100, citing Knud Rasmussen, 1931, *The Netsiluk Eskimios. Social Life and Spiritual Culture.* Copenhagen: Gyldendalske BoghAndel, Nordisk Forlag (Report of the Fifth Thule Expedition, 1921–1924, 8/1–2) at 221 f.

137 *Ibid.* citing Knud Rasmussen, 1932, *Intellectual Culture of the Copper Eskimo.* Copenhagen: Gyldendalske BoghAndel, Nordisk Forlag (Report of the Fourth Thule Expedition 1921–24) at 49.

138 *Ibid.* citing Diamond Jenness, 1922, *The Life of the Copper Eskimos.* Southern Party 1913–1916. Ottawa: F. A. Acland (Report of the Canadian Arctic Expedition, 1913–1918), 12 at 172.

139 *Ibid.* citing Franz Boas, 1907, *The Eskimo of Baffin Island and Hudson's Bay* (New York: Bulletin of the American Museum of Natural History) 15/2 at 514.

140 *Ibid.*

141 Honourable Jean-Jacques Croteau, "Final report of the Honourable Jean-Jacques Croteau, Retired Justice of the Superior Court, regarding the allegations concerning the slaughter of Inuit sled dogs in Nunavik (1950–1970)" Office of the Minister responsible for Native Affairs and Makivik Corporation, March 3, 2010.

142 Waldram, *supra* note 1 at 99.

143 John D. O'Neil & Brian D. Postl, "Community Healing and Aboriginal Self-overnment: Is the Circle Closing?" in John H. Hylton (Ed.), *Aboriginal Self-Government in Canada: Current Trends and Issues* (Saskatoon: Purich Publishing, 1994) at 79–80.

1   M. Lux, *Medicine That Walks: Disease, Medicine, and Canadian Plains Native Peoples: 1880–1940* (Toronto: University of Toronto Press, 2001). [Lux]

2   Canada, *Report of the Royal Commission on Aboriginal Peoples* (Ottawa: Supply and Services Canada, 1996), online at http://www.collectionscanada.gc.ca/webarchives/20071115053257/http://www.ainc-inac.gc.ca/ch/rcap/sg/sgmm_e.html (accessed January 5, 2014). [RCAP]

3   Noble David Cook, *Born to Die: Disease and New World Conquest, 1492–1650* (Cambridge, England: Cambridge University Press, 1998) [N. Cook] in Cynthia C. Wesley-Esquimaux & Magdalena Smolewski, *Historic Trauma and Aboriginal Healing*, prepared for the Aboriginal Healing Foundation (2004). [Historic]

4   Russell Thornton, "American Indian Holocaust and Survival: A Population History Since 1492" (Normand, OK: University of Oklahoma Press, 1987) in Historic, *ibid.* at 19.

5   N. Cook, *supra* note 3.

6   Sherbourne F. Cook (1973). The Significance of Disease in the Extinction of the New England Indians. *Human Biology* 45(3): 485–508 in Historic, *supra* note 3.

7   Martin, Calvin L. (Ed.), *The American Indian and the Problem of History* (New York: Oxford University Press, 1987) in Historic, *supra* note 3 at 19.

8   G. Graham-Cumming (1967), *Health of the Original Canadians, 1867–1967, Med. Ser. J. Can.* 23, 115–166 at 142. [Graham-Cumming]

9   *Ibid.* at 129.

10 Natural Health Publications, "Epidemics Through Time, Smallpox the Disease that Destroyed Two Empires," 2010, online: http://www.allicinfacts.com/epidemics07.htm (accessed January 5, 2014).

11 Père Biard, in R. G. Thwaites (Eds.), *Jesuit Relations and Allied Documents,* Vol. 3 (Cleveland: The Burrows Brothers, 1897) at 105.

12 Historic, *supra* note 3 at 194–196.

13 Moses Perley, *Legislative Assembly of Nova Scotia Journals*, 1843, Appendix 49 at 127.

14 Petition, in the *Acadian Recorder*, Halifax, 24 February 1849.

15 *Ibid.*

16 Historic, *supra* note 3 at 17.

17 Graham-Cumming, *supra* note 8 at 129.

18 *Ibid.*

19 Thwaites, R. G. (Ed.), *Jesuit Relations and allied Documents. . . . 1610–1791.* Cleveland, Burrows, 1896–1901, v. 6, p. 263–265, cited by Lt. Maundrell in Graham-Cumming, *supra* note 8 at 130.

20 *Ibid.*

21 H. Y. Hind, *Narrative of the Canadian Red River Exploring Expedition of 1857 and of the Assiniboine and Saskatchewan Exploring Expedition of 1858* (London, Longman, Green, Longman, & Roberts, 1860). [Hind]

22 Changed from the word rebellion as "rebellion" is a controversial term (and not applicable). Legitimate English sovereignty would first have to be established before any opposition could be characterized as a rebellion.

23 Graham-Cumming, *supra* note 8 at 130.

24 Agnes Grant, *No End of Grief: Indian Residential Schools in Canada* (Winnipeg: Pemmican Publications, 1996) at 117–118 [Grant] in Larry N. Chartrand, Tricia E. Logan, & Judy D. Daniels, *Métis History and Experience and Residential Schools in Canada*, prepared for The Aboriginal Healing Foundation (2006). [Chartrand]

25 R. G. Ferguson, *Studies in Tuberculosis* (Toronto: University of Toronto Press, 1955) at 6, cited in Graham-Cumming, *supra* note 8 at 134. By 1929 the Indian death rate in this area was 20 times greater than for the non-Aboriginal population (*ibid.* at 134).

26 J. Waldram, D. A. Herring, & T. K. Young, *Aboriginal Health in Canada. Historical, Cultural and Epidemiological Perspectives* (Toronto: University of Toronto Press, 1995) at 156. [Waldram]

27 P. H. Bryce, *The Story of a National Crime: Being a Record of the Health Conditions of the Indians of Canada from 1904–1921* (Ottawa: James Hope and Sons, 1922).

28 Brian E. Titley, *A Narrow Vision: Duncan Campbell Scott and the Administration of Indian Affairs in Canada* (Vancouver: University of British Columbia Press, 1986) at 87 [Titley] in Chartrand, *supra* note 24.

29 *Ibid.*

30 J. R. Miller, *Shingwauk's Vision: A History of Native Residential Schools* (Toronto: University of Toronto Press, 1996) at 302. [Miller]

31 Titley, *supra* note 28 at 87.

32 Miller, *supra* note 30 at 302–303. See also M. Lux, "The Great Influenza Epidemic of 1918–1920," U of S Communication: *OCN*, October 17, 1997.

33 J. S. Milloy, *A National Crime: The Canadian Government and the Residential School System: 1879–1986* (Winnipeg: University of Manitoba Press, 1999) at 3. [Milloy]

34 Memorandum, February 18, 1914 in Canada. Dept of Indian Affairs. Departmental Files (93–101) General Secretary.

35 Waldram, *supra* note 26 at 156–157 and 136.

36 *Ibid.* at 158.

37 Lux, *supra* note 1 at 201.

38 Waldram, *supra* note 26 at 160.

39 *Ibid.*

40 *Ibid.* at 159–160.

41 Lux, *supra* note 1 at 191.

42 Waldram, *supra* note 26 at 160–161.

43 Lux, *supra* note 1 at 224. See also M. Lux, "Perfect Subject: Race, Tuberculosis and the Qu'Appelle BCG Vacine Trial" CBMH/BCHM vol. 15: 1998, 277–295.

44 P. E. Moore, 1946, *Indian Health Services, Canadian Journal of Public Health* 37: 140–142.

45 Waldram, *supra* note 26 at 175–176.

46 Raymond Obomsawin, *Historical and Scientific Perspectives on the Health of Canada's First Peoples* (2007), online: http://www.soilandhealth.org/02/0203cat/020335.obomsawin.pdf at 20 (accessed January 5, 2014) at 20. [Obomsawin]

47 Métis Settlements General Council, 2012, online: http://www.msgc.ca/About+Us/History/Default.ksi (accessed October 26, 2012). See also D. N. Sprague, *Canada and the Métis, 1869–1885* (Waterloo: Wilfrid Laurier University Press, 1988).

48 Obomsawin, *supra* note 46. See also Larry Chartrand, *Maskikiwenow: The Métis Right to Health*, 2008, prepared for the National Aboriginal Health Organization.

49 *Ibid.* at 24.

50 The federal government created a scrip system for Métis by awarding a certificate redeemable for land or money of either 160 or 240 acres or dollars, depending on their circumstances. Scrip was intended to be used in Manitoba to "fulfill" the terms of the *Manitoba Act, 1870.* In 1879 the *Dominion Lands Act* authorized scrip to all of Western Canada to deal with Métis issues. See Camie Augustus, "Métis Scrip, kinanāskomitin," online: http://scaa.sk.ca/ourlegacy/exhibit_scrip (accessed January 5, 2014).

51 Justice Ewing, *Evidence and Proceedings, Half-Breed Commission*, 25 February 1935 (Edmonton: Half-Breed Commission, 1935) at 11.

52 Malcolm Norris, *Evidence and Proceedings, Half-Breed Commission*, 25 February 1935. (Edmonton: Half-Breed Commission, 1935) at 17.

53 Although twelve colonies of the Métis Settlements were originally established, four of the colonies ceased to operate because the land was unsuitable for farming. Under the 1989 Alberta Métis Settlements Accord, and resulting 1990 legislation, the Settlements collectively acquired title to the Settlement areas and were established as corporate entities, similar to municipal corporations, with broad self-governing powers. Métis Settlements are comprised of eight distinct geographic areas in northern Alberta covering approximately 1.25 million acres with a total population of 6,500 in 1995. The Settlements are governed locally by elected five-member councils and collectively by the Métis Settlements General Council. Alberta, Department of Learning, "Aboriginal Studies Glossary," in *First Nations, Métis and Inuit Education Policy Framework* (Edmonton: Government of Alberta, 2004).

54 Currently, the Inuit experience a tuberculosis rate 90 times higher than non-Inuit people. National Collaborating Centre for Aboriginal Health & UNICEF Canada, "Leaving no child behind — national spotlight on health gap for Aboriginal children in Canada" 2009, online: http://www.nccah-ccnsa.ca/88/Drawing_National_and_International_Attention_to_Aboriginal_Child_Health.nccah (accessed January 5, 2014).

55 G. Graham-Cumming, "Northern Health Services," *Canadian Medical Association Journal*, 100 (March 15, 1969), 526–531 at 526.

56 Waldram, *supra* note 26.

57 CBC Archives, "Tuberculosis: Old Disease, Continuing Threat" January 20, 1989, online: http://archives.cbc.ca/health/disease/topics/883-5325/ (accessed December 4, 2009). [CBC]

58 Pat Sandiford, *A Long Way from Home: The Tuberculosis Epidemic among the Inuit* (Montreal: McGill-Queen's University Press, 1994) at 96.

59 Waldram, *supra*, note 26 at 169.

60 CBC, *supra* note 57.

61 Northern Clipper, "Inuit families spend years looking for graves of loved ones who died from TB," May 14, 2009, online: http://mediamentor-circumpolar.blogspot.ca/2009/05/inuit-families-spend-years-looking-for.html (accessed January 5, 2014).

62 Saskatchewan Lung Association, "Tuberculosis History: the Sanatorium Age," online http://www.lung.ca/tb/tbhistory/sanatoriums/ (accessed January 5, 2014).

63 Food sovereignty is the ability to make substantive choices about what one is eating. This includes what types of foods are eaten, and where, how, and by whom they are produced. Food security, as defined at the World Food Summit in 1996, exists when all people, at all times, have physical and economic access to safe and nutritious food, which meets dietary needs and food preferences, in sufficient quantity to sustain an active and healthy lifestyle. World Food Summit, Declaration (Rome: Food and Agricultural Organization (FAO) of the United Nations, 1996).

64 Wayne Suttles, "Coast Salish resource management," in Douglas Duer & Nancy Turner (Eds.), *Keeping it Living: Traditions of Plant Use and Cultivation on the Northwest Coast of North America* (Seattle: University of Washington Press and Vancouver: UBC Press, 2005), 181–193 in Kathleen Turner, "Food Security is what is Indigenous to Our People": Colonization, Camas, and the Diet of the Coast Salish People of British Columbia, *Journal of Undergraduate Studies at Trent*, Vol. 1, 2007 at 4. [Turner]

65 Beckwith, quoting Tsartlip elder Christopher Paul, from 1967 interview with anthropology student Marguerite Babcock. Brenda R. Beckwith, "The Queen Root of this Clime:" Ethnoecological Investigations of Blue Camas (C. leichtlinii (Baker) Wats., C. quamash (Pursh) Greene (Liliaceae) and its Landscapes on Southern Vancouver Island, British Columbia (Ph.D. diss., University of Victoria at Victoria, 2004), 4 [Beckwith] in Turner, *ibid.* at 42.

66 Beckwith, *ibid.* at 15.

67   Turner, *supra* note 64.

68   *Ibid.* at 43.

69   H. Y. Hind, *North-West Territory; Reports of Progress* (Toronto: J. Lovell, 1859).

70   Lux, *supra* note 1 at 20.

71   Graham-Cumming, *supra* note 8 at 133; Waldram, *supra* note 26 at 155.

72   Graham-Cumming, *ibid.*

73   Lux, *supra* note 1 at 38.

74   *Ibid.*

75   *Ibid.* at 59. Indian History Film Project (Saskatchewan Indian Federated College Library, Regina Saskatchewan), IH 245 Interview with Tom Yellowhorn, Peigan, 7 Mar. 1975; IH 234, 234a interview with Useless Good Runner, Blood Elder; M.K. Lux Peigan Field notes, Alan Pard interview, Dec, 1999; IH233, 233a, interview with George First Rider, Blood Elder.

76   *Ibid.* at 60.

77   *Ibid.*

78   Graham-Cumming, *supra* note 8 at 157–158.

79   *Ibid.*

80   George Manuel & Michael Posluns. *The Fourth World: an Indian Reality* (Don Mills, ON: Collier-Macmillan Canada, 1974) at 65.

81   *Ibid.* at 66.

82   Jean Goodwill & Norma Sluman, *John Tootoosis: Biography of a Cree Leader* (Winnipeg: Pemmican Publications, 1984) at 100.

83   Milloy, *supra* note 33 at 143.

84   Grant, *supra* note 24 at 116.

85   David King, "A Brief Report of The Federal Government of Canada's Residential School System for Inuit," prepared for the Aboriginal Healing Foundation (2006).

86   A. Browne, & V. Smye, "A post-colonial analysis of healthcare discourses addressing aboriginal women," *Nurse Researcher* (2002) 9(3), 28–41.

87   Graham-Cumming, *supra* note 8; Waldram, *supra* note 26 at 122–123.

88   Waldram, *ibid.* at 194. See also Graham-Cumming, *ibid.* at 133.

89   Yvonne Boyer, *Discussion Paper Series in Aboriginal Health: Legal Issues no. 2 First Nations, Métis and Inuit Health Care the Crown's Fiduciary Obligation* (Ottawa: National Aboriginal Health Organization, June 2004) at 10.

90   Obomsawin, *supra* note 46.

91   Waldram, *supra* note 26 at 197.

92   Canada, *Gathering Strength: Canada's Aboriginal Action Plan*, 1998, Chapter 3.

93   Waldram, *supra* note 26 at 198.

94   Obomsawin, *supra* note 46.

95   Canada, Health Canada, *Federal Indian Health Policy*, Government of Canada, issued 1979, (2007) online: http://www.hc-sc.gc.ca/ahc-asc/branch-dirgen/fnihb-dgspni/poli_1979-eng.php (accessed February 17, 2013).

96   Canada, Indian and Northern Affairs Canada, Health and Welfare, Communiqué 1979–1988, "Statement on Indian Health Policy" (Ottawa: Canadian Government Publishing Directorate, September 19, 1979).

97   *Declaration of Alma-Ata International Conference on Primary Health Care*, Alma-Ata, USSR, 6–12 September 1978, online http://www.who.int/hpr/NPH/docs/declaration_almaata.pdf (accessed October 29, 2012).

98   T. R. Berger, *Report of the Advisory Commission on Indian and Inuit Health Consultation* (Ottawa: House of Commons, 1980).

99   House of Commons, Special Committee on *Indian Self-Government, Indian Self-Government in Canada: Report of the Special Committee* ("Penner Report"), 1983.

100   Waldram, *supra* note 26.

101   Canada, Health Canada, First Nations and Inuit Health Branch, *Ten Years of Health Transfer First Nation and Inuit Control* (Ottawa: Canadian Government Publishing Directorate) online: http://www.hc-sc.gc.ca/fniah-spnia/pubs/finance/_agree-accord/10_years_ans_trans/index-eng.php (accessed January 5, 2014).

102   Waldram, *supra* note 26 at 269–270.

103   *Ibid.* at 235–239.

104   Canada, Indian and Northern Affairs, *The Government of Canada's Approach to Implementation of the Inherent Right and the Negotiation of Aboriginal Self-Government,* (Ottawa: 2010), online: http://www.ainc-inac.gc.ca/al/ldc/ccl/pubs/sg/sg-eng.asp (accessed January 5, 2014).

105   First Ministers, First Ministers' Meeting, Ottawa: September 11, 2000 , First Ministers' Meeting, Communiqué on Health.

106   *Ibid.*

107   Canada, Health Canada, First Nations and Inuit Health Branch, *Mandate and Priorities* (Ottawa: Canadian Government Publishing Directorate, 2012), online: http://www.hc-sc.gc.ca/ahc-asc/branch-dirgen/fnihb-dgspni/mandat-eng.php (accessed February 16, 2013).

108   Canada, Health Canada, "Fact Sheet: First Nations and Inuit Health Branch" (2008), online: http://www.hc-sc.gc.ca/ahc-asc/branch-dirgen/fnihb-dgspni/fact-fiche-eng.php (accessed February 16, 2013).

109   *Ibid.*

110 National Aboriginal Health Organization, *Midwifery and Aboriginal Midwifery in Canada*, 2004, online: http://www.naho.ca/documents/naho/english/publications/DP_aboriginal_midwifery.pdf (accessed January 5, 2014). [NAHO midwifery]

111 Canadian Association of Midwives, "Midwifery in Canada: Quebec" (Quebec 2008), online: http://www.canadianmidwives.org/quebec.htm, (accessed January 5, 2014).

112 See Inuit Tuttarvingat, NAHO, Irnisuksiiniq Inuit Midwifery Network, online: http://www.naho.ca/inuitmidwifery/home/ (accessed January 5, 2014).

113 Canadian Association of Midwives, "Midwifery in Canada: Nunavut" (Quebec, 2008) online: http://www.canadianmidwives.org/nunavut.htm (accessed January 5, 2014).

114 National Aboriginal Health Organization, *An Overview of Traditional Knowledge and Medicine and Public Health in Canada* (NAHO: January 2008), online: http://www.naho.ca/publications/tkOverviewPublicHealth.pdf, (accessed January 5, 2014).

115 This is an example of the health inequities, in that an Inuit baby is 3.5 times more likely to die before his first birthday than a non-Inuit new-born — the Inuit infant mortality rate is 15.1 deaths per 1000; the national average is 5.1. (Patrick White, *Globe and Mail*, "Inuit mothers fight lonely battle for their children's health," June 5, 2010).

116 See Canadian Midwifery Consortium, *Legal Status of Midwifery in Canada*, online: http://cmrc-ccosf.ca/node/19(accessed April 28, 2013).

117 *Consolidation of Midwifery Profession Act*, S.Nu. 2008,c.18.

118 *Ibid.*

119 *Health Professions Act* [RSBC 1996] Chapter 183; the *Midwives Regulation BC* Reg 155/2009; and the College *Bylaws*.

120 Nunavut Tunngavit Submission on Bill 20, the *Midwifery Profession Act*, submitted to the Health and Education Standing Committee, January 11, 2008, Government of Nunavut.

121 Assembly of First Nations, *Residential School Update* (Ottawa: Assembly of First Nations, 1998.

122 *Ibid.*

123 RCAP, *supra* note 2.

124 Miller, *supra* note 30.

125 *Ibid.*

126 Milloy, *supra* note 33.

127 Miller, *supra* note 30.

128 Grant, *supra* note 24 at 117–118.

129 *Ibid.* at 131–132.

130   Miller, *supra* note 30, in Caroline L. Tait et al, prepared for the Aboriginal Healing Foundation, *Fetal Alcohol Syndrome Among Aboriginal People in Canada: Review and Analysis of the Intergenerational Links to Residential Schools,* Ottawa: 2003, online: http://www.ahf.ca/publications/research-series (accessed January 5, 2014) at 66, 67. [Tait]

131   S. Fournier & E. Crey, *Stolen From Our Embrace: The Abduction of First Nations Children and the Restoration of Aboriginal Communities* (Toronto: Douglas & McIntyre 1997) at 47. [Fournier and Crey]

132   *Ibid.*

133   Tait, *supra* note 129 at 73.

134   Truth and Reconciliation Commission of Canada, "TRC thanks chief coroners, chief medical examiners for commitment to help research deaths of Aboriginal children at residential schools," June 12, 2012, online: http://www.myrobust.com/websites/trcinstitution/File/pdfs/TRC%20news%20release%20re%20coroners%27%20resolution%2011%20June%202012.pdf (accessed October 27, 2012).

135   Miller, *supra* note 30 at 343–344. A more recent instance of community resistance to residential school is described in Maura Hanrahan, "Resisting Colonialism in Nova Scotia" (2008) 17:1 *Native Studies Review,* which describes the resistance of the Kesukwitk Mi'kmaq in Nova Scotia in the 1940s to centralization and to sending their children to residential school.

136   See Fournier & Crey, *supra* note 130.

137   Miller in Tait, *supra* note 129.

138   Law Reform Commission of Canada, *Sterilization: Implication for Mentally Retarded and Mentally Ill Persons* (Working Paper 24) (Ottawa: Minister of Supply and Services Canada, 1979) at 25. [Law Reform]

139   *Sexual Sterilization Act* (S.A.) (1928) c.37; *Sexual Sterilization Act* (R.S.A) (1955) c.311 [repealed 1972].

140   *Sexual Sterilization Act*, R.S.B.C. 1960, c. 353 repealed by S.B.C. 1973, *c.* 79.

141   Of patients approved for sterilization [in Alberta] 35.3% were male and 64.7% were female. Thus, not only did the Eugenics Board approve the sterilization of more females, but a disproportionately high number of them were sterilized; see Law Reform, *supra* note 137 at 42.

142   T. Christian, "The Mentally Ill and Human Rights in Alberta: a Study of the Alberta Sexual Sterilization Act" (1974) [unpublished] cited in K. G. McWirther and J. Weijer, "The Alberta Sterilization Act: A Genetic Critique" (19) 19 *University of Toronto Law Journal* 424, in Clémentine Sallée, *Reflection on The Legal Status of Sterilization in Contemporary Canada in Institute of Comparative Law*: A thesis, Master of Laws, McGill Montreal, 2002.

143   Jana Grekul, Harvey Krahn, & Dave Odynak, "Sterilizing the 'Feeble-minded': Eugenics in Alberta, Canada, 1929–1972," *Journal of Historical Sociology,* Vol. 17 No. 4, December 2004 at 363. [Grekul]

144   *Ibid.*

145   *Ibid.*

146   *Ibid.* at 375.

147   *Ibid.* at 359.

148   Wanda Vivequin, "Prof Reveals Eugenics Machine," *Express News* (July 18, 2003).

149   Grekul, *supra*, note 142.

150   Annette J. Browne and Jo-Anne Fiske, "First Nations Women's Encounters with Mainstream Health Care Services," *West J Nurs Res.*, 2001; 23; 126.

151   Robert Lechat "Intensive Sterilization for the Inuit," *Eskimo* Fall Winter 1976–1977 at 5. [Lechat]

152   *Ibid.* The original count was 23% but an official recount, made at Ottawa's request, has disclosed two more cases, which brings the proportion to 26%.

153   HR 7055.C73R37. Letter to David Lewis, from Regional Director, Alberta Regions, re: Sterilization of Eskimo Women. 1970/10/21. Deschatelets Archives — *Commission Oblats des Oeuvres Indiens & Eskimaux.*

154   Lechat, *supra* note 150 at 6.

155   *Inukshuk*, "Feature: Sterilization of Women," June 1, 1973, at 10–11.

156   Grekul, *supra* note 143 at 303.

157   M. Annette Jaimes & Theresa Halsey, "American Indian Women: At the Centre of Indigenous Resistance in Contemporary North America," in M. Annette Jaimes (Ed.), *The State of Native America: Genocide, Colonization, and Resistance* (Boston: South End Press, 1992) at 311–344.

158   *Ibid.* at 326.

159   Jane Lawrence, " The Indian Health Service and the Sterilization of Native American Women," *American Indian Quarterly*/summer 2000/vol. 24, no. 3.

160   See *Muir* v. *Alberta,* [1995] A.J. No. 1656; *Muir* v. *Alberta,* [1995] A.J. No. 658; *Muir* v. *Alberta,* [1996] A.J. No. 37.

161   James Horner, "The Sterilization of Leilani Muir," *Canadian Content* (February 1999), online: Canadian Content, http://www.canadiancontent.ca/issues/0299sterilization.html (accessed January 5, 2014).

162   *Ibid.*

163   J. Veit (1996), *Muir* v. *The Queen in Right of Alberta.* Dominion Law Reports, 132 (4th series): 695–762.

164   Southam News, the *Vancouver Sun*, "Native Kids used for experiments," April 26, 2000.

165   M. Lux, "Perfect Subjects: Race, Tuberculosis and the Qu'Appelle BCG Vaccine Trial," CBMH/BCHM vol. 15: 1998, 277–295.

166   Leilani Muir, who was wrongfully sterilized, reviewed her chart and noted that regular doses of phenobarbital, chlorpromazine, and haloperidol were tranquillizers that were administered to her without her consent or knowledge. See Heather Pringle, *Saturday Night Magazine*, June 1997, "The Mannings and Forced Sterilization in Canada," online: http://statismwatch.ca/1997/06/01/alberta-barren-the-mannings-and-forced-sterilization-in-canada/ (accessed January 5, 2014).

167   Access to Information Request of 2007, December 21, 1962, letter from Department of National Health and Welfare Dr. Cameron to A. J. MacLeod, Esq. Commissioner of Penitentiaries.

168   Dorothy Proctor & Fred Rosen, *Chameleon* (New Horizon Press: New Jersey, 1994) at 61, 62.

169   *Ibid.* at 62.

170   Interview, Monday, November 09, 1998, CBC Radio (National) *This Morning,* Rosie Rowbotham Interview with Dorothy Proctor, Allen Hornblum, & Dr. George Scott, "Secret Experiments On Canada's Convicts." [Interview]

171   *Ibid.*

172   Norbert Gilmore & Margaret Somerville, *A Review on the use of LSD and ECT at the Prison for Women in the early 1960s,* McGill Centre for Medicine, Ethics and Law, September 19, 1998 at 1.

173   *Ibid.* at 42, accessed through ATIP request 2007.

174   Bronwyn Chester, "Report on LSD raises hackles," *McGill Reporter*, Nov. 5, 1998.

175   Office of the Correctional Investigator, online: http://www.oci-bec.gc.ca/rpt/annrpt/annrpt20052006info-eng.aspx (accessed October 29, 2012).

Notes to Chapter Four

1   *Constitution Act, 1867* (U.K.), 30 & 31 Vict., c.3, reprinted in R.S.C. 1985, App. II, No. 5 (section 2.4.5). [*CA, 1867*]

2   See *RJR-MacDonald* v. *Canada (A.G.)*, [1995] 3 S.C.R. 199, 127 D.L.R. (4th) 1; *R.* v. *Wetmore*, [1983] 2 S.C.R. 284, 2 D.L.R. (4th) 577 [cited to S.C.R.].

3   Claude Emanuelli, "The Canadian Constitution and Health," in Hernan L. Fuenzalida-Puelma and Susan Scholle Conner (Eds.), *The Right to Health in the Americas: A Comparative Constitutional Study,* 138–165 (Washington: Pan American Health Organization, 1989) at 141.

4   *CA, 1867, supra* note 1.

5   R. Cheffins and R. Tucker, *The Constitutional Process in Canada,* 2nd ed. (Whitby, ON: McGraw-Hill Ryerson, 1976) at 4.

6   *Re: Canada Metal Co.* (1982), 144 D.L.R. (3d) 124 (Man.Q.B.) (upholding *Federal Clean Air Act*); *R. v. Crown Zellerbach*, [1988] 1 S.C.R. 401 (upholding *Federal Ocean Dumping Control Act*).

7   *Controlled Drugs and Substances Act*, S.C. 1996, c. 19.

8   *Food and Drugs Act*, R.S.C. 1985, c. F-27.

9   *Hazardous Products Act*, R.S.C. 1985, c. H-3.

10   Hogg notes that the existence of exclusive federal power does not exclude provincial laws from federal public property if the laws are otherwise competent to the province. P. W. Hogg, *Constitutional Law of Canada*, 4th ed.(Scarborough: Carswell, 2002) at 28.2.

11   *Canada Wildlife Act*; R.S.C. 1985, c.23.

12   *Canada National Parks Act*, S.C. 2000, c.32.

13   See Martha Jackman, "The Constitutional Basis for Federal Regulation of Health" (1996), 5 *Health L. Rev.* No. 2, 3–10.

14   *CA, 1867, supra* note 1 at s. 91(1a), 92(3), 102, 106.

15   *Reference re: Whether the Term "Indians" in s. 91(24) of the B.N.A. Act 1867, includes Eskimo Inhabitants of Quebec*, [1939] S.C.R. 104, [1939] 2 D.L.R. 417. [*Re: Eskimos*]

16   *Indian Act*, R.S.C. 1985, c.I–5 at s.6.

17   *Re: Eskimos, supra* note 15.

18   *Daniels v. Canada (Minister of Indian Affairs and Northern Development)*, [2013] F.C.J. No. 4. [Daniels]

19   *Schneider v. The Queen*, [1982] 2 S.C.R. 112.

20   *CA, 1867, supra* note 1 at s.92(2).

21   In relation to health matters, the *Indian Act* refers to s. 73(1)(f)(h)(g), s. 81 and 81(g).

22   J. Woodward, *Native Law* (Toronto: Carswell, 2002) at 5–7, at 119–128.

23   *Indian Act*, R.S., 1985, c. I-5, s. 88.

24   "Unauthorized; beyond the scope of power allowed or granted by a corporate charter or by law" (*Blacks Law Dictionary*, 7th ed. (St. Paul, MN.: West Group, 1999) *s.v.* "ultra vires.")

25   *R. v. Hill* (1907), 15 O.L.R. 406 (Ont. C.A.). [*Hill*]

26   *Medical Act.* R.S.O. 1897, ch. 176, s. 49.

27   *Hill, supra* note 25 at 407.

28   *Delgamuukw v. British Columbia*, [1993] B.C.J. No. 1395 at para 713.

29   *Four B Manufacturing v. United Garment Workers*, [1980] 1 S.C.R. 1031. *Paul v. British Columbia*, [2003] 1 S.C.R. 585.

30   In *R.* v. *Martin* (1917), 41 O.L.R. 79.

31   See *Dick* v. *The Queen*, [1985] 2 S.C.R; *Derrickson* v. *Derrickson*, [1986] 1 S.C.R. 285; *R.* v. *Francis*, [1988] 1 S.C.R. 1025, at 1030–1031.

32   *Quebec (Attorney General)* v. *Rat* [2008] Q.J. No 4120.

33   Health Council of Canada, *Empathy, dignity, and respect: Creating cultural safety for Aboriginal people in urban health care* (December 2012), online: http://healthcoun-cilcanada.ca/rpt_det.php?id=437 (accessed February 16, 2013).

34   Health Council of Canada, *Understanding and Improving Aboriginal Maternal and Child Health in Canada* (August 2011), online: http://healthcouncilcanada.ca/tree/2.01-HCC_AboriginalHealth_FINAL1.pdf at 4 (accessed February 16, 2013). In 2010, the Health Council of Canada began publishing the *Update*, a newsletter on these "serious health challenges faced by Aboriginal Peoples in Canada," online: http://healthcouncilcanada.ca/tree/2.02-AboriginalHealthUpdate_E_Oct252010.pdf (accessed January 5, 2014).

35   K. McNeil, "Section 91(24) Powers, the Inherent Right of Self Government, and Canada's Fiduciary Obligations" (Paper presented to the Canadian Aboriginal Law Conference, Vancouver: Pacific Business and Law Institute, December, 2002) at 12, 13.

36   *Indian Act,* S.C. 1906, c.81. s.1 am. S.C. 1924, c.47, s.1. [*Indian Act 1906*]

37   *Indian Act,* S.C. 1932–1933, c.42.

38   *Re: Eskimos, supra* note 15.

39   Canada, Department of Indian and Northern Affairs, *Canada's Relationship with the Inuit: A History of Policy and Program Development,* Ottawa: Minister of Supply and Services Canada, 2006 at 6.

40   *Ibid.* at 7.

41   Frank James Tester & Peter Kulchyski, *Tammarnit (Mistakes): Inuit Relocation in the Eastern Arctic 1939–1963* (Vancouver: UBC Press, 1994) at 40.

42   Clem Chartier, "'Indian': An Analysis of the Term as Used in s.91(24) of the BNA Act," (1978–1979) 43 *Sask. L. Rev.* 37.

43   First Nations Child and Family Caring Society of Canada, *Joint Declaration of Support for Jordan's Principle to Resolving Jurisdictional Disputes Affecting Services to First Nations Children,* 2012, online: http://www.fncaringsociety.com/jordans-principle (accessed January 5, 2014).

44   N. Trocmé, D. Knoke, & C. Blackstock (2004). "Pathways to overrepresentation of Aboriginal children in Canada's child welfare system." *Social Services Review, 78*(4), 577–601.

45   See the term "Indian" as defined in *An Act for the Better Protection of the Lands and Property of the Indians in Lower Canada,* S.C. 1850, c. 42, s.5.

46   *Indian Act, 1876,* S.C. 1876, c.18.

47 *Indian Act 1906, supra* note 36.

48 See, for example, *R. v. Point*, [1957] 22 W.W.R. 527, in which the court held that "the accused, on the evidence, is an Indian within the meaning of the *Indian Act*, R.S.C. 1952, c.149, and being an Indian is a person (definition in the *Indian Act*, s.2(1)(g)) and being a person is subject to the application of sec. 44(2) of the *Income Tax Act*."

49 Bill Henderson, "Notes on the *Indian Act*," online: http://www.bloorstreet. com/200block/sindact.htm (accessed January 5, 2014).

50 Canada, *Report of the Royal Commission on Aboriginal Peoples*, Vol. 3, Chap. 3: Health and Healing (Ottawa: Minister of Supply and Services Canada, 1996) at 114. [RCAP]

51 Eduardo Duran & Bonnie Duran, *Native American Postcolonial Psychology* (Albany: State University of New York Press, 1995) at 19.

52 RCAP, *supra* note 50 at Vol. 3 Appendix 3A at 1.

53 *An Act further to Amend "The Indian Act 1880,"* Ch. 27. April 19, 1884.

54 *Ibid.* Ch. 35. July 22, 1895.

55 *Ibid.* Ch. 35, s. 8. June 12, 1914.

56 RCAP, *supra* note 50 at 113.

57 *An Act to Encourage the Gradual Civilization of Indian Tribes in the Province and to amend the Laws respecting Indians*, S. Prov. C. 1857, c. 16.

58 CP, JLAC (11Vic, 24 June 1847), Report, sec III, pt. III, subsec. I: Title to Lands in Canada; J. Leslie & R. Maguire (Eds.), *The Historical Development of the Indian Act* (Ottawa: INAC, 1978) at 18, 27, 28.

59 J. Baxter & M. Trebilcock, "Formalizing" Land Tenure in First Nations: Evaluating the Case for Reserve Tenure Reform (2009) 7:2 Indigenous L .J. 45 at 72. From 1857 to 1876 only one Indian (Elias Hill, a Mohawk) applied and was granted enfranchisement under this regime. There was Indian opposition and backlash and Hill was given a cash settlement for much less than the value of the land. (J. S. Milloy, "The Era of Civilization: British Policy for the Indians of Canada, 1830–1869" PhD thesis, Oxford University, 1978 at 280).

60 RCAP, *supra* note 50 at vol. 4, ch. 2, Seven Generations, Record 19116 citing Kathleen Jamieson, *Indian Women and the Law: Citizens Minus* (Ottawa: Supply and Services, 1978). [Jamieson]

61 *A.G. Canada v. Lavell*, [1974] S.C.R. 1349; Jamieson, *ibid.* at 30.

62 *Canadian Bill of Rights*, S.C. 1960, c. 44, s. 1(b).

63 *Lovelace v. Canada*, Communication No. R.6/24, U.N. Doc. Supp. No. 40 (A/36/40) (1981) (U.N. Human Rights Committee).

64 Adopted December 16, 1966, entry into force March 23, 1976; G.A. Res. 2200A (XXI) (accession by Canada 19 May 1976) Can TS no. 47.

65 *An Act to Amend the Indian Act*, S.C. 1985, c. 27.

66   *Canadian Charter of Rights and Freedoms*, Pt. I of *Constitution Act, 1982*, being Schedule B to the Act, *Canada Act, 1982* (U.K.) 1982, c.11.

67   Sharon McIvor, Letter to Members of Parliament, May 18, 2010, Native Women's Association of Canada, online: http://www.nwac.ca/sites/default/files/imce/Sharon-May182010MPletterfinal%20%282%29.pdf (accessed October 25, 2010).

68   Canada, Indian and Northern Affairs, "Gender Equity in Indian Registration Act" May 5, 2010, online: http://www.nwac.ca/sharon-mcivor-issues-letter-urging-all-mps-defeat-bill-c-3 (accessed January 5, 2014).

69   *CA, 1867, supra* note 1.

70   See *RJR-MacDonald* v. *Canada (A.G.)*, [1995] 3 S.C.R. 199, 127 D.L.R. (4th) 1; *R.* v. *Wetmore*, [1983] 2 S.C.R. 284, 2 D.L.R. (4th) 577 [cited to S.C.R.].

71   Canada Gazette, (2003a), *Food and Drugs Act. Natural Health Products Regulations* (Part II, 137(13), June 18.

72   *Criminal Code*, R.S.C. 1985, c. C-46, s. 216; 217; 219 (1)(a)(b); 220; 221; 245 (a)(b).

73   *Controlled Drugs and Substances Act*, S.C. 1996, c-19.

74   *R.* v. *Machekequonabe* [1897] O.J. No. 98 (H.C. Just.). [*Machekequonabe*]

75   Counsel for the accused in this case described a Wendigo as "an evil spirit clothed in human form" which "attacked, killed and ate human beings" (at para. 12). "A Wendigo is also described as a spirit as distinguished from a human being" (at para. 12).

76   *Machekequonabe, supra* note 74.

77   *R.* v. *Jacko*, [1997] O.J. No. 2472; 32 O.T.C. 271; [1998] 1 C.N.L.R. 164; 35 W.C.B. (2d) 188.

78   *Ibid.*

79   NAHO Briefing Note, "Information on Ecuadorian Healers facing criminal charges." Briefing # 007/02, March 6, 2002. [NAHO BN] See also Michael Erskine, "Ecuadorian shaman speaks at Laurentian University," April 3, 2002 *Manitoulin Expositor*, online: http://www.manitoulin.ca/Expositor/oldfiles/apr3.htm (accessed January 5, 2014).

80   NAHO BN, *ibid.*

81   *Ibid.*

82   NAHO Briefing Note, "Implications of Criminal Conviction of Traditional Healers," Briefing # 063/03, April 28, 2003.

83   Noxious is defined as "harmful to health; injurious," *Blacks Law Dictionary*, 7th ed., (St. Paul, MN: West Group, 1999) *s.v.* "noxious."

84   *Thomas* v. *Norris*, [1992] 2 C.N.L.R. 139 (B.C.S.C.). [*Thomas* v. *Norris*]

85   *Ibid.* at 15.

86   *Ibid.* at 16.

87   *R.* v. *Van der Peet*, [1996] 2 S.C.R. 507, [1996] 4 C.N.L.R. 146 [cited to S.C.R.]. [*Van der Peet*]

88   *Delgamuukw* v. *British Columbia*, [1998] 1 C.N.L.R. 14.

89   *R.* v. *Marshall*, [1999] 4 C.N.L.R. 161.

90   *R.* v. *Sappier*, 2006 SCC 54.

91   *R.* v. *Morris*, [2006] 2 S.C.R. 915).

92   *Moulton Contracting Ltd.* v. *British Columbia*, [2010] B.C.J. No. 665 at para 82, citing Lewis Klar, Tort Law, 4th ed. (Toronto: Thomson Canada Ltd., 2008) at 711-12.

93   *Ibid.* at para 82.

94   *Ibid.* at para 83.

95   *Thomas* v. *Norris, supra* note 84.

96   *Ibid.* at 164.

97   *R.* v. *Cummings* (1925) 1 D.L.R. 642.

98   *Canada (AG)* v. *Cummings*, [1926] 1 D.L.R. 52 CASCC.

99   *R.* v. *Lafferty* [1992] N.W.T.J. No. 151 (S.C.).

100   *Ibid.*

101   *Johnston* v. *Wellesly Hospital*, 1971 2 O.R. 103.

102   *R.* v. *Mianskum*, [2000] O.J. No. 5802. [*Mianskum*]

103   *R.* v. *Mohan*, [1994] 2 S.C.R. 9.

104   *Mianskum, supra* note 102 at para 66, 67, 68.

105   *R.* v. *H.G.* [2003] S.J. No. 589 S.C.A.

106   *Kudaka* v. *Kudaka*, [2001] O.J. No. 712 (C.J.).

107   See, for example, *Tobacco Control Act, 1994*, S.O. 1994, c.10, s.13; Alberta Regulation 149/204 "Prevention of Youth Tobacco Use Regulations," s.4; *The Non-Smokers Health Protection Act*, C.C.S.M., c. S-125, s.7(2); *Smoke-Free Places Act*, S.N.B. 2004, ch. S-9.5, s.2(2).

108   *R.* v. *Sparrow*, [1990] 1 S.C.R. 1075, [1990] 3 C.N.L.R. 160 cited to C.N.L.R.; *Van der Peet, supra* note 87.

109   *Canada National Parks Act,* S.C. 2000, c.32. [*Parks*]

110   National Parks General Regulations, SOR/78-213.

111   National Historic Parks General Regulations, SOR/82-263.

112   *Parks, supra* note 109 at ss. 16 and 17.

113   *Species at Risk Act*, S.C. 2002, c.29.

114   National Aboriginal Council on Species at Risk 2012, online: http://www.nacosar-canep.ca/aboutus_en.php (accessed October 25, 2012).

115   *Hunt v. Halcan Log Services Ltd.*, [1987] 4 C.N.L.R. 63.

116   *MacMillan Bloedel Ltd. v. Mullin*, [1985] 3 W.W.R. 577 (B.C.C.A.).

117   *Wet'suwet'en v. British Columbia (Ministry of Water, Land and Air Protection)*, [2002] B.C.E.A. No. 49.

118   *McCrady v. Ontario*, [1991] O.J. No. 1722.

119   *Ibid.*

120   *Frontenac Ventures Corp. v. Ardoch Algonquin First Nation*, [2008] OJ No. l 2651.

121   *Platinex Inc. v. Kitchenumaykoosib Inninuwug First Nation*, [2008] OJ No. 2650.

122   *Re: Corporation of the City of Brantford v. Montour et al.*, Ontario Superior Court, CV-08-334, *Endorsement of G.E. Taylor J., June 2, 2008* and *Henco Industries Ltd. v. Haudenosaunee Six Nations Confederacy Council*, [2006] OJ 4790.

123   Helke Ferris, "On Codex," *Vitality Magazine*, February 2005.

124   Ontario, Ministry of Agriculture, CODEX Alimentarius and CODEX Commission, 2011, online: http://www.omafra.gov.on.ca/english/food/inspection/codex.htm#can (accessed October 25, 2012).

125   *Daniels, supra* note 18.

Notes to Chapter Five

1   *Constitution Act, 1982*, being Schedule B to the *Canada Act 1982* (U.K.), 1982, c.11.

2   P. W. Hogg, *Constitutional Law of Canada*, 4th ed. (Scarborough: Carswell, 2002) at 27–45.

3   M. Battiste & J. Y. Henderson, *Protecting Indigenous Knowledge and Heritage: A Global Challenge* (Saskatoon: Purich Publishing, 2000). Also confirmed in *R. v. Van der Peet*, [1996] 2 S.C.R. 507, [1996] 4 C.N.L.R. 146 [cited to S.C.R.] [*Van der Peet*]; *Delgamuukw v. British Columbia*, [1997] 3 S.C.R. 1010, [1998] 1 C.N.L.R. 14, reversing in part (1993), 10 D.L.R. (4th) 470, [1993] 5 C.N.L.R. 1 (B.C.C.A.), varying in part [1991] 3 W.W.R. 97, [1991] 5 C.N.L.R. 1 (B.C.S.C.). [*Delgamuukw*]

4   *R. v. Badger*, [1996] 1 S.C.R. 771 at para. 41, [1996] 2 C.N.L.R. 77 [cited to S.C.R.] [*Badger*]. See also James Sa'ke'j Youngblood Henderson, "Interpreting Sui Generis Treaties" (1997) 36 Alta. L. Rev. (No. 1) 46.

5   James Sa'ke'j Youngblood Henderson, *Treaty Rights in the Constitution of Canada* (Carswell: 2007); H. Cardinal and W. Hildebrandt, *Treaty Elders of Saskatchewan* (Calgary: University of Calgary Press, 2001) at 31–38.

6   *Van der Peet, supra* note 3 at para 30.

7   *Ibid.* at para 31.

8   *R. v. Sparrow*, [1990] 1 S.C.R. 1075, [1990] 3 C.N.L.R. 160 [cited to S.C.R.]. [*Sparrow*]

9   *Van der Peet, supra* note 3; *R. v. Gladstone*, [1996] 2 S.C.R. 723, [1996] 4 C.N.L.R. 65; *R. v. N.T.C. Smokehouse Ltd.*, [1996] 2 S.C.R. 672.

10   *R. v. Sappier; R. v. Gray* [2006] S.C.C. 54 [*Sappier and Gray*]; *R. v. Marshall; R. v. Bernard* [2005] 2. S.C.R. 220 at para 48. [*Marshall and Bernard*]

11   *Sparrow, supra* note 8 at 1091–1093 (footnotes omitted).

12   *Van der Peet, supra* note 3 at para 30.

13   *Ibid.* at para. 55.

14   *Ibid. at* paras. 60–62.

15   *Ibid.* at para. 73.

16   *R. v. Powley*, [2003] 2 S.C.R. 207, [2003] 4 C.N.L.R. 321 at 13 and 17. [*Powley*]

17   *Ibid.* at para. 37.

18   *Sappier and Gray, supra* note 10.

19   *Marshall and Bernard, supra* note 10 at para 34.

20   *Ibid.* at para 36.

21   *Ibid.* at para 45.

22   *Sappier and Gray, supra* note 10.

23   *Ibid.* at 22.

24   *Delgamuukw, supra* note 3 at para 198.

25   *Sappier and Gray, supra* note 10 at para 45.

26   *Van der Peet, supra* note 3 at para 48.

27   Assembly of First Nations Health Secretariat, *Treaty Right to Health approved as major focus of CCOH Strategic Plan* (2005), online at http://64.26.129.156/cmslib/general/HB04-SM.e.pdf (accessed January 5, 2014).

28   Health Council of Canada, online: http://healthcouncilcanada.ca/tree/Aboriginal_Report_EN_web_final.pdf (accessed February 16, 2013).

29   White Horse General Hospital (White Horse, 2012), online: http://www.whitehorse-hospital.ca/ (accessed January 5, 2014).

30   National Aboriginal Health Organization, *An Overview of Traditional Knowledge and Medicine and Public Health in Canada*, online: http://www.naho.ca/?s=Overview+of+Traditional+Knowledge+and+Medicine+and+Public+Health+in+Canada+, (accessed January 5, 2014) at 13.

31   All Nations' Healing Hospital, "The Staff," online: http://www.fortquappelle.com/anhh_rfpp.html (accessed February 16, 2013).

32   *Ibid.*

33   File Hills Qu'Appelle Tribal Council, *Annual Report*, online: http://fhqtc.com/wp-content/uploads/2011/10/FHQTC-Annual-Report-.pdf (accessed February 16, 2013).

34   *Marshall and Bernard, supra* note 10 at para 107.

35   James (Sa'ke'j) Youngblood Henderson & Russel Barsh, "The Supreme Court's Van der Peet Trilogy: Naïve Imperialism and Ropes of Sand" (1997) 42 *McGill L. J.* 993. [Henderson & Barsh]

36   *Van der Peet, supra* note 3 at 539–564.

37   Henderson & Barsh, *supra* note 35 at 6,

38   Johanna Lazore, "Indigenous Strategies to Protect Traditional Health Knowledge." Unpublished; on file with the author. See also Donald S. Lutz, "The Iroquois Confederation Constitution: An Analysis," *Publius*, Vol. 28, Issue 2, 99-127, 1998 (CSF Associates, Easton, PA).

39   *Powley, supra* note 16 at para. 16.

40   The utility of self government being a generic right is arguable. *Campbell* v. *British Columbia (Attorney General* (2000) BCSC 1123, 79 B.C.L.R. (3d) 122 (S.C.).

41   *R.* v. *Marshall*, [1999] 3 S.C.R. 456, [1999] 4 C.N.L.R. 161.

42   *Casimel* v. *Insurance Corp. of British Columbia* (1993), [1994] 2 C.N.L.R. 22, 82 B.C.L.R. (2d) 387, 30 B.C.A.C. 279, 49 W.A.C. 279, 18 C.C.L.I. (2d) 161, 106 D.L.R. (4th) 720 (C.A.).

43   *Delgamuukw, supra* note 3.

44   *R.* v. *Adams*, [1996] 3 S.C.R. 101, [1996] 4 C.N.L.R. 1, *R.* v. *Cote*, [1994] C.N.L.R. 98, [1993] R.J.Q. 1350, 107 D.L.R. (4th) 28 (Que. C.A.) leave to appeal refused (1994), 63 Q.A.C. 142 (note), 109 D.L.R. (4th) vii (note), 172 N.R. 90 (note) (S.C.C)..

45   *Van der Peet, supra* note 3.

46   *Van der Peet* cited by Brian Slattery, "New Developments on the Enforcement of Treaty Rights" (paper presented to the Canadian Aboriginal Law Conference, Vancouver, Pacific Business & Law institute, December 2002) [unpublished, on file with the author].

47   In *R.* v. *Cote*, the issue was that of an Algonquin fisherman being charged with not obtaining provincial licenses to fish as well as not paying the fee to enter the provincial park. The Supreme Court of Canada held that freshwater fishing had been an important source of sustenance, thereby obliterating the requirement to obtain provincial fishing licenses; however, the defendant had not been fishing for himself but to teach a younger generation how to fish. The Court confirmed incidental rights when "a substantive Aboriginal right will normally include the incidental right to teach a practice, custom and tradition to a younger generation," but may convict on other grounds.

48   J. Y. Henderson, "Treaty Rights to Health" (unpublished, Native Law Centre, University of Saskatchewan, 2002). [Treaty Rights to Health]

49   In 1970, in a congressional address, American President Richard Nixon stated, "to the extent that the government has provided health services for Indians in conjunction with treaties in which land was ceded, Indian health care represents a prepaid health plan — quite likely the first example of such a concept." R. Pfefferbaum, B. Pfefferbaum, E. Rhades, and J. Rennard, "Providing for the Health Care Needs of Native American: Policy, Programs, Procedures, and Practices" 21(1) *American Indian Law Review,* pp. 211–258 at 219.

50   *Van der Peet, supra* note 3 at paras. 52–54; *Badger, supra* note 4 at para. 76; *R. v. Sioui,* [1990] 1 S.C.R. 1025, [1990] 3 C.N.L.R. 127 at p. 1069. [*Sioui*]

51   Rene Fumoleau, *As Long as this Land Shall Last: A History of Treaty 8 and Treaty 11, 1870–1939* (Toronto: McClelland and Stewart, 1973) at 36–37. [Fumoleau]

52   *Ibid.* at 114.

53   R. Daniel, "The Spirit and Terms of Treaty Eight," in Richard Price (Ed.), *The Spirit of the Alberta Indian Treaties,* 47–100 (Montreal: Institute for Research on Public Policy, 1987) at 98. [Daniel]

54   Fumoleau, *supra* note 51 at 114.

55   W. Morrison, *Showing the Flag: The Mounted Police and Canadian Sovereignty in the North, 1894–1925* (Vancouver: University of British Columbia Press, 1985) at 149.

56   Daniel, *supra* note 53 at 142.

57   Fumoleau, *supra* note 51 at 114.

58   *R. v. Sundown,* [1999] 1 S.C.R 393, at para. 24; *Badger, supra* note 4 at para. 78; *Sioui, supra* note 50 at para. 1043; *Simon v. The Queen,* [1985] 2 S.C.R. 387, at 404. [*Simon*]

59   Chiefs of Treaty 6, 7, 8, *Declaration of Treaty 6, 7 and 7 First Nations: Treaty Right to Health* (2005) online:http://treatycouncil.info/PDF/Treaty_Rights_and_Health_Resolution.pdf (accessed October 25, 2012). [Declaration]

60   Reported by A. Morris, *The Treaties of Canada with the Indians of Manitoba and the NorthWest Territories, Including the Negotiations on Which They Were Based and Other Information Relating Thereto* (Toronto: Belfords, Clarke, 1880) commencing at 28. [Morris]

61   *Ibid.* at 92.

62   *Ibid.* at 184.

63   *Ibid.* at 211–212.

64   *Ibid.* at 132.

65   Treaty Rights to Health, *supra* note 48 at 15.

66   Morris, *supra* note 60.

67   *Ibid.* at 185.

68   *Ibid.* at 186.

69   *Ibid.* at 218.

70   Walter Hildbrandt, Dorothy First Rider, & Sarah Carter, *The True Spirit and Original intent of Treaty 7* (McGill-Queen's University Press, 1996) at 120. See also Declaration, *supra* note 59.

71   Canada, Indian and Northern Affairs, *Treaty No. 8 Made June 21, 1899 and Adhesions, Reports, Etc.* (2008), online: http://www.ainc-inac.gc.ca/al/hts/tgu/pubs/t8/trty8-eng.asp (accessed January 5, 2014).

72   Canada, Indian and Northern Affairs, *The James Bay Treaty: Treaty No. 9 (Made in 1905 and 1906) and Adhesions Made in 1929 and 1930* (2008) online at http://www.ainc-inac.gc.ca/al/hts/tgu/pubs/t9/trty9-eng.asp (accessed January 5, 2014).

73   Canada, Indian and Northern Affairs, *Treaty No. 10 and Reports of Commissioners* (2008), online at http://www.ainc-inac.gc.ca/al/hts/tgu/pubs/t10/trty10-eng.asp (accessed January 5, 2014).

74   Kenneth S. Coates & William R. Morrison, "Treaty Research Report, Treaty No. 10 (1906)," prepared for Treaties and Historical Research Centre, Indian and Northern Affairs Canada (1986), online: http://www.aadnc-aandc.gc.ca/DAM/DAM-INTER-HQ/STAGING/texte-text/tre10_1100100028871_eng.pdf (accessed April 29, 2013).

75   J. Waldram, D. A. Herring, & T. K. Young, *Aboriginal Health in Canada: Historical, Cultural and Epidemiological Perspectives* (Toronto: University of Toronto Press, 1995) at 134 and 144. [Waldram]

76   PAC, RG10, Vol. 1864, file 375, Commissioner Simpson to Secretary of State, Howe, 11 July 1871.

77   Treaty No. 6. "Between Her Majesty the Queen and the Plains and Wood Cree Indians and Other Tribes of Indians at Fort Carlton, Fort Pitt and Battle River" (Ottawa: Queen's Printer).

78   *Ibid.* at 177.

79   Fumoleau, *supra* note 51 at 36.

80   *Ibid.* at 37.

81   Waldram, *supra* note 75 at 145.

82   *Dreaver et al* v. *The King* (1935), 5 C.N.L.C. 92 Ex. Ct. Canada, online: http://library.usask.ca/native/cnlc/vol05/092.html (accessed January 5, 2014).

83   No information is reported for the decision of the Magistrate's Court in *Johnston* (i.e., date of decision, citation information, or name of the judge). This decision would have occurred sometime after the date of the information laid in relation to the charge against Johnston (22 March 1965) and the date of the appellate Court decision in *R.* v. *Johnston* (1966), 56 D.L.R. (2d) 749 (Sask. C.A.).

84   *Ibid.* at 754.

85   *Manitoba Hospital Commission* v. *Klein and Spence* (1969), 67 W.W.R. 440 (Man. Q.B.). [*Klein*]

86 Since the Saskatchewan Court of Appeal's comments concerning the interpretation of the medicine chest clause were *obiter*, the decision of the appellate Court in *Swimmer* should have become the leading case for interpreting treaty rights to free medical services and was binding on lower Courts. Interestingly, however, it is the *Johnson* case that is referenced and not the *Swimmer* decision. *R. v. Swimmer* (1970), [1971] 1 W.W.R. 756 (Sask. C.A.). [*Swimmer*]

87 *Klein , supra* note 85.

88 *Swimmer, supra* note 86.

89 *The Hospital Services Insurance Act*, S.M. 1962, c. 30.

90 *Saskatchewan Medical Care Insurance Act*, R.S.S. 1965, c. 255.

91 *Wuskwi Sipihk Cree Nation v. Canada (Minister of National Health and Welfare)* [1999] F.C.J. No. 82 (T.D.) at para 14. [*Wuskwi Sipihk*]

92 *Nowegijick v. The Queen* [1983] 1 S.C.R. 29 at 36, cited in *Wuskwi Sipihk, ibid.* at para. 13. *Sparrow, supra* note 8.

93 *Duke v. Puts* (2001), 204 Sask. R. 130 (Q.B.) at para 2.

94 Canada, Department of National Health and Welfare, *Annual Report, 1957* (Ottawa: Queen's Printer, 1958) at 76. See also Treaty No. 6. The treaties are reproduced in R. A. Reiter, *The Law of Canadian Indian Treaties* (Edmonton: Juris Analytica, 1995) at Part III.

95 James Sa'ke'j Youngblood Henderson reflects: "There has been no documented case where the two departments have ever agreed to a joint process to address the treaty right to health issue." See Treaty Rights to Health, *supra* note 48.

96 Canada, Department of National Health and Welfare, *Annual Report, 1964* (Ottawa: Queen's Printer, 1965) at 95.

97 Canada, Department of National Health and Welfare, *Annual Report, 1968* (Ottawa: Queen's Printer, 1968) at 102.

98 Canada, Department of National Health and Welfare, *Annual Report, 1969* (Ottawa: Queen's Printer, 1969) at 117

99 Canada, Department of National Health and Welfare, *Annual Report, 1971* (Ottawa: Queen's Printer, 1971) at 105.

100 Canada, Health Canada, *History of Providing Health Services to First Nations People and Inuit* (2007), online at http://www.hc-sc.gc.ca/ahc-asc/branch-dirgen/fnihb-dgspni/services-eng.php (accessed January 5, 2014).

101 Canada, Report of an Interdepartmental Working Group to the Committee of Deputy Ministers on Justice and Legal Affairs, *Fiduciary Relationship of the Crown with Aboriginal Peoples: Implementation and Management Issues: A Guide for Managers* (Ottawa: n.p., 1995) at 13.

102 Office of the Treaty Commissioner, *Statement of Treaty Issues* (1998), online at http://www.otc.ca/pdfs/OTC_STI.pdf (accessed January 5, 2014) at 36.

103 Canada, Commission on the Future of Health Care in Canada, *Building on Values: The Future of Health Care in Canada: Final Report* (Ottawa: Canadian Government Publishing, 2002), online: http://www.cbc.ca/healthcare/final_report.pdf at 212 (accessed October 24, 2012).

104 Canada, Health Canada, *Your Health Benefits: A Guide for First Nations to Access Non-Insured Health Benefits* (2012), online: http://www.hc-sc.gc.ca/fniah-spnia/alt_formats/pdf/pubs/nihb-ssna/yhb-vss/nihb-ssna-yhb-vss-eng.pdf (accessed January 5, 2014).

105 Delia Opekokew, *The First Nations: Indian Government and the Canadian Confederation* (Federation of Saskatchewan Indians, 1979) at 10.

106 Federation of Saskatchewan Indian Nations, *Statement of Treaty Principles* (2007), online at http://www.fsin.com/fsindownloads/tgo/treaty_implementation_principles.pdf (accessed January 5, 2014).

107 *Ibid.*

108 Darren Bernhardt, *Saskatoon StarPhoenix*, "Treaty Six chiefs promote Native healthcare system" (2008), online at http://www.canada.com/saskatoonstarphoenix/news/local/story.html?id=9b26cd92-f104-4953-a367-00a743e106e1 (accessed January 5, 2014).

109 Assembly of First Nations Health and Social Secretariat, *Treaty Right to Health approved as major focus of CCOH Strategic Plan* (2005), online: http://64.26.129.156/cmslib/general/HB04-SM-e.pdf (accessed January 5, 2014).

110 Assembly of First Nations, Health and Social Secretariat, *Your Health Benefits: A Guide to Accessing your Non-Insured Health Benefits*, online: http://www.hc-sc.gc.ca/fniah-spnia/pubs/nihb-ssna/yhb-vss/index-eng.php (accessed January 5, 2014).

111 *Statement of Treaty Issues*, *supra* note 102 at 33.

112 *Ibid.*

113 Canada, *Report of the Royal Commission on Aboriginal Peoples* (Ottawa: Communication Group, 1996) at vol. 2(1) at 3.

114 *Ibid.* at vol. 2(1) at 38.

115 *Ibid.* at *People to People, Nation to Nation, Highlights from the Report of the Royal Commission on Aboriginal Peoples* (Ottawa: Minister of Supply and Services Canada 1996) at 5.

Notes to Chapter Six

1 James Sa'ke'j Youngblood Henderson, "Centennial Theme: Highlighting and Animating the Aboriginal Renaissance Created by the University Of Saskatchewan," presentation to the College of Law, University of Saskatchewan, 2009, on file with the author.

2   Canada, Health Canada, *Blueprint on Aboriginal Health: A Ten Year Plan* (2005), on-line: http://www.hc-sc.gc.ca/hcs-sss/pubs/system-regime/2005-blueprint-plan-abor-auto/index-eng.php (accessed January 5, 2014).

3   Canada, First Nation and Inuit Health Branch, Specific Policy Development, *Aborigi-nal Child Rights: Special Needs Focus*, Aboriginal Head Start, 2005–2006 (on file with the author). Dawn Walker, First Nations and Inuit Health Branch, Health Canada, *Aboriginal Child's Rights Special Needs Focus*, (Ottawa: 2005–2006) [Work in Prog-ress, unpublished, on file with the author].

4   Canada, Health Canada, *Canadian Handbook on Health Impact Assessment: the Ba-sics*, online: http://dsp-psd.pwgsc.gc.ca/Collection/H46-2-99-235E-1.pdf (accessed January 5, 2014).

5   First Nations Environmental Health Innovation Network, *Human Environmental Health Impact Assessment: A Framework for Indigenous Communities* (2008), online: http://www.fnehin.ca/site.php/sitenews/human_environmental_health_impact_assessment_a_framework_for_indigenous_com/ (accessed January 5, 2014).

6   World Health Organization, "Health Impact Assessments," online: http://www.who.int/hia/about/en/ (accessed January 5, 2014. [WHO]

7   *Ibid.*

8   World Health Organization, "Health Impact Assessments, Reasons to Use HIA," on-line: http://www.who.int/hia/about/why/en/index1.html (accessed January 5, 2014).

9   *The Six Nations: Oldest Living Participatory Democracy on Earth*, online: http://www.ratical.org/many_worlds/6Nations/ (accessed January 5, 2014).

10   Office of the High Commissioner for Human Rights, "OHCHR Fact Sheet: The *UN Declaration of the Rights of Indigenous Peoples*," online: www2.ohchr.org/English/is-sues/indigenous/docs/IntDay/IndigenousDeclarationeng.pdf.

11   *United Nations Declaration of the Rights of Indigenous Peoples*, preamble para. 7 at Art. 43.

12   Jackie Hartley, Paul Joffe, & Jennifer Preston, "From Development to Implementa-tion, An Ongoing Journey," in *Realizing the UN Declaration of the Rights of Indig-enous Peoples: Triumph, Hope, and Action* (Saskatoon: Purich, 2007) at 12. [Joffe]

13   *Ibid.* at 70.

14   Canadian Human Rights Commission, Publications, *Raising Awareness. Influenc-ing Positive Change*, online: http://www.chrc-ccdp.gc.ca/publications/ar_2009_ra/page3-eng.aspx#31 (accessed January 5, 2014).

15   Letter from Minister of Indian Affairs and Northern Development Chuck Strahl to Assembly of First Nations National Chief Phil Fontaine (10 Dec. 2007) in Joffe, *supra* note 12 at 71.

16   Chuck Strahl, "Address" (Delivered at Luncheon Hosted by Canada's Permanent Mission to the United Nations, New York, 1 May 2008), online: www. Ainc-inac.gc/ai/mr/spch/2008/may0108-eng.asp in Joffe, *ibid.* at 71.

17   AANDC, FAQ, *infra*. The Declaration imposes legal obligations on States; see Claire Charters and Rodolfo Stavenhagen (Eds.) *Making the Declaration Work: The United Nations Declaration on the Rights of Indigenous Peoples*. Document No. 127 (Copenhagen: International Working Group for Indigenous Affairs, 2009) at 13. See also Joffe, *supra* note 12.

18   Once a country has voted, it cannot change the vote but can issue a Statement of Support. Canada, Aboriginal Affairs and Northern Development Canada, "Frequently Asked Questions," 2012, online: http://www.ainc-inac.gc.ca/ap/ia/dcl/faq-eng.asp (accessed January 5, 2014).

NOTES TO CONCLUSION

1   E. Geyorfi-Dyke & Bonnie Hostrawser, *Poverty and Chronic Disease: Recommendations for Action* (Chronic Disease Prevention Alliance of Canada, 2008).

2   L. Kirmayer, G. Brass, & C. Tait (2000), "The mental health of Aboriginal peoples: Transformations of identity and community," *Canadian Journal of Psychiatry*, 45, 607–615.

3   *Canada Health Act*, R.S.C. 1985, c.C-6.

Bibliography

TEXTS AND ARTICLES

Battiste, M. & J. Y. Henderson. *Protecting Indigenous Knowledge and Heritage: A Global Challenge.* Saskatoon: Purich, 2000.

Bell, Robert. "The 'medicine-man' or, Indian and Eskimo notions of medicine." Paper presented to the Bathhurst and Rideau Medical Association. Montreal: January, 1886.

Boas, Franz & Horatio Hale. *Fifth Report of the Committee: Appointed for the purpose of investigating and publishing reports on the physical characters, languages and industrial condition of the north-western tribes of the Dominion of Canada.* London: The British Association for the Advancement of Science, 1888.

Boas, Franz & Sir Daniel Wilson. "Customs regarding Birth, Puberty, Marriage and Death, "Committee on North-Western Tribes of the Dominion of Canada." *Seventh Report on the North-western tribes of Canada.* London: British Association for the Advancement of Science, 1891.

Boyer, Yvonne. "Aboriginal Health: A Constitutional Rights Analysis." Discussion Paper Series in Aboriginal Health, No. 1. National Aboriginal Health Organization and the Native Law Centre of Canada. Saskatoon: Native Law Centre, 2003.

_____. "First Nation, Métis, and Inuit Health Care: The Crown's Fiduciary Obligation." Discussion Paper Series In Aboriginal Health, No. 2. National Aboriginal Health Organization and the Native Law Centre, 2004.

Bryce, P. H. *The Story of a National Crime — Being a Record of the Health Conditions of the Indians of Canada from 1904–1921.* Ottawa: James Hope and Sons, 1922.

Canada, Royal Commission on Aboriginal Peoples. *Report of the Royal Commission on Aboriginal Peoples: Gathering Strength.* Ottawa: Supply and Services Canada, 1996.

Canada, Health Canada. *Blueprint on Aboriginal Health: A Ten Year Plan 2005,* online: http://www.hc-sc.gc.ca/hcs-sss/pubs/system-regime/2005-blueprint-plan-abor-auto/index-eng.php (accessed January 5, 2014).

Cardinal, H. & W. Hildebrandt. *Treaty Elders of Saskatchewan.* Calgary: University of Calgary Press, 2001.

Carroll, D. & C. Benoit. "Aboriginal Midwifery in Canada: Blending Traditional and Modern Forms." (2001) 4:3 *The Canadian Women's Health Network Magazine.*

Chartrand, Larry N., Tricia E. Logan, & Judy D. Daniels. "Métis History and Experience in Residential Schools in Canada." Ottawa: Aboriginal Healing Foundation, 2006.

Colhoun, James Edward, William H. Keating, & Stephen Harriman Long. *Narrative of an expedition to the source of St. Peter's River, Lake Winnepeek, Lake of the Woods, &c. &c.: performed in the year 1823 by order of the Hon. J. C. Calhoun, secretary of war, under the command of Stephen H. Long, major U.S. T.E.* Philadelphia: H. C. Carey and I. Lea, 1824.

Cook, N. D. *Born to Die: Disease and New World Conquest, 1492–1650.* Cambridge: Cambridge University Press, 1998.

Dickason, O. P. *Canada's First Nations: A History of Founding Peoples from Earliest Times.* Toronto: McClelland and Stewart, 1992.

Duran, Eduardo & Bonnie Duran. *Native American Postcolonial Psychology.* Albany: State University of New York Press, 1995.

Ewing, Justice. *Evidence and Proceedings, Half-Breed Commission.* 25 February 1935. Edmonton: Half-Breed Commission, 1935.

Ferguson, R. G. *Studies in Tuberculosis.* Toronto: University of Toronto Press, 1955.

First Nations Centre. *First Nations Regional Longitudinal Health Survey (RHS) 2002/2003: Results for Adults, Youth and Children Living in First Nations Communities.* Ottawa: First Nations Centre at the National Aboriginal Health Organization, 2005.

Fournier, S. & E. Crey. *Stolen from Our Embrace: The Abduction of First Nations Children and the Restoration of Aboriginal Communities.* Toronto: Douglas & McIntyre, 1997.

Fumoleau, R. *As Long as the Land Shall Last.* Toronto: McLelland & Stewart, 1973.

Graham-Cumming, G. "Northern Health Services." *Canadian Medical Association Journal,* (1969) 100:11.

_____. "Health of the Original Canadians, 1867–1967." (1967) Med. Serv. J. Can. (23)22.

Grant, A. *No End of Grief: Indian Residential Schools in Canada.* Winnipeg: Pemmican Publications, 1996.

Grekul, Jana, et al. "Sterilizing the 'Feeble-minded': Eugenics in Alberta, Canada, 1929-1972." (2004) 17:4 *Journal of Historical Sociology,* 359.

Grygier, P. S. *A Long Way from Home: The Tuberculosis Epidemic among the Inuit.* Montreal: McGill Queens University Press, 1997.

Hartley, Jackie, Paul Joffe, & Jennifer Preston, "From Development to Implementation, An Ongoing Journey," in *Realizing the UN Declaration of the Rights of Indigenous Peoples: Triumph, Hope, and Action,* 12–16 (Saskatoon: Purich, 2007).

Henderson, J. Sa'ke'j. "Treaty Rights to Health." Native Law Centre, University of Saskatchewan, 2002 [unpublished].

Henderson, James (Sa'ke'j) Youngblood & Russel Barsh. "The Supreme Court's Van der Peet Trilogy: Naïve Imperialism and Ropes of Sand." (1997) 42 *McGill L.J.* 993.

Hildebrandt, Walter, Dorothy First Rider, & Sarah Carter. *The True Spirit and Original Intent of Treaty 7.* Montreal: McGill Queen's University Press, 1996.

Hind, H. Y. & W. G. R. Hind. *Explorations in the Interior of the Labrador Peninsula: The Country of the Montagnais and Nasquapee Indians.* London: Longman, Green, Longman, Roberts & Green, 1863.

Hoffman, Walter J. *The Midewiwin or "Grand Medicine Society" of the Ojibway,* Seventh Annual Report of the Bureau of American Ethnology, 1885–1886, pp. 149–300. Washington, D.C.: Government Printing Office, 1891.

Hogg, P. W. *Constitutional Law of Canada,* 4th ed. Scarborough: Carswell, 2002.

Jackman, Martha. "The Constitutional Basis for Federal Regulation of Health." (1996) 5 Health L. Rev. 2.

Jenness, Diamond. *Eskimo Administration: I I,* Canada. Arctic Institute of North America Technical Paper No. 14. Montreal: Arctic Institute of North America, 1964.

The Jesuit Relations and Allied Documents. "Travels and Explorations of the Jesuit Missionaries in New France 1610–1791." Cleveland: Burrows Brothers, 1818–1896.

Jones, J. A. *Traditions of the North American Indians: Being a Second and Revised Edition of "Tales of an Indian Camp."* London: H. Colburn and R. Bentley, 1830.

Kirmayer, Laurence, J. Gregory, M. Brass & Tara Holton. "Suicide Among Aboriginal People in Canada." Aboriginal Healing Foundation, 2007.

Laugrand, F. & J. Oosten. "Canicide and Healing: The Position of the Dog in the Inuit Cultures of the Canadian Arctic/Canicide Et Guérison: La Position Du Chien Dans Les Cultures Inuit De L'arctique Canadien." (2002) 97:1 *Anthropos.*

Levesque, Francis. "The Inuit, Their Dogs and the Northern Administration, from 1950 to 2007." (2008) *Anthropology of a Contemporary Inuit Claim.*

Lux, M. *Medicine That Walks: Disease, Medicine, and Canadian Plains Native Peoples: 1880–1940.* Toronto, University of Toronto Press, 2001.

Miller, J. R. *Shingwauk's Vision: A History of Native Residential Schools.* Toronto: University of Toronto Press, 1996.

Milloy, J. S. *A National Crime: The Canadian Government and the Residential School System, 1879–1986.* Winnipeg: University of Manitoba Press, 1999.

Morantz-Ornstein, Gillian & Louis-Patrick Haraoui, "Emerging Patterns in the Resistance to the Medicalization of Birth in North America." (2003) 7:1 *McGill Journal of Medicine.*

Morris, A. *The Treaties of Canada with the Indians of Manitoba and the NorthWest Territories, Including the Negotiations on Which They Were Based and Other Information Relating Thereto.* Toronto: Belfords, Clarke, 1880.

Norris, Malcolm. *Evidence and Proceedings, Half-Breed Commission,* 25 February 1935. Edmonton: Half-Breed Commission, 1935.

O'Neil, John D. "Self-Determination, Medical Ideology and Health Services in Inuit Communities." In Gurston Dacks and Ken Coates (Eds.) *Northern Communities: The Prospects for Empowerment,* Edmonton: Boreal Institute for Northern Studies, 1988.

Ootoova, I., Q.T. Atagutsiak, T. Ijjangiaq, J.Pitseolak, Aa.Joamie, Ak.Joamie, & M. Papatsie. *Interviewing Inuit Elders*. Vol. 5. Perspectives on traditional health. Iqaluit: Nunavut Arctic College, 2001.

Paleah L. Black, John T. Arnason, & Alain Cuerrier. "Medicinal plants used by the Inuit of Qikiqtaaluk" (Baffin Island, Nunavut) 86 (2008) *Botany*.

Pfefferbaum R., B. Pfefferbaum, E. Rhades, & J. Rennard. "Providing for the Health Care Needs of Native Americans: Policy, Programs, Procedures, and Practices." 21:1 *American Indian Law Review*.

Razack, Sherene H. *Looking White People in the Eye: Gender, Race and Culture in Courtrooms and Classrooms*. Toronto: University of Toronto Press, 1998.

Reading, J. L. & University of Victoria, Centre for Aboriginal Health Research. *The Crisis of Chronic Disease among Aboriginal Peoples: A Challenge for Public Health, Population Health and Social Policy*. Victoria: University of Victoria, Centre for Aboriginal Health Research, 2009.

Reiter, R. A. *The Law of Canadian Indian Treaties*. Edmonton: *Juris Analytica*, 1995.

Shannon, K. A. "The Unique Role of Sled Dogs in Inuit Culture: An Examination of the Relationship between Inuit and Sled Dogs in the Changing North." (Thesis, University of Alberta, 1997).

Slattery, B. "New Developments of the Enforcement of Treaty Rights." Paper presented to the Canadian Aboriginal Law Conference. Vancouver: Pacific Business and Law Institute.

Suttles, Wayne. "Coast Salish resource management." In Douglas Deur & Nancy Turner (Eds.), *Keeping it Living: Traditions of Plant Use and Cultivation on the Northwest Coast of North America*. Seattle: University of Washington Press, and Vancouver: UBC Press, 2005.

Talbot, E. A. *Five Years' Residence in the Canadas: Including a Tour through Part of the United States of America, in the Year 1823*. London: Longman, Hurst, Rees, Orme, Brown and Green, 1824.

Taylor, J. G. "Canicide in Labrador: Function and Meaning of an Inuit Killing Ritual." (1993) 17:1 *Études Inuit Studies*.

Tester, Frank James & Peter Kulchyski. *Tammarnit (Mistakes): Inuit Relocation in the Eastern Arctic 1939–63*. Vancouver: UBC Press, 1994.

Thornton, R. *American Indian Holocaust and Survival: A Population History since 1492*. Normand: Univ of Oklahoma Press, 1987.

Thwaites , R. G. (Ed.). *Jesuit Relations and Allied Documents, 1634–1635, vol. VII*. Cleveland: The Burrows Brothers, 1897.

Titley, Brian E. *A Narrow Vision: Duncan Campbell Scott and the Administration of Indian Affairs in Canada*. Vancouver: University of British Columbia Press (1986).

Treaties and Historical Research Centre. *The Historical Development of the Indian Act*. 2nd ed. Ottawa: Indian and Northern Affairs, 1978.

Valaskakis, G. G. *Indian Country: Essays on Contemporary Native Culture.* Waterloo: Wilfrid Laurier University Press, 2005.

Waldram, J., D. A. Herring, & T. K. Young. *Aboriginal Health in Canada. Historical, Cultural and Epidemiological Perspectives.* Toronto: University of Toronto Press, 1995.

Woodward, J. *Native Law.* Toronto: Carswell, 2002.

INTERNATIONAL DECLARATIONS

United Nations Declaration on the Rights of Indigenous Peoples (2007) United Nations A/61/L.67.

TREATIES

Treaty No. 6. "Between Her Majesty the Queen and the Plains and Wood Cree Indians and Other Tribes of Indians at Fort Carlton, Fort Pitt and Battle River" (Ottawa: Queen's Printer).

Treaty No. 7. "Between Her Majesty the Queen and the Blackfeet and other Indian Tribes, at the Blackfoot Crossing of Bow River and Fort MacLeod" (Ottawa: Queen's Printer).

Treaty No. 8. (Ottawa: Queen's Printer).

Treaty No. 10. (Ottawa: Queen's Printer).

Treaty No. 11. (Ottawa: Queen's Printer).

LEGISLATION

Canada Health Act, R.S.C. 1985, c.C-6.

Consolidation of Midwifery Profession Act, S.Nu. 2008, c. 18.

Constitution Act, 1867 (U.K.), 30 & 31 Vict., c.3, reprinted in R.S.C. 1985, App. II, No. 5.

Constitution Act, 1982, being Schedule B to the *Canada Act 1982* (U.K.), 1982, c. 11.

Indian Act, 1876, S.C. 1876, c. 18.

Indian Act, S.C. 1906, c. 81 am. S.C. 1924, c. 47.

Indian Act, S.C. 1932-33, c. 42.

Indian Act, R.S.C. 1985, *c.* I-5.

Sexual Sterilization Act (S.A.) (1928) c. 37.

Sexual Sterilization Act (R.S.A) (1955) c. 311 [repealed 1972].

Sexual Sterilization Act, R.S.B.C. 1960, c. 353 repealed by S.B.C. 1973, *c.* 79.

CASE LAW

Daniels v. Canada (Minister of Indian Affairs and Northern Development), [2013] F.C.J. No. 4.

Delgamuukw v. British Columbia, [1997] 3 S.C.R. 1010, [1998] 1 C.N.L.R. 14 (S.C.C.), reversing in part (1993) 10 D.L.R. (4th) 470, [1993] 5 C.N.L.R. 1 (B.C.C.A.), varying in part [1991] 3 W.W.R. 97, [1991] 5 C.N.L.R. 1 (B.C.S.C.).

Dreaver v. The King (1935), 5 C.N.L.C. 92 (Exch.).

Duke v. Puts (2001), 204 Sask. R. 130 (Sask. Q.B.).

Frontenac Ventures Corp. v. Ardoch Algonquin First Nation, [2008] OJ No. l 2651.

Lovelace v. Canada, Communication No. R.6/24, U.N. Doc. Supp. No. 40 (A/36/40) (1981) (U.N. Human Rights Committee).

Johnston v. Wellesly Hospital, 1971 2 O.R. 103.

Manitoba Hospital Commission v. Klein and Spence (1969), 67 W.W.R. 440 (Man. Q.B.).

Mikisew Cree First Nation v. Canada, 214 F.T.R. 48, [2002] 1 C.N.L.R. 169 (F.C.T.D.).

Mitchell v. Peguis Indian Band, [1990] 2 S.C.R. 85, [1990] 3 C.N.L.R. 46.

Nowegijick v. R., [1983] 1 S.C.R. 29, [1983] 2 C.N.L.R. 89.

Platinex Inc. v. Kitchenumaykoosib Inninuwug First Nation, [2008] OJ No. 2650.

Re: Eskimos, [1939] S.C.R. 104, [1939] 2 D.L.R. 417.

R. v. Badger, [1996] 1 S.C.R. 771, [1996] 2 C.N.L.R. 77.

R. v. Côté, [1996] 3 S.C.R. 139, [1996] 4 C.N.L.R. 26.

R. v. Gladstone, [1996] 2 S.C.R. 723, [1996] 4 C.N.L.R. 65.

R. v. Hill (1907), 15 O.L.R. 406 (Ont. C.A.) .

R. v. Horseman, [1990] 1 S.C.R. 901, [1990] 3 C.N.L.R. 95.

R. v. Johnston (1966), 56 D.L.R. (2d) 749 (Sask. C.A.).

R. v. Marshall, [1999] 3 S.C.R. 456, [1999] 4 C.N.L.R. 161. .

R. v. Powley, [2003] 2 S.C.R. 207, [2003] 4 C.N.L.R. 321.

R. v. Sioui, [1990] 1 S.C.R. 1025, [1990] 3 C.N.L.R. 127.

R. v. Sparrow, [1990] 1 S.C.R. 1075, [1990] 3 C.N.L.R. 160.

R. v. Sundown, [1999] 1 S.C.R. 393, [1999] 2 C.N.L.R. 289.

R. v. Swimmer (1970), [1971] 1 W.W.R. 756 (Sask. C.A.).

R. v. Van der Peet, [1996] 2 S.C.R. 507, [1996] 4 C.N.L.R. 146.

Simon v. The Queen, [1985] 2 S.C.R. 387, [1986] 1 C.N.L.R. 153.

Thomas v. Norris, [1992] 2 C.N.L.R. 139 (B.C.S.C.).

Wuskwi Sipihk Cree Nation v. *Canada (Minister of National Health and Welfare)* (1999), 164 F.T.R. 276, [1999] 4 C.N.L.R. 293.

Index

Yvonne Boyer currently holds the Canada Research Chair in Aboriginal Health and Wellness at Brandon University. She is a member of the Métis Nation of Saskatchewan and owns Boyer Law Office, where she specializes in providing holistic services that blend mainstream law with Indigenous laws. With a background in nursing, she has more than 15 years of experience practicing law and publishing extensively on the topics of Aboriginal health and how Aboriginal and treaty law intersects on the health of First Nations, Métis, and Inuit.

Yvonne received her Bachelor of Laws from the University of Saskatchewan, Master of Laws and Doctorate of Laws from the University of Ottawa, and in 2012 completed a post-doctoral fellowship at the Indigenous People's Health Research Centre. Yvonne volunteers her time and expertise with several organizations, and most notably she is a mother to four children, with one grandchild, and more on the way.